NON SANZ DROICT.

THE TRAGEDIE OF
IVLIVS CÆSAR.

Decorative headband and title from the earliest printed edition of
Julius Caesar, in the First Folio (1623)

William Shakespeare

The Tragedy of Julius Caesar

With New and Updated
Critical Essays
and a Revised Bibliography

Edited by William and Barbara Rosen

THE SIGNET CLASSIC SHAKESPEARE
General Editor: Sylvan Barnet

A SIGNET CLASSIC

SIGNET CLASSIC
Published by the Penguin Group
Penguin Putnam Inc., 375 Hudson Street, New York, New York 10014, U.S.A.
Penguin Books Ltd, 27 Wrights Lane, London W8 5TZ, England
Penguin Books Australia Ltd, Ringwood, Victoria, Australia
Penguin Books Canada Ltd, 10 Alcorn Avenue, Toronto, Ontario, Canada M4V 3B2
Penguin Books (N.Z.) Ltd, 182–190 Wairau Road, Auckland 10, New Zealand

Penguin Books Ltd, Registered Offices:
Harmondsworth, Middlesex, England

Published by Signet Classic, an imprint of Dutton NAL,
a member of Penguin Putnam Inc.
The Signet Classic edition of *Julius Caesar* was first published in 1963, and an updated
edition was published in 1986.

First Signet Classic Printing (Second Revised Edition), August, 1998
10 9 8 7 6 5 4 3 2 1

Library of Congress Catalog Card Number: 97-38430

Printed in the United States of America

BOOKS ARE AVAILABLE AT QUANTITY DISCOUNTS WHEN USED TO PROMOTE PRODUCTS OR
SERVICES. FOR INFORMATION PLEASE WRITE TO PREMIUM MARKETING DIVISION, PENGUIN
PUTNAM INC., 375 HUDSON STREET, NEW YORK, NEW YORK 10014.

Contents

Shakespeare: An Overview

Biographical Sketch

Between the record of his baptism in Stratford on 26 April 1564 and the record of his burial in Stratford on 25 April 1616, some forty official documents name Shakespeare, and many others name his parents, his children, and his grandchildren. Further, there are at least fifty literary references to him in the works of his contemporaries. More facts are known about William Shakespeare than about any other playwright of the period except Ben Jonson. The facts should, however, be distinguished from the legends. The latter, inevitably more engaging and better known, tell us that the Stratford boy killed a calf in high style, poached deer and rabbits, and was forced to flee to London, where he held horses outside a playhouse. These traditions are only traditions; they may be true, but no evidence supports them, and it is well to stick to the facts.

Mary Arden, the dramatist's mother, was the daughter of a substantial landowner; about 1557 she married John Shakespeare, a tanner, glove-maker, and trader in wool, grain, and other farm commodities. In 1557 John Shakespeare was a member of the council (the governing body of Stratford), in 1558 a constable of the borough, in 1561 one of the two town chamberlains, in 1565 an alderman (entitling him to the appellation of "Mr."), in 1568 high bailiff—the town's highest political office, equivalent to mayor. After 1577, for an unknown reason he drops out of local politics. What *is* known is that he had to mortgage his wife's property, and that he was involved in serious litigation.

The birthday of William Shakespeare, the third child and the eldest son of this locally prominent man, is unrecorded, but the Stratford parish register records that the infant was baptized on 26 April 1564. (It is quite possible that he was born on 23 April, but this date has probably been assigned by tradition because it is the date on which, fifty-two years later, he died, and perhaps because it is the feast day of St. George, patron saint of England.) The attendance records of the Stratford grammar school of the period are not extant, but it is reasonable to assume that the son of a prominent local official attended the free school—it had been established for the purpose of educating males precisely of his class—and received substantial training in Latin. The masters of the school from Shakespeare's seventh to fifteenth years held Oxford degrees; the Elizabethan curriculum excluded mathematics and the natural sciences but taught a good deal of Latin rhetoric, logic, and literature, including plays by Plautus, Terence, and Seneca.

On 27 November 1582 a marriage license was issued for the marriage of Shakespeare and Anne Hathaway, eight years his senior. The couple had a daughter, Susanna, in May 1583. Perhaps the marriage was necessary, but perhaps the couple had earlier engaged, in the presence of witnesses, in a formal "troth plight" which would render their children legitimate even if no further ceremony were performed. In February 1585, Anne Hathaway bore Shakespeare twins, Hamnet and Judith.

That Shakespeare was born is excellent; that he married and had children is pleasant; but that we know nothing about his departure from Stratford to London or about the beginning of his theatrical career is lamentable and must be admitted. We would gladly sacrifice details about his children's baptism for details about his earliest days in the theater. Perhaps the poaching episode is true (but it is first reported almost a century after Shakespeare's death), or perhaps he left Stratford to be a schoolmaster, as another tradition holds; perhaps he was moved (like Petruchio in *The Taming of the Shrew*) by

> Such wind as scatters young men through the world,
> To seek their fortunes farther than at home
> Where small experience grows.   (1.2.49–51)

In 1592, thanks to the cantankerousness of Robert Greene, we have our first reference, a snarling one, to Shakespeare as an actor and playwright. Greene, a graduate of St. John's College, Cambridge, had become a playwright and a pamphleteer in London, and in one of his pamphlets he warns three university-educated playwrights against an actor who has presumed to turn playwright:

> There is an upstart crow, beautified with our feathers, that with his *tiger's heart wrapped in a player's hide* supposes he is as well able to bombast out a blank verse as the best of you, and being an absolute Johannes-factotum [i.e., jack-of-all-trades] is in his own conceit the only Shake-scene in a country.

The reference to the player, as well as the allusion to Aesop's crow (who strutted in borrowed plumage, as an actor struts in fine words not his own), makes it clear that by this date Shakespeare had both acted and written. That Shakespeare is meant is indicated not only by *Shake-scene* but also by the parody of a line from one of Shakespeare's plays, *3 Henry VI*: "O, tiger's heart wrapped in a woman's hide" (1.4.137). If in 1592 Shakespeare was prominent enough to be attacked by an envious dramatist, he probably had served an apprenticeship in the theater for at least a few years.

In any case, although there are no extant references to Shakespeare between the record of the baptism of his twins in 1585 and Greene's hostile comment about "Shake-scene" in 1592, it is evident that during some of these "dark years" or "lost years" Shakespeare had acted and written. There are a number of subsequent references to him as an actor. Documents indicate that in 1598 he is a "principal comedian," in 1603 a "principal tragedian," in 1608 he is one of the "men players." (We do not have, however, any solid information about which roles he may have played; later traditions say he played Adam in *As You Like It* and the ghost in *Hamlet*, but nothing supports the assertions. Probably his role as dramatist came to supersede his role as actor.) The profession of actor was not for a gentleman, and it occasionally drew the scorn of university men like Greene who resented writing speeches for persons less educated than themselves, but it was respectable enough; players, if prosperous, were in effect members of the bourgeoisie, and there is nothing to suggest that Stratford considered William Shakespeare less than a solid citizen. When, in 1596, the Shakespeares were granted a coat of arms—i.e., the right to be considered gentlemen— the grant was made to Shakespeare's father, but probably William Shakespeare had arranged the matter on his own behalf. In subsequent transactions he is occasionally styled a gentleman.

Although in 1593 and 1594 Shakespeare published two narrative poems dedicated to the Earl of Southampton, *Venus and Adonis* and *The Rape of Lucrece*, and may well have written most or all of his sonnets in the middle nineties, Shakespeare's literary activity seems to have been almost entirely devoted to the theater. (It may be significant that the two narrative poems were written in years when the plague closed the theaters for several months.) In 1594 he was a charter member of a theatrical company called the Chamberlain's Men, which in 1603 became the royal company, the King's Men, making Shakespeare the king's playwright. Until he retired to Stratford (about 1611, apparently), he was with this remarkably stable company. From 1599 the company acted primarily at the Globe theater, in which Shakespeare held a one-tenth interest. Other Elizabethan dramatists are known to have acted, but no other is known also to have been entitled to a share of the profits.

Shakespeare's first eight published plays did not have his name on them, but this is not remarkable; the most popular play of the period, Thomas Kyd's *The Spanish Tragedy*, went through many editions without naming Kyd, and Kyd's authorship is known only because a book on the profession of acting happens to quote (and attribute to Kyd) some lines on the interest of Roman emperors in the drama. What is remarkable is that after 1598 Shakespeare's name commonly appears on printed plays—some of which are not his. Presumably his name was a drawing card, and publishers used it to attract potential buyers. Another indication of his popularity comes from Francis Meres, author of *Palladis Tamia: Wit's Treasury* (1598). In this anthology of snippets accompanied by an essay on literature, many playwrights are mentioned, but Shakespeare's name occurs more often than any other, and Shakespeare is the only playwright whose plays are listed.

From his acting, his play writing, and his share in a playhouse, Shakespeare seems to have made considerable money. He put it to work, making substantial investments in Stratford real estate. As early as 1597 he bought New Place, the second-largest house in Stratford. His family moved in soon afterward, and the house remained in the family until a granddaughter died in 1670. When Shakespeare made his will in 1616, less than a month before he died, he sought to leave his property intact to his descendants. Of small bequests to relatives and to friends (including three actors, Richard Burbage, John Heminges, and Henry Condell), that to his wife of the second-best bed has provoked the most comment. It has sometimes been taken as a sign of an unhappy marriage (other supposed signs are the apparently hasty marriage, his wife's seniority of eight years, and his residence in London without his family). Perhaps the second-best bed was the bed the couple had slept in, the best bed being reserved for visitors. In any case, had Shakespeare not excepted it, the bed would have gone (with the rest of his household possessions) to his daughter and her husband.

On 25 April 1616 Shakespeare was buried within the chancel of the church at Stratford. An unattractive monument to his memory, placed on a wall near the grave, says that he died on 23 April. Over the grave itself are the lines, perhaps by Shakespeare, that (more than his literary fame) have kept his bones undisturbed in the crowded burial ground where old bones were often dislodged to make way for new:

> Good friend, for Jesus' sake forbear
> To dig the dust enclosed here.
> Blessed be the man that spares these stones
> And cursed be he that moves my bones.

A Note on the Anti-Stratfordians, Especially Baconians and Oxfordians

Not until 1769—more than a hundred and fifty years after Shakespeare's death—is there any record of anyone expressing doubt about Shakespeare's authorship of the plays and poems. In 1769, however, Herbert Lawrence nominated Francis Bacon (1561–1626) in *The Life and Adventures of Common Sense*. Since then, at least two dozen other nominees have been offered, including Christopher Marlowe, Sir Walter Raleigh, Queen Elizabeth I, and Edward de Vere, 17th earl of Oxford. The impulse behind all anti-Stratfordian movements is the scarcely concealed snobbish opinion that "the man from Stratford" simply could not have written the plays because he was a country fellow without a university education and without access to high society. Anyone, the argument goes, who used so many legal terms, medical terms, nautical terms, and so forth, and who showed some familiarity with classical writing, must have attended a university, and anyone who knew so much about courtly elegance and courtly deceit must himself have moved among courtiers. The plays do indeed reveal an author whose interests were exceptionally broad, but specialists in any given field—law, medicine, arms and armor, and so on—soon find that the plays do not reveal deep knowledge in specialized matters; indeed, the playwright often gets technical details wrong.

The claim on behalf of Bacon, forgotten almost as soon as it was put forth in 1769, was independently reasserted by Joseph C. Hart in 1848. In 1856 it was reaffirmed by W. H. Smith in a book, and also by Delia Bacon in an article; in 1857 Delia Bacon published a book, arguing that Francis Bacon had directed a group of intellectuals who wrote the plays.

Francis Bacon's claim has largely faded, perhaps because it was advanced with such evident craziness by Ignatius Donnelly, who in *The Great Cryptogram* (1888) claimed to break a code in the plays that proved Bacon had written not only the plays attributed to Shakespeare but also other Renaissance works, for instance the plays of Christopher Marlowe and the essays of Montaigne.

Consider the last two lines of the Epilogue in *The Tempest*:

As you from crimes would pardoned be,
Let your indulgence set me free.

What was Shakespeare—sorry, Francis Bacon, Baron Verulam—*really* saying in these two lines? According to Baconians, the lines are an anagram reading, "Tempest of Francis Bacon, Lord Verulam; do ye ne'er divulge me, ye words." Ingenious, and it is a pity that in the quotation the letter *a* appears only twice in the cryptogram, whereas in the deciphered message it appears three times. Oh, no problem; just alter "Verulam" to "Verul'm" and it works out very nicely.

Most people understand that with sufficient ingenuity one can torture any text and find in it what one wishes. For instance: Did Shakespeare have a hand in the King James Version of the Bible? It was nearing completion in 1610, when Shakespeare was forty-six years old. If you look at the 46th Psalm and count forward for forty-six words, you will find the word *shake*. Now if you go to the end of the psalm and count backward forty-six words, you will find the word *spear*. Clear evidence, according to some, that Shakespeare slyly left his mark in the book.

Bacon's candidacy has largely been replaced in the twentieth century by the candidacy of Edward de Vere (1550–1604), 17th earl of Oxford. The basic ideas behind the Oxford theory, advanced at greatest length by Dorothy and Charlton Ogburn in *This Star of England* (1952, rev. 1955), a book of 1297 pages, and by Charlton Ogburn in *The Mysterious William Shakespeare* (1984), a book of 892 pages, are these: (1) The man from Stratford could not possibly have had the mental equipment and the experience to have written the plays—only a courtier could have written them; (2) Oxford had the requisite background (social position, education, years at Queen Elizabeth's court); (3) Oxford did not wish his authorship to be known for two basic reasons: writing for the public theater was a vulgar pursuit, and the plays show so much courtly and royal disreputable behavior that they would have compromised Oxford's position at court. Oxfordians offer countless details to support the claim. For example, Hamlet's phrase "that ever I was born to set it right" (1.5.89) barely conceals "E. Ver, I was born to set it right," an unambiguous announcement of de Vere's authorship, according to *This Star of England* (p. 654). A second example: Consider

Ben Jonson's poem entitled "To the Memory of My Beloved Master William Shakespeare," prefixed to the first collected edition of Shakespeare's plays in 1623. According to Oxfordians, when Jonson in this poem speaks of the author of the plays as the "swan of Avon," he is alluding not to William Shakespeare, who was born and died in Stratford-on-Avon and who throughout his adult life owned property there; rather, he is alluding to Oxford, who, the Ogburns say, used "William Shakespeare" as his pen name, and whose manor at Bilton was on the Avon River. Oxfordians do not offer any evidence that Oxford took a pen name, and they do not mention that Oxford had sold the manor in 1581, forty-two years before Jonson wrote his poem. Surely a reference to the Shakespeare who was born in Stratford, who had returned to Stratford, and who had died there only seven years before Jonson wrote the poem is more plausible. And exactly why Jonson, who elsewhere also spoke of Shakespeare as a playwright, and why Heminges and Condell, who had acted with Shakespeare for about twenty years, should speak of Shakespeare as the author in their dedication in the 1623 volume of collected plays is never adequately explained by Oxfordians. Either Jonson, Heminges and Condell, and numerous others were in on the conspiracy, or they were all duped—equally unlikely alternatives. Another difficulty in the Oxford theory is that Oxford died in 1604, and some of the plays are clearly indebted to works and events later than 1604. Among the Oxfordian responses are: At his death Oxford left some plays, and in later years these were touched up by hacks, who added the material that points to later dates. *The Tempest*, almost universally regarded as one of Shakespeare's greatest plays and pretty clearly dated to 1611, does indeed date from a period after the death of Oxford, but it is a crude piece of work that should not be included in the canon of works by Oxford.

The anti-Stratfordians, in addition to assuming that the author must have been a man of rank and a university man, usually assume two conspiracies: (1) a conspiracy in Elizabethan and Jacobean times, in which a surprisingly large number of persons connected with the theater knew that the actor Shakespeare did not write the plays attributed to him but for some reason or other pretended that he did; (2) a conspiracy of today's Stratfordians, the professors who teach Shakespeare in the colleges and universities, who are said to have a vested interest in preserving Shakespeare as the author of the plays they teach. In fact, (1) it is inconceivable that the secret of Shakespeare's non-authorship could have been preserved by all of the people who supposedly were in on the conspiracy, and (2) academic fame awaits any scholar today who can disprove Shakespeare's authorship.

The Stratfordian case is convincing not only because hundreds or even thousands of anti-Stratford arguments—of the sort that say "ever I was born"—has the secret double meaning "E. Ver, I was born"—add up to nothing at all but also because irrefutable evidence connects the man from Stratford with the London theater and with the authorship of particular plays. The anti-Stratfordians do not seem to understand that it is not enough to dismiss the Stratford case by saying that a fellow from the provinces simply couldn't have written the plays. Nor do they understand that it is not enough to dismiss all of the evidence connecting Shakespeare with the plays by asserting that it is perjured.

The Shakespeare Canon

We return to William Shakespeare. Thirty-seven plays as well as some nondramatic poems are generally held to constitute the Shakespeare canon, the body of authentic works. The exact dates of composition of most of the works are highly uncertain, but evidence of a starting point and/or of a final limiting point often provides a framework for informed guessing. For example, *Richard II* cannot be earlier than 1595, the publication date of some material to which it is indebted; *The Merchant of Venice* cannot be later than 1598, the year Francis Meres mentioned it. Sometimes arguments for a date hang on an alleged topical allusion, such as the lines about the unseasonable weather in *A Midsummer Night's Dream*, 2.1.81–117, but such an allusion, if indeed it is an allusion to an event in the real world, can be variously interpreted, and in any case there is always the possibility that a topical allusion was inserted years later, to bring the play up to date. (The issue of alterations in a text between the time that Shakespeare drafted it and the time that it was printed—alterations due to censorship or playhouse practice or Shakespeare's own second thoughts—will be discussed in "The Play Text as a Collaboration" later in this overview.) Dates are often attributed on the basis of style, and although conjectures about style usually rest on other conjectures (such as Shakespeare's development as a playwright, or the appropriateness of lines to character), sooner or later one must rely on one's literary sense. There is no documentary proof, for example, that *Othello* is not as early as *Romeo and Juliet*, but one feels that *Othello* is a later, more mature work, and because the first record of its performance is 1604, one is glad enough to set its composition at that date and not push it back into Shakespeare's early years. (*Romeo and Juliet* was first published in 1597, but evidence suggests that it was written a little earlier.) The following chronology, then, is indebted not only to facts but also to informed guesswork and sensitivity. The dates, necessarily imprecise for some works, indicate something like a scholarly consensus concerning the time of original composition. Some plays show evidence of later revision.

Plays. The first collected edition of Shakespeare, published in 1623, included thirty-six plays. These are all accepted as Shakespeare's, though for one of them, *Henry VIII*, he is thought to have had a collaborator. A thirty-seventh play, *Pericles*, published in 1609 and attributed to Shakespeare on the title page, is also widely accepted as being partly by Shakespeare even though it is not included in the 1623 volume. Still another play not in the 1623 volume, *The Two Noble Kinsmen*, was first published in 1634, with a title page attributing it to John Fletcher and Shakespeare. Probably most students of the subject now believe that Shakespeare did indeed have a hand in it. Of the remaining plays attributed at one time or another to Shakespeare, only one, *Edward III*, anonymously published in 1596, is now regarded by some scholars as a serious candidate. The prevailing opinion, however, is that this rather simpleminded play is not

Shakespeare's; at most he may have revised some passages, chiefly scenes with the Countess of Salisbury. We include *The Two Noble Kinsmen* but do not include *Edward III* in the following list.

1588–94	*The Comedy of Errors*
1588–94	*Love's Labor's Lost*
1589–91	*2 Henry VI*
1590–91	*3 Henry VI*
1589–92	*1 Henry VI*
1592–93	*Richard III*
1589–94	*Titus Andronicus*
1593–94	*The Taming of the Shrew*
1592–94	*The Two Gentlemen of Verona*
1594–96	*Romeo and Juliet*
1595	*Richard II*
1595–96	*A Midsummer Night's Dream*
1596–97	*King John*
1594–96	*The Merchant of Venice*
1596–97	*1 Henry IV*
1597	*The Merry Wives of Windsor*
1597–98	*2 Henry IV*
1598–99	*Much Ado About Nothing*
1598–99	*Henry V*
1599	*Julius Caesar*
1599–1600	*As You Like It*
1599–1600	*Twelfth Night*
1600–1601	*Hamlet*
1601–1602	*Troilus and Cressida*
1602–1604	*All's Well That Ends Well*
1603–1604	*Othello*
1604	*Measure for Measure*
1605–1606	*King Lear*
1605–1606	*Macbeth*
1606–1607	*Antony and Cleopatra*
1605–1608	*Timon of Athens*
1607–1608	*Coriolanus*
1607–1608	*Pericles*
1609–10	*Cymbeline*

1610–11	*The Winter's Tale*
1611	*The Tempest*
1612–13	*Henry VIII*
1613	*The Two Noble Kinsmen*

Poems. In 1989 Donald W. Foster published a book in which he argued that "A Funeral Elegy for Master William Peter," published in 1612, ascribed only to the initials W.S., *may* be by Shakespeare. Foster later published an article in a scholarly journal, *PMLA* 111 (1996), in which he asserted the claim more positively. The evidence begins with the initials, and includes the fact that the publisher and the printer of the elegy had published Shakespeare's *Sonnets* in 1609. But such facts add up to rather little, especially because no one has found any connection between Shakespeare and William Peter (an Oxford graduate about whom little is known, who was murdered at the age of twenty-nine). The argument is based chiefly on statistical examinations of word patterns, which are said to correlate with Shakespeare's known work. Despite such correlations, however, many readers feel that the poem does not sound like Shakespeare. True, Shakespeare has a great range of styles, but consistently his work is imaginative and interesting. Many readers find neither of these qualities in "A Funeral Elegy."

1592–93	*Venus and Adonis*
1593–94	*The Rape of Lucrece*
1593–1600	*Sonnets*
1600–1601	*The Phoenix and the Turtle*

Shakespeare's English

1. Spelling and Pronunciation. From the philologist's point of view, Shakespeare's English is modern English. It requires footnotes, but the inexperienced reader can comprehend substantial passages with very little help, whereas for the same reader Chaucer's Middle English is a foreign language. By the beginning of the fifteenth century the chief grammatical changes in English had taken place, and the final unaccented

-e of Middle English had been lost (though it survives even today in spelling, as in *name*); during the fifteenth century the dialect of London, the commercial and political center, gradually displaced the provincial dialects, at least in writing; by the end of the century, printing had helped to regularize and stabilize the language, especially spelling. Elizabethan spelling may seem erratic to us (there were dozens of spellings of *Shakespeare*, and a simple word like *been* was also spelled *beene* and *bin*), but it had much in common with our spelling. Elizabethan spelling was conservative in that for the most part it reflected an older pronunciation (Middle English) rather than the sound of the language as it was then spoken, just as our spelling continues to reflect medieval pronunciation—most obviously in the now silent but formerly pronounced letters in a word such as *knight*. Elizabethan pronunciation, though not identical with ours, was much closer to ours than to that of the Middle Ages. Incidentally, though no one can be certain about what Elizabethan English sounded like, specialists tend to believe it was rather like the speech of a modern stage Irishman (*time* apparently was pronounced *toime*, *old* pronounced *awld*, *day* pronounced *die*, and *join* pronounced *jine*) and not at all like the Oxford speech that most of us think it was.

An awareness of the difference between our pronunciation and Shakespeare's is crucial in three areas—in accent, or number of syllables (many metrically regular lines may look irregular to us); in rhymes (which may not look like rhymes); and in puns (which may not look like puns). Examples will be useful. Some words that were at least on occasion stressed differently from today are *aspèct*, *còmplete*, *fòrlorn*, *revènue*, and *sepùlcher*. Words that sometimes had an additional syllable are *emp[e]ress*, *Hen[e]ry*, *mon[e]th*, and *villain* (three syllables, *vil-lay-in*). An additional syllable is often found in possessives, like *moon*'s (pronounced *moones*) and in words ending in *-tion* or *-sion*. Words that had one less syllable than they now have are *needle* (pronounced *neel*) and *violet* (pronounced *vilet*). Among rhymes now lost are *one* with *loan*, *love* with *prove*, *beast* with *jest*, *eat* with *great*. (In reading, trust your sense of metrics and your ear, more than your eye.) An example of a pun that has become obliterated by a

change in pronunciation is Falstaff's reply to Prince Hal's
"Come, tell us your reason" in *1 Henry IV*: "Give you a reason on compulsion? If reasons were as plentiful as blackberries, I would give no man a reason upon compulsion, I"
(2.4.237–40). The *ea* in *reason* was pronounced rather like a
long *a*, like the *ai* in *raisin*, hence the comparison with
blackberries.

Puns are not merely attempts to be funny; like metaphors
they often involve bringing into a meaningful relationship
areas of experience normally seen as remote. In *2 Henry IV,*
when Feeble is conscripted, he stoically says, "I care not. A
man can die but once. We owe God a death" (3.2.242–43),
punning on *debt,* which was the way *death* was pronounced.
Here an enormously significant fact of life is put into simple
commercial imagery, suggesting its commonplace quality.
Shakespeare used the same pun earlier in *1 Henry IV,* when
Prince Hal says to Falstaff, "Why, thou owest God a death,"
and Falstaff replies, " 'Tis not due yet: I would be loath to
pay him before his day. What need I be so forward with him
that calls not on me?" (5.1.126–29).

Sometimes the puns reveal a delightful playfulness; sometimes they reveal aggressiveness, as when, replying to
Claudius's "But now, my cousin Hamlet, and my son," Hamlet says, "A little more than kin, and less than kind!"
(1.2.64–65). These are Hamlet's first words in the play, and
we already hear him warring verbally against Claudius.
Hamlet's "less than kind" probably means (1) Hamlet is not
of Claudius's family or nature, *kind* having the sense it still
has in our word *mankind*; (2) Hamlet is not kindly (affection-
ately) disposed toward Claudius; (3) Claudius is not naturally
(but rather unnaturally, in a legal sense incestuously) Hamlet's father. The puns evidently were not put in as sops to the
groundlings; they are an important way of communicating a
complex meaning.

2. *Vocabulary.* A conspicuous difficulty in reading Shakespeare is rooted in the fact that some of his words are no
longer in common use—for example, words concerned with
armor, astrology, clothing, coinage, hawking, horsemanship,
law, medicine, sailing, and war. Shakespeare had a large

vocabulary—something near thirty thousand words—but it was not so much a vocabulary of big words as a vocabulary drawn from a wide range of life, and it is partly his ability to call upon a great body of concrete language that gives his plays the sense of being in close contact with life. When the right word did not already exist, he made it up. Among words thought to be his coinages are *accommodation, all-knowing, amazement, bare-faced, countless, dexterously, dislocate, dwindle, fancy-free, frugal, indistinguishable, lackluster, laughable, overawe, premeditated, sea change, star-crossed*. Among those that have not survived are the verb *convive*, meaning to feast together, and *smilet*, a little smile.

Less overtly troublesome than the technical words but more treacherous are the words that seem readily intelligible to us but whose Elizabethan meanings differ from their modern ones. When Horatio describes the Ghost as an "erring spirit," he is saying not that the ghost has sinned or made an error but that it is wandering. Here is a short list of some of the most common words in Shakespeare's plays that often (but not always) have a meaning other than their most usual modern meaning:

'a	he
abuse	deceive
accident	occurrence
advertise	inform
an, and	if
annoy	harm
appeal	accuse
artificial	skillful
brave	fine, splendid
censure	opinion
cheer	(1) face (2) frame of mind
chorus	a single person who comments on the events
closet	small private room
competitor	partner
conceit	idea, imagination
cousin	kinsman

cunning	skillful
disaster	evil astrological influence
doom	judgment
entertain	receive into service
envy	malice
event	outcome
excrement	outgrowth (of hair)
fact	evil deed
fancy	(1) love (2) imagination
fell	cruel
fellow	(1) companion (2) low person (often an insulting term if addressed to someone of approximately equal rank)
fond	foolish
free	(1) innocent (2) generous
glass	mirror
hap, haply	chance, by chance
head	army
humor	(1) mood (2) bodily fluid thought to control one's psychology
imp	child
intelligence	news
kind	natural, acting according to nature
let	hinder
lewd	base
mere(ly)	utter(ly)
modern	commonplace
natural	a fool, an idiot
naughty	(1) wicked (2) worthless
next	nearest
nice	(1) trivial (2) fussy
noise	music
policy	(1) prudence (2) stratagem
presently	immediately
prevent	anticipate
proper	handsome
prove	test

quick	alive
sad	serious
saw	proverb
secure	without care, incautious
silly	innocent
sensible	capable of being perceived by the senses
shrewd	sharp
so	provided that
starve	die
still	always
success	that which follows
tall	brave
tell	count
tonight	last night
wanton	playful, careless
watch	keep awake
will	lust
wink	close both eyes
wit	mind, intelligence

All glosses, of course, are mere approximations; sometimes one of Shakespeare's words may hover between an older meaning and a modern one, and as we have seen, his words often have multiple meanings.

3. Grammar. A few matters of grammar may be surveyed, though it should be noted at the outset that Shakespeare sometimes made up his own grammar. As E. A. Abbott says in *A Shakespearian Grammar,* "Almost any part of speech can be used as any other part of speech": a noun as a verb ("he childed as I fathered"); a verb as a noun ("She hath made compare"); or an adverb as an adjective ("a seldom pleasure"). There are hundreds, perhaps thousands, of such instances in the plays, many of which at first glance would not seem at all irregular and would trouble only a pedant. Here are a few broad matters.

Nouns: The Elizabethans thought the *-s* genitive ending for nouns (as in *man's*) derived from *his*; thus the line " 'gainst the count his galleys I did some service," for "the count's galleys."

Adjectives: By Shakespeare's time adjectives had lost the endings that once indicated gender, number, and case. About the only difference between Shakespeare's adjectives and ours is the use of the now redundant *more* or *most* with the comparative ("some more fitter place") or superlative ("This was the most unkindest cut of all"). Like double comparatives and double superlatives, double negatives were acceptable; Mercutio "will not budge for no man's pleasure."

Pronouns: The greatest change was in pronouns. In Middle English *thou, thy,* and *thee* were used among familiars and in speaking to children and inferiors; *ye, your,* and *you* were used in speaking to superiors (servants to masters, nobles to the king) or to equals with whom the speaker was not familiar. Increasingly the "polite" forms were used in all direct address, regardless of rank, and the accusative *you* displaced the nominative *ye.* Shakespeare sometimes uses *ye* instead of *you,* but even in Shakespeare's day *ye* was archaic, and it occurs mostly in rhetorical appeals.

Thou, thy, and *thee* were not completely displaced, however, and Shakespeare occasionally makes significant use of them, sometimes to connote familiarity or intimacy and sometimes to connote contempt. In *Twelfth Night* Sir Toby advises Sir Andrew to insult Cesario by addressing him as *thou*: "If thou thou'st him some thrice, it shall not be amiss" (3.2.46–47). In *Othello* when Brabantio is addressing an unidentified voice in the dark he says, "What are you?" (1.1.91), but when the voice identifies itself as the foolish suitor Roderigo, Brabantio uses the contemptuous form, saying, "I have charged thee not to haunt about my doors" (93). He uses this form for a while, but later in the scene, when he comes to regard Roderigo as an ally, he shifts back to the polite *you,* beginning in line 163, "What said she to you?" and on to the end of the scene. For reasons not yet satisfactorily explained, Elizabethans used *thou* in addresses to God— "O God, thy arm was here," the king says in *Henry V* (4.8.108)—and to supernatural characters such as ghosts and witches. A subtle variation occurs in *Hamlet.* When Hamlet first talks with the Ghost in 1.5, he uses *thou,* but when he sees the Ghost in his mother's room, in 3.4, he uses *you,* presumably because he is now convinced that the ghost is not a counterfeit but is his father.

Perhaps the most unusual use of pronouns, from our point of view, is the neuter singular. In place of our *its, his* was often used, as in "How far that little candle throws *his* beams." But the use of a masculine pronoun for a neuter noun came to seem unnatural, and so *it* was used for the possessive as well as the nominative: "The hedge-sparrow fed the cuckoo so long / That it had it head bit off by it young." In the late sixteenth century the possessive form *its* developed, apparently by analogy with the *-s* ending used to indicate a genitive noun, as in *book*'s, but *its* was not yet common usage in Shakespeare's day. He seems to have used *its* only ten times, mostly in his later plays. Other usages, such as "you have seen Cassio and she together" or the substitution of *who* for *whom,* cause little problem even when noticed.

Verbs, Adverbs, and Prepositions: Verbs cause almost no difficulty: The third person singular present form commonly ends in *-s,* as in modern English (e.g., "He blesses"), but sometimes in *-eth* (Portia explains to Shylock that mercy "blesseth him that gives and him that takes"). Broadly speaking, the *-eth* ending was old-fashioned or dignified or "literary" rather than colloquial, except for the words *doth, hath,* and *saith.* The *-eth* ending (regularly used in the King James Bible, 1611) is very rare in Shakespeare's dramatic prose, though not surprisingly it occurs twice in the rather formal prose summary of the narrative poem *Lucrece.* Sometimes a plural subject, especially if it has collective force, takes a verb ending in *-s,* as in "My old bones aches." Some of our strong or irregular preterites (such as *broke*) have a different form in Shakespeare (*brake*); some verbs that now have a weak or regular preterite (such as *helped*) in Shakespeare have a strong or irregular preterite (*holp*). Some adverbs that today end in *-ly* were not inflected: "grievous sick," "wondrous strange." Finally, prepositions often are not the ones we expect: "We are such stuff as dreams are made on," "I have a king here to my flatterer."

Again, none of the differences (except meanings that have substantially changed or been lost) will cause much difficulty. But it must be confessed that for some elliptical passages there is no widespread agreement on meaning. Wise editors resist saying more than they know, and when they are uncertain they add a question mark to their gloss.

Shakespeare's Theater

In Shakespeare's infancy, Elizabethan actors performed wherever they could—in great halls, at court, in the courtyards of inns. These venues implied not only different audiences but also different playing conditions. The innyards must have made rather unsatisfactory theaters: on some days they were unavailable because carters bringing goods to London used them as depots; when available, they had to be rented from the innkeeper. In 1567, presumably to avoid such difficulties, and also to avoid regulation by the Common Council of London, which was not well disposed toward theatricals, one John Brayne, brother-in-law of the carpenter turned actor James Burbage, built the Red Lion in an eastern suburb of London. We know nothing about its shape or its capacity; we can say only that it may have been the first building in Europe constructed for the purpose of giving plays since the end of antiquity, a thousand years earlier. Even after the building of the Red Lion theatrical activity continued in London in makeshift circumstances, in marketplaces and inns, and always uneasily. In 1574 the Common Council required that plays and playing places in London be licensed because

> sundry great disorders and inconveniences have been found to ensue to this city by the inordinate haunting of great multitudes of people, specially youth, to plays, interludes, and shows, namely occasion of frays and quarrels, evil practices of incontinency in great inns having chambers and secret places adjoining to their open stages and galleries.

The Common Council ordered that innkeepers who wished licenses to hold performance put up a bond and make contributions to the poor.

The requirement that plays and innyard theaters be licensed, along with the other drawbacks of playing at inns and presumably along with the success of the Red Lion, led James Burbage to rent a plot of land northeast of the city walls, on property outside the jurisdiction of the city. Here he built England's second playhouse, called simply the Theatre. About all that is known of its construction is that it was wood. It soon had imitators, the most famous being the Globe (1599), essentially an amphitheater built across the Thames (again outside the city's jurisdiction), constructed with timbers of the Theatre, which had been dismantled when Burbage's lease ran out.

Admission to the theater was one penny, which allowed spectators to stand at the sides and front of the stage that jutted into the yard. An additional penny bought a seat in a covered part of the theater, and a third penny bought a more comfortable seat and a better location. It is notoriously difficult to translate prices into today's money, since some things that are inexpensive today would have been expensive in the past and vice versa—a pipeful of tobacco (imported, of course) cost a lot of money, about three pennies, and an orange (also imported) cost two or three times what a chicken cost—but perhaps we can get some idea of the low cost of the penny admission when we realize that a penny could also buy a pot of ale. An unskilled laborer made about five or sixpence a day, an artisan about twelve pence a day, and the hired actors (as opposed to the sharers in the company, such as Shakespeare) made about ten pence a performance. A printed play cost five or sixpence. Of course a visit to the theater (like a visit to a baseball game today) usually cost more than the admission since the spectator probably would also buy food and drink. Still, the low entrance fee meant that the theater was available to all except the very poorest people, rather as movies and most athletic events are today. Evidence indicates that the audience ranged from apprentices who somehow managed to scrape together the minimum entrance fee and to escape from their masters for a few hours, to prosperous members of the middle class and aristocrats who paid the additional fee for admission to the galleries.

The exact proportion of men to women cannot be determined, but women of all classes certainly were present. Theaters were open every afternoon but Sundays for much of the year, except in times of plague, when they were closed because of fear of infection. By the way, no evidence suggests the presence of toilet facilities. Presumably the patrons re-

Johannes de Witt, a Continental visitor to London, made a drawing of the Swan theater in about the year 1596. The original drawing is lost; this is Aernout van Buchell's copy of it.

lieved themselves by making a quick trip to the fields surrounding the playhouses.

There are four important sources of information about the structure of Elizabethan public playhouses—drawings, a contract, recent excavations, and stage directions in the plays. Of drawings, only the so-called de Witt drawing (c. 1596) of the Swan—really his friend Aernout van Buchell's copy of Johannes de Witt's drawing—is of much significance. The drawing, the only extant representation of the interior of an Elizabethan theater, shows an amphitheater of three tiers, with a stage jutting from a wall into the yard or center of the building. The tiers are roofed, and part of the stage is covered by a roof that projects from the rear and is supported at its front on two posts, but the groundlings, who paid a penny to stand in front of the stage or at its sides, were exposed to the sky. (Performances in such a playhouse were held only in the daytime; artificial illumination was not used.) At the rear of the stage are two massive doors; above the stage is a gallery.

The second major source of information, the contract for the Fortune (built in 1600), specifies that although the Globe (built in 1599) is to be the model, the Fortune is to be square, eighty feet outside and fifty-five inside. The stage is to be forty-three feet broad, and is to extend into the middle of the yard, i.e., it is twenty-seven and a half feet deep.

The third source of information, the 1989 excavations of the Rose (built in 1587), indicate that the Rose was fourteen-sided, about seventy-two feet in diameter with an inner yard almost fifty feet in diameter. The stage at the Rose was about sixteen feet deep, thirty-seven feet wide at the rear, and twenty-seven feet wide downstage. The relatively small dimensions and the tapering stage, in contrast to the rectangular stage in the Swan drawing, surprised theater historians and have made them more cautious in generalizing about the Elizabethan theater. Excavations at the Globe have not yielded much information, though some historians believe that the fragmentary evidence suggests a larger theater, perhaps one hundred feet in diameter.

From the fourth chief source, stage directions in the plays, one learns that entrance to the stage was by the doors at the rear (*"Enter one citizen at one door, and another at the other"*). A curtain hanging across the doorway—or a curtain hanging between the two doorways—could provide a place where a character could conceal himself, as Polonius does, when he wishes to overhear the conversation between Hamlet and Gertrude. Similarly, withdrawing a curtain from the doorway could "discover" (reveal) a character or two. Such discovery scenes are very rare in Elizabethan drama, but a good example occurs in *The Tempest* (5.1.171), where a stage direction tells us, *"Here Prospero discovers Ferdinand and Miranda playing at chess."* There was also some sort of playing space "aloft" or "above" to represent, for instance, the top of a city's walls or a room above the street. Doubtless each theater had its own peculiarities, but perhaps we can talk about a "typical" Elizabethan theater if we realize that no theater need exactly fit the description, just as no mother is the average mother with 2.7 children.

This hypothetical theater is wooden, round, or polygonal (in *Henry V* Shakespeare calls it a "wooden *O*") capable of holding some eight hundred spectators who stood in the yard around the projecting elevated stage—these spectators were the "groundlings"—and some fifteen hundred additional spectators who sat in the three roofed galleries. The stage, protected by a "shadow" or "heavens" or roof, is entered from two doors; behind the doors is the "tiring house" (attiring house, i.e., dressing room), and above the stage is some sort of gallery that may sometimes hold spectators but can be used (for example) as the bedroom from which Romeo—according to a stage direction in one text—"goeth down." Some evidence suggests that a throne can be lowered onto the platform stage, perhaps from the "shadow"; certainly characters can descend from the stage through a trap or traps into the cellar or "hell." Sometimes this space beneath the stage accommodates a sound-effects man or musician (in *Antony and Cleopatra "music of the hautboys* [oboes] *is under the stage"*) or an actor (in *Hamlet* the *"Ghost cries under the stage"*). Most characters simply walk on and off through the doors, but because there is no curtain in front of the platform, corpses will have to be carried off (Hamlet obligingly clears the stage of Polonius's corpse, when he says, "I'll lug the guts into the neighbor room"). Other characters may have fallen at the rear, where a curtain on a doorway could be drawn to conceal them.

Such may have been the "public theater," so called because its inexpensive admission made it available to a wide range of the populace. Another kind of theater has been called the "private theater" because its much greater admission charge (sixpence versus the penny for general admission at the public theater) limited its audience to the wealthy or the prodigal. The private theater was basically a large room, entirely roofed and therefore artificially illuminated, with a stage at one end. The theaters thus were distinct in two ways: One was essentially an amphitheater that catered to the general public; the other was a hall that catered to the wealthy. In 1576 a hall theater was established in Blackfriars, a Dominican priory in London that had been suppressed in 1538 and confiscated by the Crown and thus was not under the city's jurisdiction. All the actors in this Blackfriars theater were boys about eight to thirteen years old (in the public theaters similar boys played female parts; a boy Lady Macbeth played to a man Macbeth). Near the end of this section on Shakespeare's theater we will talk at some length about possible implications in this convention of using boys to play female roles, but for the moment we should say that it doubtless accounts for the relative lack of female roles in Elizabethan drama. Thus, in *A Midsummer Night's Dream*, out of twenty-one named roles, only four are female; in *Hamlet*, out of twenty-four, only two (Gertrude and Ophelia) are female. Many of Shakespeare's characters have fathers but no mothers—for instance, King Lear's daughters. We need not bring in Freud to explain the disparity; a dramatic company had only a few boys in it.

To return to the private theaters, in some of which all of the performers were children—the "eyrie of . . . little eyases" (nest of unfledged hawks—2.2.347–48) which Rosencrantz mentions when he and Guildenstern talk with Hamlet. The theater in Blackfriars had a precarious existence, and ceased operations in 1584. In 1596 James Burbage, who had already made theatrical history by building the Theatre, began to construct a second Blackfriars theater. He died in 1597, and

for several years this second Blackfriars theater was used by
a troupe of boys, but in 1608 two of Burbage's sons and five
other actors (including Shakespeare) became joint operators
of the theater, using it in the winter when the open-air Globe
was unsuitable. Perhaps such a smaller theater, roofed, artificially illuminated, and with a tradition of a wealthy audience,
exerted an influence in Shakespeare's late plays.

Performances in the private theaters may well have had in-
termissions during which music was played, but in the public
theaters the action was probably uninterrupted, flowing from
scene to scene almost without a break. Actors would enter,
speak, exit, and others would immediately enter and establish
(if necessary) the new locale by a few properties and by
words and gestures. To indicate that the scene took place at
night, a player or two would carry a torch. Here are some
samples of Shakespeare establishing the scene:

This is Illyria, lady.   (*Twelfth Night,* 1.2.2)

Well, this is the Forest of Arden.   (*As You Like It,* 2.4.14)

This castle has a pleasant seat; the air
Nimbly and sweetly recommends itself
Unto our gentle senses.   (*Macbeth,* 1.6.1–3)

The west yet glimmers with some streaks of day.
                                                        (*Macbeth,* 3.3.5)

Sometimes a speech will go far beyond evoking the minimal
setting of place and time, and will, so to speak, evoke the social world in which the characters move. For instance, early
in the first scene of *The Merchant of Venice* Salerio suggests
an explanation for Antonio's melancholy. (In the following
passage, *pageants* are decorated wagons, floats, and *cursy* is
the verb "to curtsy," or "to bow.")

Your mind is tossing on the ocean,
There where your argosies with portly sail—
Like signiors and rich burghers on the flood,

Or as it were the pageants of the sea—
Do overpeer the petty traffickers
That cursy to them, do them reverence,
As they fly by them with their woven wings.   (1.1.8–14)

Late in the nineteenth century, when Henry Irving produced
the play with elaborate illusionistic sets, the first scene
showed a ship moored in the harbor, with fruit vendors and
dock laborers, in an effort to evoke the bustling and exotic life
of Venice. But Shakespeare's words give us this exotic, rich
world of commerce in his highly descriptive language when
Salerio speaks of "argosies with portly sail" that fly with
"woven wings"; equally important, through Salerio Shakespeare conveys a sense of the orderly, hierarchical society in
which the lesser ships, "the petty traffickers," curtsy and
thereby "do . . . reverence" to their superiors, the merchant
prince's ships, which are "Like signiors and rich burghers."

On the other hand, it is a mistake to think that except for
verbal pictures the Elizabethan stage was bare. Although
Shakespeare's Chorus in *Henry V* calls the stage an "unworthy scaffold" (Prologue 1.10) and urges the spectators to
"eke out our performance with your mind" (Prologue 3.35),
there was considerable spectacle. The last act of *Macbeth,*
for instance, has five stage directions calling for *"drum and
colors,"* and another sort of appeal to the eye is indicated by
the stage direction *"Enter Macduff, with Macbeth's head."*
Some scenery and properties may have been substantial;
doubtless a throne was used, but the pillars supporting the
roof would have served for the trees on which Orlando pins
his poems in *As You Like It.*

Having talked about the public theater—"this wooden
O"—at some length, we should mention again that Shakespeare's plays were performed also in other locales. Alvin
Kernan, in *Shakespeare, the King's Playwright: Theater in
the Stuart Court 1603–1613* (1995) points out that "several
of [Shakespeare's] plays contain brief theatrical performances, set always in a court or some noble house. When
Shakespeare portrayed a theater, he did not, except for the
choruses in *Henry V,* imagine a public theater" (p. 195). (Ex-

amples include episodes in *The Taming of the Shrew*, *A Midsummer Night's Dream*, *Hamlet*, and *The Tempest*.)

A Note on the Use of Boy Actors in Female Roles

Until fairly recently, scholars were content to mention that the convention existed; they sometimes also mentioned that it continued the medieval practice of using males in female roles, and that other theaters, notably in ancient Greece and in China and Japan, also used males in female roles. (In classical Noh drama in Japan, males still play the female roles.) Prudery may have been at the root of the academic failure to talk much about the use of boy actors, or maybe there really is not much more to say than that it was a convention of a male-centered culture (Stephen Greenblatt's view, in *Shakespearean Negotiations* [1988]). Further, the very nature of a convention is that it is not thought about: Hamlet is a Dane and Julius Caesar is a Roman, but in Shakespeare's plays they speak English, and we in the audience never give this odd fact a thought. Similarly, a character may speak in the presence of others and we understand, again without thinking about it, that he or she is not heard by the figures on the stage (the aside); a character alone on the stage may speak (the soliloquy), and we do not take the character to be unhinged; in a realistic (box) set, the fourth wall, which allows us to see what is going on, is miraculously missing. The nononsense view, then, is that the boy actor was an accepted convention, accepted unthinkingly—just as today we know that Kenneth Branagh is not Hamlet, Al Pacino is not Richard III, and Denzel Washington is not the Prince of Aragon. In this view, the audience takes the performer for the role, and that is that; such is the argument we now make for race-free casting, in which African-Americans and Asians can play roles of persons who lived in medieval Denmark and ancient Rome. But gender perhaps is different, at least today. It is a matter of abundant academic study: The Elizabethan theater is now sometimes called a transvestite theater, and we hear much about cross-dressing.

Shakespeare himself in a very few passages calls attention to the use of boys in female roles. At the end of *As You Like*

It the boy who played Rosalind addresses the audience, and
says, "O men, ... if I were a woman, I would kiss as many
of you as had beards that pleased me." But this is in the Epilogue; the plot is over, and the actor is stepping out of the
play and into the audience's everyday world. A second reference to the practice of boys playing female roles occurs in
Antony and Cleopatra, when Cleopatra imagines that she and
Antony will be the subject of crude plays, her role being performed by a boy:

> The quick comedians
> Extemporally will stage us, and present
> Our Alexandrian revels: Antony
> Shall be brought drunken forth, and I shall see
> Some squeaking Cleopatra boy my greatness.   (5.2.216–20)

In a few other passages, Shakespeare is more indirect. For
instance, in *Twelfth Night* Viola, played of course by a boy,
disguises herself as a young man and seeks service in the
house of a lord. She enlists the help of a Captain, and (by
way of explaining away her voice and her beardlessness)
says,

> I'll serve this duke
> Thou shalt present me as an eunuch to him.   (1.2.55–56)

In *Hamlet*, when the players arrive in 2.2, Hamlet jokes with
the boy who plays a female role. The boy has grown since
Hamlet last saw him: "By'r Lady, your ladyship is nearer to
heaven than when I saw you last by the altitude of a cho-
pine" (a lady's thick-soled shoe). He goes on: "Pray God
your voice ... be not cracked" (434–38).

Exactly how sexual, how erotic, this material was and is,
is now much disputed. Again, the use of boys may have been
unnoticed, or rather not thought about—an unexamined
convention—by most or all spectators most of the time, perhaps *all* of the time, except when Shakespeare calls the convention to the attention of the audience, as in the passages
just quoted. Still, an occasional bit seems to invite erotic
thoughts. The clearest example is the name that Rosalind

takes in *As You Like It*, Ganymede—the beautiful youth whom Zeus abducted. Did boys dressed to play female roles carry homoerotic appeal for straight men (Lisa Jardine's view, in *Still Harping on Daughters* [1983]), or for gay men, or for some or all women in the audience? Further, when the boy actor played a woman who (for the purposes of the plot) disguised herself as a male, as Rosalind, Viola, and Portia do—so we get a boy playing a woman playing a man—what sort of appeal was generated, and for what sort of spectator?

Some scholars have argued that the convention empowered women by letting female characters display a freedom unavailable in Renaissance patriarchal society; the convention, it is said, undermined rigid gender distinctions. In this view, the convention (along with plots in which female characters for a while disguised themselves as young men) allowed Shakespeare to say what some modern gender critics say: Gender is a constructed role rather than a biological given, something we make, rather than a fixed binary opposition of male and female (see Juliet Dusinberre, in *Shakespeare and the Nature of Women* [1975]). On the other hand, some scholars have maintained that the male disguise assumed by some female characters serves only to reaffirm traditional social distinctions since female characters who don male garb (notably Portia in *The Merchant of Venice* and Rosalind in *As You Like It*) return to their female garb and at least implicitly (these critics say) reaffirm the status quo. (For this last view, see Clara Claiborne Park, in an essay in *The Woman's Part*, ed. Carolyn Ruth Swift Lenz et al. [1980].) Perhaps no one answer is right for all plays; in *As You Like It* cross-dressing empowers Rosalind, but in *Twelfth Night* cross-dressing comically traps Viola.

Shakespeare's Dramatic Language: Costumes, Gestures and Silences; Prose and Poetry

Because Shakespeare was a dramatist, not merely a poet, he worked not only with language but also with costume, sound effects, gestures, and even silences. We have already discussed some kinds of spectacle in the preceding section, and now we will begin with other aspects of visual language; a theater, after all, is literally a "place for seeing." Consider the opening stage direction in *The Tempest*, the first play in the first published collection of Shakespeare's plays: *"A tempestuous noise of thunder and Lightning heard: Enter a Shipmaster, and a Boteswain."*

Costumes: What did that shipmaster and that boatswain wear? Doubtless they wore something that identified them as men of the sea. Not much is known about the costumes that Elizabethan actors wore, but at least three points are clear: (1) many of the costumes were splendid versions of contemporary Elizabethan dress; (2) some attempts were made to approximate the dress of certain occupations and of antique or exotic characters such as Romans, Turks, and Jews; (3) some costumes indicated that the wearer was supernatural. Evidence for elaborate Elizabethan clothing can be found in the plays themselves and in contemporary comments about the "sumptuous" players who wore the discarded clothing of noblemen, as well as in account books that itemize such things as "a scarlet cloak with two broad gold laces, with gold buttons down the sides."

The attempts at approximation of the dress of certain occupations and nationalities also can be documented from the plays themselves, and it derives additional confirmation from a drawing of the first scene of Shakespeare's *Titus Andronicus*—the only extant Elizabethan picture of an identifiable episode in a play. (See pp. xxxviii–xxxix.) The drawing, probably done in 1594 or 1595, shows Queen Tamora pleading for mercy. She wears a somewhat medieval-looking robe and a crown; Titus wears a toga and a wreath, but two soldiers behind him wear costumes fairly close to Elizabethan dress. We do not know, however, if the drawing represents an actual stage production in the public theater, or perhaps a private production, or maybe only a reader's visualization of an episode. Further, there is some conflicting evidence: In *Julius Caesar* a reference is made to Caesar's doublet (a close-fitting jacket), which, if taken literally, suggests that even the protagonist did not wear Roman clothing;

and certainly the lesser characters, who are said to wear hats, did not wear Roman garb.

It should be mentioned, too, that even ordinary clothing can be symbolic: Hamlet's "inky cloak," for example, sets him apart from the brightly dressed members of Claudius's court and symbolizes his mourning; the fresh clothes that are put on King Lear partly symbolize his return to sanity. Consider, too, the removal of disguises near the end of some plays. For instance, Rosalind in *As You Like It* and Portia and Nerissa in *The Merchant of Venice* remove their male attire, thus again becoming fully themselves.

Gestures and Silences: Gestures are an important part of a dramatist's language. King Lear kneels before his daughter Cordelia for a benediction (4.7.57–59), an act of humility that contrasts with his earlier speeches banishing her and that contrasts also with a comparable gesture, his ironic kneeling before Regan (2.4.153–55). Northumberland's failure to kneel before King Richard II (3.3.71–72) speaks volumes. As

for silences, consider a moment in *Coriolanus*: Before the protagonist yields to his mother's entreaties (5.3.182), there is this stage direction: *"Holds her by the hand, silent."* Another example of "speech in dumbness" occurs in *Macbeth*, when Macduff learns that his wife and children have been murdered. He is silent at first, as Malcolm's speech indicates: "What, man! Ne'er pull your hat upon your brows. Give sorrow words" (4.3.208–09). (For a discussion of such moments, see Philip C. McGuire's *Speechless Dialect: Shakespeare's Open Silences* [1985].)

Of course when we think of Shakespeare's work, we think primarily of his language, both the poetry and the prose.

Prose: Although two of his plays (*Richard II* and *King John*) have no prose at all, about half the others have at least one quarter of the dialogue in prose, and some have notably more: *1 Henry IV* and *2 Henry IV*, about half; *As You Like It* and *Twelfth Night*, a little more than half; *Much Ado About Nothing*, more than three quarters; and *The Merry Wives of Windsor*, a little more than five sixths. We should remember that despite Molière's joke about M. Jourdain, who was amazed to learn that he spoke prose, most of us do not speak prose. Rather, we normally utter repetitive, shapeless, and often ungrammatical torrents; prose is something very different—a sort of literary imitation of speech at its most coherent.

Today we may think of prose as "natural" for drama; or even if we think that poetry is appropriate for high tragedy we may still think that prose is the right medium for comedy. Greek, Roman, and early English comedies, however, were written in verse. In fact, prose was not generally considered a literary medium in England until the late fifteenth century; Chaucer tells even his bawdy stories in verse. By the end of the 1580s, however, prose had established itself on the English comic stage. In tragedy, Marlowe made some use of prose, not simply in the speeches of clownish servants but even in the speech of a tragic hero, Doctor Faustus. Still, before Shakespeare, prose normally was used in the theater only for special circumstances: (1) letters and proclamations, to set them off from the poetic dialogue; (2) mad characters, to indicate that normal thinking has become disordered; and (3) low comedy, or speeches uttered by clowns even when they are not being comic. Shakespeare made use of these conventions, but he also went far beyond them. Sometimes he begins a scene in prose and then shifts into verse as the emotion is heightened; or conversely, he may shift from verse to prose when a speaker is lowering the emotional level, as when Brutus speaks in the Forum.

Shakespeare's prose usually is not prosaic. Hamlet's prose includes not only small talk with Rosencrantz and Guildenstern but also princely reflections on "What a piece of work is a man" (2.2.312). In conversation with Ophelia, he shifts from light talk in verse to a passionate prose denunciation of women (3.1.103), though the shift to prose here is perhaps also intended to suggest the possibility of madness. (Consult Brian Vickers, *The Artistry of Shakespeare's Prose* [1968].)

Poetry: Drama in rhyme in England goes back to the Middle Ages, but by Shakespeare's day rhyme no longer dominated poetic drama; a finer medium, blank verse (strictly speaking, unrhymed lines of ten syllables, with the stress on every second syllable) had been adopted. But before looking at unrhymed poetry, a few things should be said about the chief uses of rhyme in Shakespeare's plays. (1) A couplet (a pair of rhyming lines) is sometimes used to convey emotional heightening at the end of a blank verse speech; (2) characters sometimes speak a couplet as they leave the stage, suggesting closure; (3) except in the latest plays, scenes fairly often conclude with a couplet, and sometimes, as in *Richard II*, 2.1.145–46, the entrance of a new character within a scene is preceded by a couplet, which wraps up the earlier portion of that scene; (4) speeches of two characters occasionally are linked by rhyme, most notably in *Romeo and Juliet*, 1.5.95–108, where the lovers speak a sonnet between them; elsewhere a taunting reply occasionally rhymes with the previous speaker's last line; (5) speeches with sententious or gnomic remarks are sometimes in rhyme, as in the duke's speech in *Othello* (1.3.199–206); (6) speeches of sardonic mockery are sometimes in rhyme—for example, Iago's speech on women in *Othello* (2.1.146–58)—and they sometimes conclude with an emphatic couplet, as in Bolingbroke's speech on comforting words in *Richard II* (1.3.301–2); (7) some characters are associated with rhyme, such as the fairies in *A Midsummer Night's Dream*; (8) in the early plays, especially *The Comedy of Errors* and *The Taming of the Shrew*, comic scenes that in later plays would be in prose are in jingling rhymes; (9) prologues, choruses, plays-within-the-play, inscriptions, vows, epilogues, and so on are often in rhyme, and the songs in the plays are rhymed.

Neither prose nor rhyme immediately comes to mind when we first think of Shakespeare's medium: It is blank verse, unrhymed iambic pentameter. (In a mechanically exact line there are five iambic feet. An iambic foot consists of two syllables, the second accented, as in *away*; five feet make a pentameter line. Thus, a strict line of iambic pentameter contains ten syllables, the even syllables being stressed more heavily than the odd syllables. Fortunately, Shakespeare usually varies the line somewhat.) The first speech in *A Midsummer*

Night's Dream, spoken by Duke Theseus to his betrothed, is
an example of blank verse:

> Now, fair Hippolyta, our nuptial hour
> Draws on apace. Four happy days bring in
> Another moon; but, O, methinks, how slow
> This old moon wanes! She lingers my desires,
> Like to a stepdame, or a dowager,
> Long withering out a young man's revenue.   (1.1.1–6)

As this passage shows, Shakespeare's blank verse is not mechanically unvarying. Though the predominant foot is the
iamb (as in *apace* or *desires*), there are numerous variations.
In the first line the stress can be placed on "fair," as the regular metrical pattern suggests, but it is likely that "Now" gets
almost as much emphasis; probably in the second line
"Draws" is more heavily emphasized than "on," giving us a
trochee (a stressed syllable followed by an unstressed one);
and in the fourth line each word in the phrase "This old
moon wanes" is probably stressed fairly heavily, conveying
by two spondees (two feet, each of two stresses) the oppres-
sive tedium that Theseus feels.

   In Shakespeare's early plays much of the blank verse is
end-stopped (that is, it has a heavy pause at the end of each
line), but he later developed the ability to write iambic pentameter verse paragraphs (rather than lines) that give the il-
lusion of speech. His chief techniques are (1) enjambing, i.e.,
running the thought beyond the single line, as in the first
three lines of the speech just quoted; (2) occasionally replacing an iamb with another foot; (3) varying the position of the
chief pause (the caesura) within a line; (4) adding an occasional unstressed syllable at the end of a line, traditionally
called a feminine ending; (5) and beginning or ending a
speech with a half line.

   Shakespeare's mature blank verse has much of the rhyth-
mic flexibility of his prose; both the language, though richly
figurative and sometimes dense, and the syntax seem natural.
It is also often highly appropriate to a particular character.
Consider, for instance, this speech from *Hamlet*, in which
Claudius, King of Denmark ("the Dane"), speaks to Laertes:

And now, Laertes, what's the news with you?
You told us of some suit. What is't, Laertes?
You cannot speak of reason to the Dane
And lose your voice. What wouldst thou beg, Laertes,
That shall not be my offer, not thy asking? (1.2.42–46)

Notice the short sentences and the repetition of the name "Laertes," to whom the speech is addressed. Notice, too, the shift from the royal "us" in the second line to the more intimate "my" in the last line, and from "you" in the first three lines to the more intimate "thou" and "thy" in the last two lines. Claudius knows how to ingratiate himself with Laertes.

For a second example of the flexibility of Shakespeare's blank verse, consider a passage from *Macbeth*. Distressed by the doctor's inability to cure Lady Macbeth and by the imminent battle, Macbeth addresses some of his remarks to the doctor and others to the servant who is arming him. The entire speech, with its pauses, interruptions, and irresolution (in "Pull't off, I say," Macbeth orders the servant to remove the armor that the servant has been putting on him), catches Macbeth's disintegration. (In the first line, *physic* means "medicine," and in the fourth and fifth lines, *cast the water* means "analyze the urine.")

Throw physic to the dogs, I'll none of it.
Come, put mine armor on. Give me my staff.
Seyton, send out.—Doctor, the thanes fly from me.—
Come, sir, dispatch. If thou couldst, doctor, cast
The water of my land, find her disease
And purge it to a sound and pristine health,
I would applaud thee to the very echo,
That should applaud again.—Pull't off, I say.—
What rhubarb, senna, or what purgative drug,
Would scour these English hence? Hear'st thou of them?
(5.3.47–56)

Blank verse, then, can be much more than unrhymed iambic pentameter, and even within a single play Shakespeare's blank verse often consists of several styles, depending on the speaker and on the speaker's emotion at the moment.

The Play Text as a Collaboration

Shakespeare's fellow dramatist Ben Jonson reported that the actors said of Shakespeare, "In his writing, whatsoever he penned, he never blotted out line," i.e., never crossed out material and revised his work while composing. None of Shakespeare's plays survives in manuscript (with the possible exception of a scene in *Sir Thomas More*), so we cannot fully evaluate the comment, but in a few instances the published work clearly shows that he revised his manuscript. Consider the following passage (shown here in facsimile) from the best early text of *Romeo and Juliet*, the Second Quarto (1599):

Ro. Would I were sleepe and peace so sweet to rest
The grey eyde morne smiles on the frowning night,
Checkring the Easterne Clouds with streaks of light,
And darknesse fleckted like a drunkard reeles,
From forth daies pathway, made by *Tytans* wheeles.
Hence will I to my ghostly Friers close cell,
His helpe to craue, and my deare hap to tell.

                                                    Exit.

Enter Frier alone with a basket.   (night,
Fri. The grey-eyed morne smiles on the frowning
Checking the Easterne clowdes with streaks of light:
And fleckeld darknesse like a drunkard reeles,
From forth daies path, and *Titans* burning wheeles:
Now ere the sun aduance his burning eie,

Romeo rather elaborately tells us that the sun at dawn is dispelling the night (morning is smiling, the eastern clouds are checked with light, and the sun's chariot—Titan's wheels—advances), and he will seek out his spiritual father, the Friar. He exits and, oddly, the Friar enters and says pretty much the same thing about the sun. Both speakers say that "the gray-eyed morn smiles on the frowning night," but there are small differences, perhaps having more to do with the business of printing the book than with the author's composition: For Romeo's "checkring," "fleckted," and "pathway," we get the Friar's "checking," "fleckeld," and "path." (Notice, by the way, the inconsistency in Elizabethan spelling: Romeo's "clouds" become the Friar's "clowdes.")

Both versions must have been in the printer's copy, and it seems safe to assume that both were in Shakespeare's manuscript. He must have written one version—let's say he first wrote Romeo's closing lines for this scene—and then he decided, no, it's better to give this lyrical passage to the Friar, as the opening of a new scene, but he neglected to delete the first version. Editors must make a choice, and they may feel that the reasonable thing to do is to print the text as Shakespeare intended it. But how can we know what he intended? Almost all modern editors delete the lines from Romeo's speech, and retain the Friar's lines. They don't do this because they know Shakespeare's intention, however. They give the lines to the Friar because the first published version (1597) of *Romeo and Juliet* gives only the Friar's version, and this text (though in many ways inferior to the 1599 text) is thought to derive from the memory of some actors, that is, it is thought to represent a performance, not just a script. Maybe during the course of rehearsals Shakespeare—an actor as well as an author—unilaterally decided that the Friar should speak the lines; if so (remember that we don't know this to be a fact) his final intention was to give the speech to the Friar. Maybe, however, the actors talked it over and settled on the Friar, with or without Shakespeare's approval. On the other hand, despite the 1597 version, one might argue (if only weakly) on behalf of giving the lines to Romeo rather than to the Friar, thus: (1) Romeo's comment on the coming of the daylight emphasizes his separation from Juliet, and (2) the figurative language seems more appropriate to Romeo than to the Friar. Having said this, in the Signet edition we have decided in this instance to draw on the evidence provided by earlier text and to give the lines to the Friar, on the grounds that since Q1 reflects a production, in the theater (at least on one occasion) the lines were spoken by the Friar.

A playwright sold a script to a theatrical company. The script thus belonged to the company, not the author, and author and company alike must have regarded this script not as a literary work but as the basis for a play that the actors would create on the stage. We speak of Shakespeare as the author of the plays, but readers should bear in mind that the texts they read, even when derived from a single text, such as the First Folio (1623), are inevitably the collaborative work not simply of Shakespeare with his company— doubtless during rehearsals the actors would suggest alterations—but also with other forces of the age. One force was governmental censorship. In 1606 parliament passed "an Act to restrain abuses of players," prohibiting the utterance of oaths and the name of God. So where the earliest text of *Othello* gives us "By heaven" (3.3.106), the first Folio gives "Alas," presumably reflecting the compliance of stage practice with the law. Similarly, the 1623 version of *King Lear* omits the oath "Fut"(probably from "By God's foot") at 1.2.142, again presumably reflecting the line as it was spoken on the stage. Editors who seek to give the reader the play that Shakespeare initially conceived—the "authentic" play conceived by the solitary Shakespeare—probably will restore the missing oaths and references to God. Other editors, who see the play as a collaborative work, a construction made not only by Shakespeare but also by actors and compositors and even government censors, may claim that what counts is the play as it was actually performed. Such editors regard the censored text as legitimate, since it is the play that was (presumably) finally put on. A performed text, they argue, has more historical reality than a text produced by an editor who has sought to get at what Shakespeare initially wrote. In this view, the text of a play is rather like the script of a film; the script is not the film, and the play text is not the performed play. Even if we want to talk about the play that Shakespeare "intended," we will find ourselves talking about a script that he handed over to a company with the intention that it be implemented by actors. The "intended" play is the one that the actors—we might almost say "society"—would help to construct.

Further, it is now widely held that a play is also the work of readers and spectators, who do not simply receive meaning, but who create it when they respond to the play. This idea is fully in accord with contemporary post-structuralist critical thinking, notably Roland Barthes's "The Death of the Author," in *Image-Music-Text* (1977) and Michel Foucault's "What Is an Author?," in *The Foucault Reader* (1984). The gist of the idea is that an author is not an isolated genius; rather, authors are subject to the politics and other social structures of their age. A dramatist especially is a worker in a collaborative project, working most obviously with actors—parts may be written for particular actors—but working also with the audience. Consider the words of Samuel Johnson, written to be spoken by the actor David Garrick at the opening of a theater in 1747:

> The stage but echoes back the public voice;
> The drama's laws, the drama's patrons give,
> For we that live to please, must please to live.

The audience—the public taste as understood by the playwright—helps to determine what the play is. Moreover, even members of the public who are not part of the playwright's immediate audience may exert an influence through censorship. We have already glanced at governmental censorship, but there are also other kinds. Take one of Shakespeare's most beloved characters, Falstaff, who appears in three of Shakespeare's plays, the two parts of *Henry IV* and *The Merry Wives of Windsor*. He appears with this name in the earliest printed version of the first of these plays, *1 Henry IV*, but we know that Shakespeare originally called him (after an historical figure) Sir John Oldcastle. Oldcastle appears in Shakespeare's source (partly reprinted in the Signet edition of *1 Henry IV*), and a trace of the name survives in Shakespeare's play, 1.2.43–44, where Prince Hal punningly addresses Falstaff as "my old lad of the castle." But for some reason—perhaps because the family of the historical Oldcastle complained—Shakespeare had to change the name. In short, the play as we have it was (at least in this detail) subject to some sort of censorship. If we think that a text should present what we take to be the author's intention, we probably will want to replace *Falstaff* with *Oldcastle*. But if we recognize that a play is a collaboration, we may welcome the change, even if it was forced on Shakespeare. Somehow *Falstaff*, with its hint of *false-staff*, i.e., inadequate prop, seems just right for this fat knight who, to our delight, entertains the young prince with untruths. We can go as far as saying that, at least so far as a play is concerned, an insistence on the author's original intention (even if we could know it) can sometimes impoverish the text.

The tiny example of Falstaff's name illustrates the point that the text we read is inevitably only a version—something in effect produced by the collaboration of the playwright with his actors, audiences, compositors, and editors—of a fluid text that Shakespeare once wrote, just as the *Hamlet* that we see on the screen starring Kenneth Branagh is not the *Hamlet* that Shakespeare saw in an open-air playhouse starring Richard Burbage. *Hamlet* itself, as we shall note in a moment, also exists in several versions. It is not surprising that there is now much talk about the *instability* of Shakespeare's texts.

Because he was not only a playwright but was also an actor and a shareholder in a theatrical company, Shakespeare probably was much involved with the translation of the play from a manuscript to a stage production. He may or may not have done some rewriting during rehearsals, and he may or may not have been happy with cuts that were made. Some plays, notably *Hamlet* and *King Lear*, are so long that it is most unlikely that the texts we read were acted in their entirety. Further, for both of these plays we have more than one early text that demands consideration. In *Hamlet*, the Second Quarto (1604) includes some two hundred lines not found in the Folio (1623). Among the passages missing from the Folio are two of Hamlet's reflective speeches, the "dram of evil" speech (1.4.13–38) and "How all occasions do inform against me" (4.4.32–66). Since the Folio has more numerous and often fuller stage directions, it certainly looks as though in the Folio we get a theatrical version of the play, a text whose cuts were probably made—this is only a hunch, of course— not because Shakespeare was changing his conception of Hamlet but because the playhouse demanded a modified play. (The problem is complicated, since the Folio not only cuts some of the Quarto but adds some material. Various explanations have been offered.)

Or take an example from *King Lear*. In the First and Second Quarto (1608, 1619), the final speech of the play is given to Albany, Lear's surviving son-in-law, but in the First Folio version (1623), the speech is given to Edgar. The Quarto version is in accord with tradition—usually the highest-ranking character in a tragedy speaks the final words. Why does the Folio give the speech to Edgar? One possible answer is this: The Folio version omits some of Albany's speeches in earlier scenes, so perhaps it was decided (by Shakespeare? by the players?) not to give the final lines to so pale a character. In fact, the discrepancies are so many between the two texts, that some scholars argue we do not simply have texts showing different theatrical productions. Rather, these scholars say, Shakespeare substantially revised the play, and we really have two versions of *King Lear* (and of *Othello* also, say some)—two different plays—not simply two texts, each of which is in some ways imperfect.

In this view, the 1608 version of *Lear* may derive from Shakespeare's manuscript, and the 1623 version may derive from his later revision. The Quartos have almost three hundred lines not in the Folio, and the Folio has about a hundred lines not in the Quartos. It used to be held that all the texts were imperfect in various ways and from various causes—some passages in the Quartos were thought to have been set from a manuscript that was not entirely legible, other passages were thought to have been set by a compositor who was new to setting plays, and still other passages were thought to have been provided by an actor who misremembered some of the lines. This traditional view held that an editor must draw on the Quartos and the Folio in order to get Shakespeare's "real" play. The new argument holds (although not without considerable strain) that we have two authentic plays, Shakespeare's early version (in the Quarto) and Shakespeare's—or his theatrical company's—revised version (in the Folio). Not only theatrical demands but also Shakespeare's own artistic sense, it is argued, called for extensive revisions. Even the titles vary: Q1 is called *True Chronicle Historie of the life and death of King Lear and his three*

Daughters, whereas the Folio text is called *The Tragedie of King Lear*. To combine the two texts in order to produce what the editor thinks is the play that Shakespeare intended to write is, according to this view, to produce a text that is false to the history of the play. If the new view is correct, and we do have texts of two distinct versions of *Lear* rather than two imperfect versions of one play, it supports in a textual way the poststructuralist view that we cannot possibly have an unmediated vision of (in this case) a play by Shakespeare; we can only recognize a plurality of visions.

Editing Texts

Though eighteen of his plays were published during his lifetime, Shakespeare seems never to have supervised their publication. There is nothing unusual here; when a playwright sold a play to a theatrical company he surrendered his ownership to it. Normally a company would not publish the play, because to publish it meant to allow competitors to acquire the piece. Some plays did get published: Apparently hard-up actors sometimes pieced together a play for a publisher; sometimes a company in need of money sold a play; and sometimes a company allowed publication of a play that no longer drew audiences. That Shakespeare did not concern himself with publication is not remarkable; of his contemporaries, only Ben Jonson carefully supervised the publication of his own plays.

In 1623, seven years after Shakespeare's death, John Heminges and Henry Condell (two senior members of Shakespeare's company, who had worked with him for about twenty years) collected his plays—published and unpublished—into a large volume, of a kind called a folio. (A folio is a volume consisting of large sheets that have been folded once, each sheet thus making two leaves, or four pages. The size of the page of course depends on the size of the sheet—a folio can range in height from twelve to sixteen inches, and in width from eight to eleven; the pages in the 1623 edition of Shakespeare, commonly called the First Folio, are approximately thirteen inches tall and eight inches wide.) The eighteen plays published during Shakespeare's lifetime had been issued one play per volume in small formats called quartos. (Each sheet in a quarto has been folded twice, making four leaves, or eight pages, each page being about nine inches tall and seven inches wide, roughly the size of a large paperback.)

Heminges and Condell suggest in an address "To the great variety of readers" that the republished plays are presented in better form than in the quartos:

> Before you were abused with diverse stolen and surreptitious copies, maimed and deformed by the frauds and stealths of injurious impostors that exposed them; even those, are now offered to your view cured and perfect of their limbs, and all the rest absolute in their numbers, as he [i.e., Shakespeare] conceived them.

There is a good deal of truth to this statement, but some of the quarto versions are better than others; some are in fact preferable to the Folio text.

Whoever was assigned to prepare the texts for publication in the first Folio seems to have taken the job seriously and yet not to have performed it with uniform care. The sources of the texts seem to have been, in general, good unpublished copies or the best published copies. The first play in the collection, *The Tempest*, is divided into acts and scenes, has unusually full stage directions and descriptions of spectacle, and concludes with a list of the characters, but the editor was not able (or willing) to present all of the succeeding texts so fully dressed. Later texts occasionally show signs of carelessness: in one scene of *Much Ado About Nothing* the names of actors, instead of characters, appear as speech prefixes, as they had in the Quarto, which the Folio reprints; proofreading throughout the Folio is spotty and apparently was done without reference to the printer's copy; the pagination of *Hamlet* jumps from 156 to 257. Further, the proofreading was done while the presses continued to print, so that each play in each volume contains a mix of corrected and uncorrected pages.

Modern editors of Shakespeare must first select their copy; no problem if the play exists only in the Folio, but a considerable problem if the relationship between a Quarto and the Folio—or an early Quarto and a later one—is unclear. In the case of *Romeo and Juliet*, the First Quarto (Q1), published in 1597, is vastly inferior to the Second (Q2), published in 1599. The basis of Q1 apparently is a version put together from memory by some actors. Not surprisingly, it garbles many passages and is much shorter than Q2. On the other hand, occasionally Q1 makes better sense than Q2. For instance, near the end of the play, when the parents have assembled and learned of the deaths of Romeo and Juliet, in Q2 the Prince says (5.3.208–9),

Come, *Montague;* for thou art early vp
To see thy sonne and heire, now earling downe.

The last three words of this speech surely do not make sense, and many editors turn to Q1, which instead of "now earling downe" has "more early downe." Some modern editors take only "early" from Q1, and print "now early down"; others take "more early," and print "more early down." Further, Q1 (though, again, quite clearly a garbled and abbreviated text) includes some stage directions that are not found in Q2, and today many editors who base their text on Q2 are glad to add these stage directions, because the directions help to give us a sense of what the play looked like on Shakespeare's stage. Thus, in 4.3.58, after Juliet drinks the potion, Q1 gives us this stage direction, not in Q2: *"She falls upon her bed within the curtains."*

In short, an editor's decisions do not end with the choice of a single copy text. First of all, editors must reckon with Elizabethan spelling. If they are not producing a facsimile, they probably modernize the spelling, but ought they to preserve the old forms of words that apparently were pronounced quite unlike their modern forms—*lanthorn, alablaster*? If they preserve these forms are they really preserving Shakespeare's forms or perhaps those of a compositor in the printing house? What is one to do when one finds *lanthorn* and *lantern* in adjacent lines? (The editors of this series in general, but not invariably, assume that words should be spelled in their modern form, unless, for instance, a rhyme is involved.) Elizabethan punctuation, too, presents problems. For example, in the First Folio, the only text for the play, Macbeth rejects his wife's idea that he can wash the blood from his hand (2.2.60–62):

> No: this my Hand will rather
> The multitudinous Seas incarnardine,
> Making the Greene one, Red.

Obviously an editor will remove the superfluous capitals, and will probably alter the spelling to "incarnadine," but what about the comma before "Red"? If we retain the comma, Macbeth is calling the sea "the green one." If we drop the comma, Macbeth is saying that his bloody hand will make the sea ("the Green") *uniformly* red.

An editor will sometimes have to change more than spelling and punctuation. Macbeth says to his wife (1.7.46–47):

> I dare do àll that may become a man,
> Who dares no more, is none.

For two centuries editors have agreed that the second line is unsatisfactory, and have emended "no" to "do": "Who dares do more is none." But when in the same play (4.2.21–22) Ross says that fearful persons

> Floate vpon a wilde and violent Sea
> Each way, and moue,

need we emend the passage? On the assumption that the compositor misread the manuscript, some editors emend "each way, and move" to "and move each way"; others emend "move" to "none" (i.e., "Each way and none"). Other editors, however, let the passage stand as in the original. The editors of the Signet Classic Shakespeare have restrained themselves from making abundant emendations. In their minds they hear Samuel Johnson on the dangers of emendation: "I have adopted the Roman sentiment, that it is more honorable to save a citizen than to kill an enemy." Some departures (in addition to spelling, punctuation, and lineation) from the copy text have of course been made, but the original readings are listed in a note following the play, so that readers can evaluate the changes for themselves.

Following tradition, the editors of the Signet Classic Shakespeare have prefaced each play with a list of characters, and throughout the play have regularized the names of the speakers. Thus, in our text of *Romeo and Juliet*, all speeches by Juliet's mother are prefixed "Lady Capulet," although the 1599 Quarto of the play, which provides our copy text, uses at various points seven speech tags for this one character: *Capu. Wi.* (i.e., Capulet's wife), *Ca. Wi., Wi., Wife, Old La.* (i.e., Old Lady), *La.,* and *Mo.* (i.e., Mother). Similarly, in *All's Well That Ends Well*, the character whom we regularly call "Countess" is in the Folio (the copy text) variously identified as *Mother, Countess, Old Countess, Lady,* and *Old Lady*. Admittedly there is some loss in regularizing, since the various prefixes may give us a hint of the way Shakespeare (or a scribe who copied Shakespeare's manuscript) was thinking of the character in a particular scene— for instance, as a mother, or as an old lady. But too much can be made of these differing prefixes, since the social relationships implied are *not* always relevant to the given scene.

We have also added line numbers and in many cases act and scene divisions as well as indications of locale at the beginning of scenes. The Folio divided most of the plays into acts and some into scenes. Early eighteenth-century editors increased the divisions. These divisions, which provide a convenient way of referring to passages in the plays, have been retained, but when not in the text chosen as the basis for the Signet Classic text they are enclosed within square brackets, [ ], to indicate that they are editorial additions. Similarly, though no play of Shakespeare's was equipped with indications of the locale at the heads of scene divisions, locales have here been added in square brackets for the convenience of readers, who lack the information that costumes, properties, gestures, and scenery afford to spectators. Spectators can tell at a glance they are in the throne room, but without an editorial indication the reader may be puzzled for a while. It should be mentioned, incidentally, that there are a few authentic stage directions—perhaps Shakespeare's, perhaps a prompter's—that suggest locales, such as *"Enter Brutus in his orchard,"* and *"They go up into the Senate house."* It is hoped that the bracketed additions in the Signet text will provide readers with the sort of help provided by these two authentic directions, but it is equally hoped that the reader will remember that the stage was not loaded with scenery.

Shakespeare on the Stage

Each volume in the Signet Classic Shakespeare includes a brief stage (and sometimes film) history of the play. When we read about earlier productions, we are likely to find them eccentric, obviously wrongheaded—for instance, Nahum Tate's version of *King Lear*, with a happy ending, which held the stage for about a century and a half, from the late seventeenth century until the end of the first quarter of the nineteenth. We see engravings of David Garrick, the greatest actor of the eighteenth century, in eighteenth-century garb as King Lear, and we smile, thinking how absurd the production must have been. If we are more thoughtful, we say, with the English novelist L. P. Hartley, "The past is a foreign country: they do things differently there." But if the eighteenth-century staging is a foreign country, what of the plays of the late sixteenth and seventeenth centuries? A foreign language, a foreign theater, a foreign audience.

Probably all viewers of Shakespeare's plays, beginning with Shakespeare himself, at times have been unhappy with the plays on the stage. Consider three comments about production that we find in the plays themselves, which suggest Shakespeare's concerns. The Chorus in *Henry V* complains that the heroic story cannot possibly be adequately staged:

> But pardon, gentles all,
> The flat unraisèd spirits that hath dared
> On this unworthy scaffold to bring forth
> So great an object. Can this cockpit hold
> The vasty fields of France? Or may we cram
> Within this wooden *O* the very casques

That did affright the air at Agincourt?

. . . .

Piece out our imperfections with your thoughts.

(Prologue 1.8–14,23)

Second, here are a few sentences (which may or may not represent Shakespeare's own views) from Hamlet's longish lecture to the players:

Speak the speech, I pray you, as I pronounced it to you, trippingly on the tongue. But if you mouth it, as many of our players do, I had as lief the town crier spoke my lines. . . . O, it offends me to the soul to hear a robustious periwig-pated fellow tear a passion to tatters, to very rags, to split the ears of the groundlings. . . . And let those that play your clowns speak no more than is set down for them, for there be of them that will themselves laugh, to set on some quantity of barren spectators to laugh too, though in the meantime some necessary question of the play be then to be considered. That's villainous and shows a most pitiful ambition in the fool that uses it. (3.2.1–47)

Finally, we can quote again from the passage cited earlier in this introduction, concerning the boy actors who played the female roles. Cleopatra imagines with horror a theatrical version of her activities with Antony:

            The quick comedians
Extemporally will stage us, and present
Our Alexandrian revels: Antony
Shall be brought drunken forth, and I shall see
Some squeaking Cleopatra boy my greatness
I' th' posture of a whore.   (5.2.216–21)

It is impossible to know how much weight to put on such passages—perhaps Shakespeare was just being modest about his theater's abilities—but it is easy enough to think that he was unhappy with some aspects of Elizabethan production. Probably no production can fully satisfy a playwright, and for that matter, few productions can fully satisfy *us;* we regret this or that cut, this or that way of costuming the play, this or that bit of business.

One's first thought may be this: Why don't they just do "authentic" Shakespeare, "straight" Shakespeare, the play as Shakespeare wrote it? But as we read the plays—words written to be performed—it sometimes becomes clear that we do not know *how* to perform them. For instance, in *Antony and Cleopatra* Antony, the Roman general who has succumbed to Cleopatra and to Egyptian ways, says, "The nobleness of life / Is to do thus" (1.1.36–37). But what is "thus"? Does Antony at this point embrace Cleopatra? Does he embrace and kiss her? (There are, by the way, very few scenes of kissing on Shakespeare's stage, possibly because boys played the female roles.) Or does he make a sweeping gesture, indicating the Egyptian way of life?

This is not an isolated example; the plays are filled with lines that call for gestures, but we are not sure what the gestures should be. *Interpretation* is inevitable. Consider a passage in *Hamlet*. In 3.1, Polonius persuades his daughter, Ophelia, to talk to Hamlet while Polonius and Claudius eavesdrop. The two men conceal themselves, and Hamlet encounters Ophelia. At 3.1.131 Hamlet suddenly says to her, "Where's your father?" Why does Hamlet, apparently out of nowhere—they have not been talking about Polonius—ask this question? Is this an example of the "antic disposition" (fantastic behavior) that Hamlet earlier (1.5.172) had told Horatio and others—including us—he would display? That is, is the question about the whereabouts of her father a seemingly irrational one, like his earlier question (3.1.103) to Ophelia, "Ha, ha! Are you honest?" Or, on the other hand, has Hamlet (as in many productions) suddenly glimpsed Polonius's foot protruding from beneath a drapery at the rear? That is, does Hamlet ask the question because he has suddenly seen something suspicious and now is testing Ophelia? (By the way, in productions that do give Hamlet a physical cue, it is almost always Polonius rather than Claudius who provides the clue. This itself is an act of interpretation on the part of the director.) Or (a third possibility) does Hamlet get a clue from Ophelia, who inadvertently betrays the spies by nervously glancing at their place of hiding? This is the interpretation used in the BBC television version, where Ophelia glances in fear toward the hiding place just after Hamlet says "Why wouldst thou be a breeder of sinners?" (121–22). Hamlet, realizing that he is being observed, glances here and there *before* he asks "Where's your father?" The question thus is a climax to what he has been doing while speaking the preceding lines. Or (a fourth interpretation) does Hamlet suddenly, without the aid of any clue whatsoever, intuitively (insightfully, mysteriously, wonderfully) sense that someone is spying? Directors must decide, of course—and so must readers.

Recall, too, the preceding discussion of the texts of the plays, which argued that the texts—though they seem to be before us in permanent black on white—are unstable. The Signet text of *Hamlet*, which draws on the Second Quarto (1604) and the First Folio (1623) is considerably longer than any version staged in Shakespeare's time. Our version, even if spoken very briskly and played without any intermission, would take close to four hours, far beyond "the two hours' traffic of our stage" mentioned in the Prologue to *Romeo and Juliet*. (There are a few contemporary references to the duration of a play, but none mentions more than three hours.) Of Shakespeare's plays, only *The Comedy of Errors*, *Macbeth*, and *The Tempest* can be done in less than three hours without cutting. And even if we take a play that exists only in a short text, *Macbeth*, we cannot claim that we are experiencing the very play that Shakespeare conceived, partly because some of the Witches' songs almost surely are non-Shakespearean additions, and partly because we are not willing to watch the play performed without an intermission and with boys in the female roles.

Further, as the earlier discussion of costumes mentioned, the plays apparently were given chiefly in contemporary, that is, in Elizabethan dress. If today we give them in the costumes that Shakespeare probably saw, the plays seem not contemporary but curiously dated. Yet if we use our own dress, we find lines of dialogue that are at odds with what we see; we may feel that the language, so clearly not our own, is inappropriate coming out of people in today's dress. A common solution, incidentally, has been to set the plays in the nineteenth century, on the grounds that this attractively distances the plays (gives them a degree of foreignness, allowing for interesting costumes) and yet doesn't put them into a museum world of Elizabethan England.

Inevitably our productions are adaptations, *our* adaptations, and inevitably they will look dated, not in a century but in twenty years, or perhaps even in a decade. Still, we cannot escape from our own conceptions. As the director Peter Brook has said, in *The Empty Space* (1968):

> It is not only the hair-styles, costumes and make-ups that look dated. All the different elements of staging—the shorthands of behavior that stand for emotions; gestures, gesticulations and tones of voice—are all fluctuating on an invisible stock exchange all the time. . . . A living theatre that thinks it can stand aloof from anything as trivial as fashion will wilt. (p. 16)

As Brook indicates, it is through today's hairstyles, costumes, makeup, gestures, gesticulations, tones of voice—this includes our *conception* of earlier hairstyles, costumes, and so forth if we stage the play in a period other than our own—that we inevitably stage the plays.

It is a truism that every age invents its own Shakespeare, just as, for instance, every age has invented its own classical world. Our view of ancient Greece, a slave-holding society in which even free Athenian women were severely circumscribed, does not much resemble the Victorians' view of ancient Greece as a glorious democracy, just as, perhaps, our view of Victorianism itself does not much resemble theirs. We cannot claim that the Shakespeare on our stage is the true Shakespeare, but in our stage productions we find a Shakespeare that speaks to us, a Shakespeare that our ancestors doubtless did not know but one that seems to us to be the true Shakespeare—at least for a while.

Our age is remarkable for the wide variety of kinds of staging that it uses for Shakespeare, but one development deserves special mention. This is the now common practice of race-blind or color-blind or nontraditional casting, which allows persons who are not white to play in Shakespeare. Previously blacks performing in Shakespeare were limited to a

mere three roles, Othello, Aaron (in *Titus Andronicus*), and
the Prince of Morocco (in *The Merchant of Venice*), and
there were no roles at all for Asians. Indeed, African-
Americans rarely could play even one of these three roles,
since they were not welcome in white companies. Ira
Aldridge (c.1806–1867), a black actor of undoubted talent,
was forced to make his living by performing Shakespeare in
England and in Europe, where he could play not only
Othello but also—in whiteface—other tragic roles such as
King Lear. Paul Robeson (1898–1976) made theatrical history when he played Othello in London in 1930, and there
was some talk about bringing the production to the United
States, but there was more talk about whether American audiences would tolerate the sight of a black man—a real black
man, not a white man in blackface—kissing and then killing
a white woman. The idea was tried out in summer stock in
1942, the reviews were enthusiastic, and in the following
year Robeson opened on Broadway in a production that ran
an astounding 296 performances. An occasional all-black
company sometimes performed Shakespeare's plays, but
otherwise blacks (and other minority members) were in effect shut out from performing Shakespeare. Only since about
1970 has it been common for nonwhites to play major roles
along with whites. Thus, in a 1996–97 production of *Antony
and Cleopatra*, a white Cleopatra, Vanessa Redgrave, played
opposite a black Antony, David Harewood. Multiracial casting is now especially common at the New York Shakespeare
Festival, founded in 1954 by Joseph Papp, and in England,
where even siblings such as Claudio and Isabella in *Measure
for Measure* or Lear's three daughters may be of different
races. Probably most viewers today soon stop worrying about
the lack of realism, and move beyond the color of the performers' skin to the quality of the performance.

Nontraditional casting is not only a matter of color or race;
it includes sex. In the past, occasionally a distinguished
woman of the theater has taken on a male role—Sarah
Bernhardt (1844–1923) as Hamlet is perhaps the most famous example—but such performances were widely regarded as eccentric. Although today there have been some
performances involving cross-dressing (a drag *As You Like It*

staged by the National Theatre in England in 1966 and in the United States in 1974 has achieved considerable fame in the annals of stage history), what is more interesting is the casting of women in roles that traditionally are male but that need not be. Thus, a 1993–94 English production of *Henry V* used a woman—*not* cross-dressed—in the role of the governor of Harfleur. According to Peter Holland, who reviewed the production in *Shakespeare Survey* 48 (1995), "having a female Governor of Harfleur feminized the city and provided a direct response to the horrendous threat of rape and murder that Henry had offered, his language and her body in direct connection and opposition" (p. 210). Ten years from now the device may not play so effectively, but today it speaks to us. Shakespeare, born in the Elizabethan Age, has been dead nearly four hundred years, yet he is, as Ben Jonson said, "not of an age but for all time." We must understand, however, that he is "for all time" precisely because each age finds in his abundance something for itself and something of itself.

And here we come back to two issues discussed earlier in this introduction—the instability of the text and, curiously, the Bacon/Oxford heresy concerning the authorship of the plays. *Of course* Shakespeare wrote the plays, and we should daily fall on our knees to thank him for them—and yet there is something to the idea that he is not their only author. Every editor, every director and actor, and every reader to some degree shapes them, too, for when we edit, direct, act, or read, we inevitably become Shakespeare's collaborator and re-create the plays. The plays, one might say, are so cunningly contrived that they guide our responses, tell us how we ought to feel, and make a mark on us, but (for better or for worse) we also make a mark on them.

—Sylvan Barnet
Tufts University

Introduction

Thomas Platter, a Swiss traveler to England, recorded his visit of September 21, 1599, to a London theater: at about two o'clock, after lunch, he and his party crossed the river, and in a house with a thatched roof saw an excellent performance of the tragedy of the first Emperor Julius Caesar. (Platter was mistaken in giving to Caesar the title of "Emperor," either because he was weak in history or because he was impressed by the imperious portrayal of the title role.) He went on to note that there was a cast of about fifteen, and that after the play, according to custom, there was a most elegant and curious dance, two participants being dressed in men's clothes, and two in women's.

The dance that Platter saw was the jig, and the play was undoubtedly Shakespeare's *The Tragedy of Julius Caesar*, performed at the newly constructed Globe Theatre. It is quite probable that Shakespeare wrote the play early in 1599, and it marks an important stage in his development. His previous work, *Henry V* (1599), was the last of a long series of English history plays; and while attention shifts to Roman times in *Julius Caesar*, Shakespeare incorporates those ideas of history that grew through the English plays. Starting as a chronicle of wars and bloody events, the histories progressively move toward a recognition of tragedy through historical progress. As the histories unfold, Shakespeare's horror of civil war becomes increasingly apparent; and as the focus narrows to individual rulers, we see the development of his intense belief in the divine quality of kingship as the only possible safeguard against civil dissension.

In *Julius Caesar* Shakespeare continues to explore the

drama of power politics and personal conscience; only now, as if to gain perspective on the great issues of the histories, he moves the setting to a more distant time. The shift to ancient history would have sharpened rather than blunted the play's contemporary relevance because of the acknowledged Elizabethan habit of viewing history as a series of object lessons for present conduct.

We must not forget how widespread was the longing for unshakable rule and how overwhelming was the dread of civil war at the time *Julius Caesar* was first performed. Elizabeth I had come to the throne in 1558 when the country was in such a state of rebellion and confusion that it seemed likely to slip back into the horrors of the Wars of the Roses. Elizabeth had given her subjects peace, and the nation had prospered; for many years she had been a strong ruler, despite the repeated Catholic claims that she was illegitimate and therefore not a true successor. Attempts at assassination had been many. By 1599 she was old and visibly failing. She had no direct heir; there was no one whose claim to the throne after her was beyond dispute. Childless like Caesar, she could pass on the office only by naming an heir, and this she refused to do, perhaps in order to prevent the growth of factions. The shadow of war and dissension grew ominous. In such circumstances, we see first among the issues of *Julius Caesar* the very topical and concrete problem of a disputed succession, and the more abstract problem of killing—and replacing—the ruler.

Even without Machiavelli many Elizabethans knew that the moral problems of government are not necessarily the same as the moral problems of men. It was precisely because Elizabeth had compromised her personal beliefs whenever the public interest demanded it that she had been so successful a ruler; indeed, in many cases it is still impossible to know what she as a private person believed. Mary Tudor, who had tried to rule in accordance with religious principles, had brought about years of bloodshed. The theory of divine grace accorded to the public actions of a duly appointed ruler was not childish authoritarianism but a philosophical way of resolving the well-perceived gap between what the man might believe and what the ruler must do.

When we view *Julius Caesar* in the light of the political considerations of its own time, many of the difficulties of the play can be seen in perspective. Caesar *is* proud, and destined for the punishment of *hubris*; he is, nonetheless, "the ruler" by ability as well as power, as Plutarch himself suggests in *The Life of Julius Caesar*, a primary source for Shakespeare's work:

> The Romans, inclining to Caesar's prosperity and taking the bit in the mouth, supposing that to be ruled by one man alone, it would be a good mean for them to take breath a little, after so many troubles and miseries as they had abidden in these civil wars, they chose him perpetual Dictator. . . . And now for himself, after he had ended his civil wars, he did so honorably behave himself, that there was no fault to be found in him.

Plutarch goes on to list Caesar's achievements and enterprises, and suggests that his only failing is a desire to be *called* king. However, Caesar's personal faults have no bearing upon his public abilities.

Brutus is high-minded and disinterested, even though his love of political liberty leads him to transgress the rules of allegiance to a ruler and gratitude to a benefactor. His personal virtues, however, have no bearing upon his public abilities. He is naïve enough to believe that a republic needs no power structure, that the removal of Caesar will simply allow power to flow back to the officers of the republic. But of course events prove otherwise, and he and Cassius are forced in their turn to assume power against those who would "destroy the revolution." Neither Brutus nor Cassius has the ability—or the right—to rule, and both are defeated. Yet the man who ultimately replaces them is not the man who roused the public against them, but the one whose impersonal manner from the beginning marks him as the next possessor of the power to rule—Octavius Caesar.

Brutus, Octavius, and Antony all become guilty as men. Brutus kills his friend; Octavius joins the others of the Triumvirate in condemning innocent men to death; Antony deliberately rouses a mob and turns it loose to do what mischief it will. What they do, however, does not matter in considering the fitness of each to rule. Personal innocence or guilt is not in question, and we are not asked to feel that one man or another is "right." We are asked to see that while a just man in private life is to be praised, a just man in public life may very well bring about catastrophe. The wicked—or, like Caesar, the conceited and superstitious—may be the genius as a ruler. Man's worth as a private individual does not necessarily ensure his value as a public ruler. Less sentimental than many of his critics, Shakespeare sees that a morally repulsive act may at times be a politically desirable one; that a man who acts from the highest of motives may be too busy keeping his conscience clean to lead well; that a man who once does evil in the expectation that good will be the final result may be forced more deeply into self-deception and impotence than a man who acts simply from expediency. But he also sees that the pursuit of expediency and lack of scruple do not in themselves guarantee ability to govern—else why not, ultimately, an Antony in command?

There is a natural inclination to desire unequivocal answers and absolute judgments, to simplify events until they can be seen as black or white; and we are naturally bewildered when forced into a position that requires us to judge but forbids us the use of simple terms of reference. It is not surprising, therefore, that we may be confounded by *Julius Caesar*, for often we confront situations in which personalities and actions are neither wholly right nor wholly wrong. We cannot feel unreserved hate or love for any character; each seems to call for a different response as he reacts to the seemingly irreconcilable demands of public and private life. Caesar is deaf, aging, subject to epileptic fits, inclined to superstition, warmhearted to his friends in private yet inflexible in public. But if we can believe Antony at all, Caesar has a genuine love of his country. His fault is a kind of ecstasy that the exercise of his office brings upon him. As a private individual he shows many weaknesses; as a public institution he sees himself superior to all ordinary dangers, and believes that his office is a power that must not be opposed. Indeed, Caesar constantly uses his name to speak of his alter ego, the Dictator, and in an early speech to Antony, in which he reveals his distrust of Cassius, he sums up the two views of himself as he unwittingly contrasts two attitudes: the public office that is perfect, and the private individual who is defective. It is as though his public self is quite dissociated from his personal weaknesses:

> I rather tell thee what is to be feared
> Than what I fear; for always I am Caesar.
> Come on my right hand, for this ear is deaf,
> And tell me truly what thou think'st of him.

                                        (1.2.211–14)

Caesar may have a number of weaknesses, but none of the personal defects impairs the spirit of Caesar—the capacity to rule. The play vividly demonstrates that there is more stability, freedom, and justice in Rome with Caesar alive than with Caesar dead.

We may be far more sympathetic to the personality of Brutus; yet we must admit that neither he nor Cassius has any specific charges that would warrant the killing of Caesar. Cassius derides Caesar's weaknesses. His attacks are the result of personal envy—why should the fact that Caesar failed in a swimming contest, or suffered from fever, make him contemptible as a ruler? And Brutus admits that he has no immediate cause for indicting his friend. His soliloquy at the beginning of Act 2 is an agonized attempt to reconcile the idea of tyranny with the personal Caesar he knows. He begins his analysis of the situation with the conclusion—"It must be by his death" (10)—and then, unable to find anything concrete for which Caesar deserves death, he has to resort to possibilities and probabilities: "He would be crowned. / How that might change his nature, there's the question" (12–13). In the end he convinces himself of the necessity of murder by thinking not of what is but what might be, by imagining the future abuse of power, and finally, by employing false analogy:

> And therefore think him as a serpent's egg
> Which hatched, would as his kind grow mischievous,
> And kill him in the shell.

                                        (32–34)

But Caesar is a man, not a serpent's egg; and Brutus is no less mistaken when he tries to kill the spirit of Caesar by doing away with the man. He only succeeds in killing the man, not his spirit—and this is forcefully dramatized when, after the assassination, the people are eager to transfer their allegiance to Brutus, just as they had abandoned Pompey for Caesar:

> *Third Plebeian.* Let him be Caesar.
> *Fourth Plebeian.*   Caesar's better parts
>   Shall be crowned in Brutus.
>
> (3.2.52–53)

It is not only Brutus' misfortune but his fault that his achievements turn out, ironically, to be the reverse of his best intentions. He brings to Rome anarchy and the horrors of civil war, not "Peace, freedom, and liberty."

In dramatizing the complex issues of power politics, *Julius Caesar* offers no easy solution to problems that are no less baffling to our own age. Many will find that this work is one of Shakespeare's most perplexing, for it is disconcerting when a play—or history itself—appeals to man's earnest desire to judge actions in terms of simple, personal standards of right and wrong and then betrays and mocks his deepest convictions by suggesting that Power is better than Virtue, that efficiency may be preferable to goodness, or that conscience may be dangerously inadequate in determining political action.

An individual's scrupulous concern for morality may, indeed, be disastrously impolitic. Cassius leads Brutus to an abhorrent deed, but when the consequences involve Brutus in the exercise of power, Brutus continues to think and act in accordance with private morality. His scruples about killing Antony or about unjustly raising money hinder the success of the conspiracy. His wish to fight a pitched battle, to decide the matter once and for all, instead of following stratagems and winning by attrition, is also the decision of a man who refuses to take on the role of politician. It is noteworthy that Cassius, after his initial victory, consistently defers to Brutus' moral scruples; knowing him to be wrong in his strategy, he is still swayed by the very image of nobility for which Brutus was chosen as the figurehead of the conspiracy. The irony is unmistakable: the politic man sets up an image of virtue, dissociated from politics, to serve his own purposes, to endear him to the populace; but once that image is established, his freedom to act without it is curbed, and he is hampered in the achievement of his political ends by the very image he has fostered.

The spirit of Caesar that dominates the play is to be associated, finally, with the exercise of supreme power. When Caesar dies, power is without a master, and as such, indiscriminately destructive. Each man in his turn tries to grasp the lightning that has been set free, and is fearfully transformed, until finally it comes to rest upon the man who alone, by gift of personality and legitimate succession, may wield it unscathed.

Shakespeare fully delineates the intriguing pattern of shifting power as an old Caesar is succeeded by a young one. The politic Cassius gives in to an impolitic Brutus and both fail as a result. Antony, Octavius, and Lepidus begin with complete ruthlessness; however, this does not guarantee them power or even win the battle for them—their opponents defeat themselves through mistakes. Lepidus, the "straw man," is first burdened with responsibility, then eliminated; and afterward, effortlessly, Antony, the ruthless and emotional partner, is displaced by the man without a temperament, the personification of impersonal rule.

The transfer of power from Antony to Octavius is subtly and swiftly dramatized in Act 5, Scene 1, when Octavius suddenly opposes Antony's command and leads his troops in his own way—"I do not cross you," he tells Antony, "but I will do so." (20) From this point Antony refers to his partner as "Caesar," whereas until that moment he had called him only "Octavius." Even when Octavius asks for advice immediately after he has asserted his independence (23), Antony calls him "Caesar" before bidding him "Make forth." And soon afterward Octavius is seen as the one who is beginning to prevail; it is he who gives directions: "Come, Antony; away!" (63) In the last scene of the play Octavius is in total charge of the action, while Antony is returned to his first prominent role, that of funeral orator. Antony may deliver the wonderful eulogy for Brutus, but Octavius, in businesslike fashion, gives the orders for burial, and without consulting or mentioning Antony, says to his former adversaries: "All that served Brutus, I will entertain them" (5.5.60), as if he were in sole command. Finally, Octavius renders the play's concluding speech, which is conventionally given by the person of highest rank, whose task is to restore order to the state.

In portraying Octavius and describing his rise to power, Shakespeare departs from his primary source, Plutarch's *Lives*, and his changes are important for our understanding of the play. Plutarch's Octavius is not an exceptional soldier but an outwardly pleasant person of charm and wit, the very opposite of Shakespeare's characterization. And whereas Shakespeare's Octavius gains stature at the battle of Philippi, in Plutarch's *The Life of Marcus Antonius* he is sick at this time, and Antony "had the chiefest glory of all this victory." In Plutarch's *Life of Marcus Brutus* it is further reported that Octavius was absent from the battle; he had himself carried from his camp because of a friend's ominous dream, "and no man could tell what became of Octavius Caesar after he was carried out of his camp."

Shakespeare's independent treatment of Octavius reveals his conception of the kind of man who can wield power in the spirit of Caesar. Brutus, Cassius, and Antony grasp at power and are unable to retain it, perhaps because in exercising it they are more swayed by personal passions than Caesar. Octavius had no part in the murder; he is the only person in the play as free of the passions of love or hate as Caesar claimed to be. In his speech at the beginning of Act 5 he identifies himself with the spirit of Caesar, makes himself spiritually his heir, and assumes the duty of revenge:

> Look,
> I draw a sword against conspirators.
> When think you that the sword goes up again?
> Never, till Caesar's three and thirty wounds
> Be well avenged; or till another Caesar
> Have added slaughter to the sword of traitors.

> (50–55)

At the close of the play we are meant to feel that the exercise of power necessary for these times has once more been placed in adequate hands. The spirit of Caesar, for good or ill, has not been put to rest.

Nevertheless, those who distrust established power will generally respond more strongly to the play's subversive rendering of both rule and the status quo. "Marullus and Flavius," we are told at the beginning of the play, "for pulling scarfs off Caesar's images, are put to silence" (1.2. 285–86). In contrast to a Caesar whose strength of purpose is needed to maintain stability and justice in Rome, there is Caesar, the possible tyrant, who seems intent on establishing a dynasty, and whose actions cause Brutus to fear that power corrupts and absolute power corrupts absolutely. "He would be crowned. / How that might change his nature, there's the question" (2.1.12–13). For Brutus and the conspirators, the assassination of Caesar is the deed of patriots who take part in a ritual sacrifice to cleanse Rome and restore ideals of the past: "Liberty! Freedom! Tyranny is dead!" But for Antony, it is the murderous act of "butchers."

Seemingly contradictory views are found in the literature of the Renaissance, in Shakespeare's play, and in Plutarch: Caesar is the murdered benefactor of Rome; he is also the tyrannical usurper who threatens Rome's liberties. One way of incorporating these opposites is to assent to the view that for Shakespeare—and Elizabethans in general—established order is preferable to chaotic and violent change. However imperfect, Caesar's strong leadership is needed to maintain Rome's liberties. By recovering Shakespeare's intention, it would be argued, we re-establish his true meaning. Formalists—now regarded as "old style" literary critics—assumed that a text had an organizing principle and embodied a coherent meaning. Contradictions, when encountered, were integrated into a unified whole. Deconstructionists, on the other hand, assume that a text is indeterminate; it has no unified meaning; and contradictions, when revealed, are not resolved, for they point to what is subversive in the text. The *uncertainty of certainty*, now an established principle in critical theories that have gained prominence in recent years, claims that an author's intention, even if openly stated, cannot be established because the work may have eluded the author's purpose. Furthermore, some argue, a text has no meaning in and of itself. It is the reader or the director of a play who provides meaning to a text.

The conviction that there can be no single interpretation of a text and no way of establishing objective truth in historical and literary studies gives license to multiple views and voices, and enlarges our awareness of what others see and respond to in Shakespeare's plays. In the midst of new and changing methodologies, Shakespeare's plays maintain their own integrity and interest because they dramatize the concerns and human predicaments that are ours. A dramatist always alert to what succeeds on stage, Shakespeare was probably influenced by the popularity of revenge drama when he wrote *Julius Caesar*. The blood of Caesar cries out for revenge; but the play goes beyond conventional revenge formulas and presents more than Elizabethan worries about disputed succession and the necessities of legitimate rule. Deeply concerned with the nature of justice, with changing realities beneath the same appearance, and with the tricks played by the human mind under stress, the drama raises to a level of consciousness many of the profound concerns of the Elizabethan age, which recur in all ages—the battle of opposing truths, and whether, in a world of shifting appearances and loyalties, real truth can be known, and action for a cause, validated.

—WILLIAM ROSEN
BARBARA ROSEN
University of Connecticut

The Tragedy of
JULIUS CAESAR

Julius Caesar
Octavius Caesar ⎫
Marcus Antonius ⎬ triumvirs after
M. Aemilius Lepidus ⎭   the death of Julius Caesar
Cicero ⎫
Publius ⎬ senators
Popilius Lena ⎭
Marcus Brutus ⎫
Cassius │
Casca │
Trebonius │
Ligarius ⎬ conspirators against Julius Caesar
Decius Brutus │
Metellus Cimber │
Cinna ⎭
Flavius ⎫ tribunes
Marullus ⎭
Artemidorus of Cnidos, a teacher of rhetoric
A Soothsayer
Cinna, a poet
Another Poet
Lucilius ⎫
Titinius │
Messala ⎬ friends to Brutus and Cassius
Young Cato │
Volumnius ⎭
Varro ⎫
Clitus │
Claudius │
Strato ⎬ servants to Brutus
Lucius │
Dardanius ⎭
Pindarus, servant to Cassius
Calphurnia, wife to Caesar
Portia, wife to Brutus
Senators, Citizens, Guards, Attendants, &c.

Scene: During most of the play, at Rome;
afterward near Sardis, and near Philippi]

The Tragedy of Julius Caesar

ACT 1

Scene 1. [*Rome. A street.*]

Enter Flavius, Marullus, and certain Commoners over the stage.

Flavius. Hence! Home, you idle creatures, get you home!
Is this a holiday? What, know you not,
Being mechanical,°¹ you ought not walk
Upon a laboring day without the sign
Of your profession?° Speak, what trade art thou?   5

Carpenter. Why, sir, a carpenter.

Marullus. Where is thy leather apron and thy rule?
What dost thou with thy best apparel on?
You, sir, what trade are you?

Cobbler. Truly, sir, in respect of a fine° workman, I am   10
but, as you would say, a cobbler.°

Marullus. But what trade art thou? Answer me directly.°

Cobbler. A trade, sir, that, I hope, I may use with a safe

---

¹ The degree sign (°) indicates a footnote, which is keyed to the text by line number. Text references are printed in **boldface** type; the annotation follows in roman type.
1.1.3 **mechanical** of the working class
mark of your trade, i.e., working clothes
parison with a skilled   11 **cobbler**
12 **directly** straightforwardly
4–5 **sign/Of your profession**
10 **in respect of a fine** in comparison
(1) shoemaker (2) bungler

3

15   conscience, which is indeed, sir, a mender of bad
      soles.°

Flavius. What trade, thou knave? Thou naughty° knave,
      what trade?

Cobbler. Nay, I beseech you, sir, be not out° with me:
      yet, if you be out,° sir, I can mend you.°

20 *Marullus.* What mean'st thou by that? Mend me, thou
      saucy fellow?

Cobbler. Why, sir, cobble you.

Flavius. Thou art a cobbler, art thou?

Cobbler. Truly, sir, all that I live by is with the awl: I
25   meddle with no tradesman's matters, nor women's
      matters; but withal,° I am indeed, sir, a surgeon to old
      shoes: when they are in great danger, I recover° them.
      As proper men as ever trod upon neat's leather° have
      gone upon my handiwork.

30 *Flavius.* But wherefore art not in thy shop today?
      Why dost thou lead these men about the streets?

Cobbler. Truly, sir, to wear out their shoes, to get myself
      into more work. But indeed, sir, we make holiday to
      see Caesar and to rejoice in his triumph.°

Marullus. Wherefore rejoice? What conquest brings he
35   home?
      What tributaries° follow him to Rome,
      To grace in captive bonds his chariot wheels?
      You blocks, you stones, you worse than senseless
          things!
      O you hard hearts, you cruel men of Rome,
40   Knew you not Pompey?° Many a time and oft
      Have you climbed up to walls and battlements,
      To tow'rs and windows, yea, to chimney tops,

---

15 **soles** (pun on "souls")   16 **naughty** worthless   18 **out** angry   19 **be
out** i.e., have worn-out shoes   19 **mend you** (1) mend your shoes (2) improve your character   26 **withal** (1) nevertheless (2) with awl (3) with
all   27 **recover** (1) resole (2) cure   28 **neat's leather** cattle's hide
34 **triumph** triumphal celebration   36 **tributaries** captives   40 **Pompey** (defeated by Caesar in 48 B.C., later murdered)

Your infants in your arms, and there have sat
The livelong day, with patient expectation,
To see great Pompey pass the streets of Rome.   45
And when you saw his chariot but appear,
Have you not made an universal shout,
That Tiber trembled underneath her banks
To hear the replication° of your sounds
Made in her concave shores?°   50
And do you now put on your best attire?
And do you now cull out a holiday?
And do you now strew flowers in his way
That comes in triumph over Pompey's blood?°
Be gone!   55
Run to your houses, fall upon your knees,
Pray to the gods to intermit° the plague
That needs must light on this ingratitude.

Flavius. Go, go, good countrymen, and, for this fault,
Assemble all the poor men of your sort;   60
Draw them to Tiber banks and weep your tears
Into the channel, till the lowest stream
Do kiss the most exalted shores of all.°
                                  Exeunt all the Commoners.
See, whe'r° their basest mettle° be not moved;
They vanish tongue-tied in their guiltiness.   65
Go you down that way towards the Capitol;
This way will I. Disrobe the images,
If you do find them decked with ceremonies.°

Marullus. May we do so?
You know it is the feast of Lupercal.°   70

Flavius. It is no matter; let no images
Be hung with Caesar's trophies. I'll about

49 **replication** echo   50 **concave shores** hollowed-out banks   54 **in triumph over Pompey's blood** as the conqueror of Pompey's sons   57 **intermit** hold back   63 **most exalted shores of all** highest water mark   64 **whe'r** whether   64 **mettle** (1) substance (2) disposition   68 **ceremonies** robes (or ornaments)   70 **Lupercal** (fertility festival held on February 15; Caesar's triumph really took place in the preceding October, but Shakespeare combines events and shortens time spans for dramatic effect)

And drive away the vulgar° from the streets;
So do you too, where you perceive them thick.
75   These growing feathers plucked from Caesar's wing
Will make him fly an ordinary pitch,°
Who else would soar above the view of men
And keep us all in servile fearfulness.   *Exeunt.*

[Scene 2. *A public place.*]

*Enter Caesar, Antony (for the course), Calphurnia,
Portia, Decius, Cicero, Brutus, Cassius, Casca, a
Soothsayer; after them, Marullus and Flavius.*

Caesar. Calphurnia!

Casca.   Peace, ho! Caesar speaks.

Caesar.   Calphurnia!

Calphurnia. Here, my lord.

Caesar. Stand you directly in Antonius' way
When he doth run his course. Antonius!

5   *Antony.* Caesar, my lord?

Caesar. Forget not in your speed, Antonius,
To touch Calphurnia; for our elders say
The barren, touchèd in this holy chase,
Shake off their sterile curse.

Antony.   I shall remember:
10   When Caesar says "Do this," it is performed.

Caesar. Set on, and leave no ceremony out.

Soothsayer. Caesar!

Caesar. Ha! Who calls?

73 **vulgar** common people   76 **pitch** height

Casca. Bid every noise be still; peace yet again!

Caesar. Who is it in the press° that calls on me?   *15*
   I hear a tongue, shriller than all the music,
   Cry "Caesar." Speak; Caesar is turned to hear.

Soothsayer. Beware the ides of March.°

Caesar.   What man is that?

Brutus. A soothsayer bids you beware the ides of March.

Caesar. Set him before me; let me see his face.   *20*

Cassius. Fellow, come from the throng; look upon
   Caesar.

Caesar. What say'st thou to me now? Speak once again.

Soothsayer. Beware the ides of March.

Caesar. He is a dreamer, let us leave him. Pass.
      Sennet.° Exeunt. Mane[n]t° Brutus and Cassius.

Cassius. Will you go see the order of the course?°   *25*

Brutus. Not I.

Cassius. I pray you do.

Brutus. I am not gamesome:° I do lack some part
   Of that quick spirit° that is in Antony.
   Let me not hinder, Cassius, your desires;   *30*
   I'll leave you.

Cassius. Brutus, I do observe you now of late;
   I have not from your eyes that gentleness
   And show of love as I was wont° to have;
   You bear too stubborn and too strange a hand°   *35*
   Over your friend that loves you.

1.2.15 **press** crowd   18 **ides of March** March 15   24 s.d. **Sennet** flourish
of trumpets marking ceremonial entrance or exit   24 s.d. **Mane[n]t** (they)
remain   25 **order of the course** progress of the race   28 **gamesome** (1)
fond of sport (2) merry   29 **quick spirit** (1) lively nature (2) prompt
obedience   34 **wont** accustomed   35 **bear . . . hand** treat too haughtily
and distantly, keep at arm's length (the metaphor is from horsemanship)

Brutus.   Cassius,
Be not deceived: if I have veiled my look,
I turn the trouble of my countenance
Merely upon myself.° Vexèd I am
40   Of late with passions of some difference,°
Conceptions only proper to myself,°
Which give some soil,° perhaps, to my behaviors;
But let not therefore my good friends be grieved
(Among which number, Cassius, be you one)
45   Nor construe° any further my neglect
Than that poor Brutus, with himself at war,
Forgets the shows° of love to other men.

Cassius. Then, Brutus, I have much mistook your pas-
     sion;°
By means whereof° this breast of mine hath buried
50   Thoughts of great value, worthy cogitations.
Tell me, good Brutus, can you see your face?

Brutus. No, Cassius; for the eye sees not itself
But by reflection, by some other things.

Cassius. 'Tis just:°
55   And it is very much lamented, Brutus,
That you have no such mirrors as will turn
Your hidden worthiness into your eye,
That you might see your shadow.° I have heard
Where many of the best respect° in Rome
60   (Except immortal Caesar), speaking of Brutus,
And groaning underneath this age's yoke,
Have wished that noble Brutus had his eyes.

Brutus. Into what dangers would you lead me, Cassius,
That you would have me seek into myself
65   For that which is not in me?

37–39 **if I have . . . upon myself** i.e., if I have seemed withdrawn, it is because I am displeased with myself and no one else (*Merely* =
wholly)· 40 **passions of some difference** conflicting emotions
41 **Conceptions . . . myself** ideas concerning me only   42 **soil** blem-
ish   45 **construe** interpret   47 **shows** manifestations   48 **passion** feelings   49 **By means whereof** as a consequence of which   54 **just**
true   58 **shadow** reflection, i.e., yourself as others see you   59 **best respect** highest reputation

Cassius. Therefore, good Brutus, be prepared to hear;
   And since you know you cannot see yourself
   So well as by reflection, I, your glass°
   Will modestly discover to yourself
   That of yourself which you yet know not of.   *70*
   And be not jealous on° me, gentle Brutus:
   Were I a common laughter,° or did use
   To stale with ordinary oaths my love
   To every new protester;° if you know
   That I do fawn on men and hug them hard,   *75*
   And after scandal° them; or if you know
   That I profess myself° in banqueting
   To all the rout,° then hold me dangerous.
                          Flourish° and shout.

Brutus. What means this shouting? I do fear the people
   Choose Caesar for their king.

Cassius.   Ay, do you fear it?   *80*
   Then must I think you would not have it so.

Brutus. I would not, Cassius, yet I love him well.
   But wherefore do you hold me here so long?
   What is it that you would impart to me?
   If it be aught toward the general good,°   *85*
   Set honor in one eye and death i' th' other,
   And I will look on both indifferently;°
   For let the gods so speed me,° as I love
   The name of honor more than I fear death.

Cassius. I know that virtue to be in you, Brutus,   *90*
   As well as I do know your outward favor.°
   Well, honor is the subject of my story.
   I cannot tell what you and other men
   Think of this life, but for my single self,

---

68 **glass** mirror   71 **jealous on** suspicious of   72 **laughter** object of
mockery   72–74 **did use ... protester** were accustomed to make cheap
with glib and frequent avowals to every new promiser of friendship (*ordinary* = [1] tavern [2] everyday)   76 **scandal** slander   77 **profess myself**
declare my friendship   78 **rout** vulgar crowd   78 s.d. **Flourish** ceremonial sounding of trumpets   85 **general good** public welfare   87 **indifferently** impartially   88 **speed me** make me prosper   91 **favor** appearance

95   I had as lief not be,° as live to be
In awe of such a thing as I myself.°
I was born free as Caesar; so were you:
We both have fed as well, and we can both
Endure the winter's cold as well as he:
100   For once, upon a raw and gusty day,
The troubled Tiber chafing with° her shores,
Caesar said to me "Dar'st thou, Cassius, now
Leap in with me into this angry flood,
And swim to yonder point?" Upon the word,
105   Accout'red° as I was, I plungèd in
And bade him follow: so indeed he did.
The torrent roared, and we did buffet it
With lusty sinews, throwing it aside
And stemming it with hearts of controversy.°
110   But ere we could arrive the point proposed,
Caesar cried "Help me, Cassius, or I sink!"
I, as Aeneas,° our great ancestor,
Did from the flames of Troy upon his shoulder
The old Anchises bear, so from the waves of Tiber
115   Did I the tired Caesar. And this man
Is now become a god, and Cassius is
A wretched creature, and must bend his body
If Caesar carelessly but nod on him.
He had a fever when he was in Spain,
120   And when the fit was on him, I did mark
How he did shake; 'tis true, this god did shake.
His coward lips did from their color fly,°
And that same eye whose bend° doth awe the world
Did lose his° luster; I did hear him groan;
125   Ay, and that tongue of his, that bade the Romans
Mark him and write his speeches in their books,
Alas, it cried, "Give me some drink, Titinius,"

95 **as lief not be** just as soon not exist   96 **such a thing as I myself** i.e.,
another human being (Caesar)   101 **chafing with** raging against
105 **Accout'red** fully armed   109 **stemming . . . controversy** moving
forward against it (1) aggressively (2) in rivalry   112 **Aeneas** (legendary
founder of the Roman state, and hero of Vergil's *Aeneid*. Anchises was his
feeble father)   122 **His coward . . . fly** the color fled from his lips like a
deserter fleeing from his banner in battle (*color* = [1] hue [2]
banner)   123 **bend** glance   124 **his** its

As a sick girl. Ye gods! It doth amaze me,
A man of such a feeble temper° should
So get the start of° the majestic world,   *130*
And bear the palm° alone.   *Shout. Flourish.*

Brutus. Another general shout?
      I do believe that these applauses are
      For some new honors that are heaped on Caesar.

Cassius. Why, man, he doth bestride the narrow world   *135*
      Like a Colossus,° and we petty men
      Walk under his huge legs and peep about
      To find ourselves dishonorable° graves.
      Men at some time are masters of their fates:
      The fault, dear Brutus, is not in our stars,°   *140*
      But in ourselves, that we are underlings.
      Brutus and Caesar: what should be in that "Caesar"?
      Why should that name be sounded° more than yours?
      Write them together, yours is as fair a name;
      Sound them, it doth become the mouth as well;   *145*
      Weigh them, it is as heavy; conjure with 'em,
      "Brutus" will start° a spirit as soon as "Caesar."
      Now, in the names of all the gods at once,
      Upon what meat doth this our Caesar feed,
      That he is grown so great? Age, thou art shamed!   *150*
      Rome, thou hast lost the breed of noble bloods!
      When went there by an age, since the great flood,°
      But it was famed with° more than with one man?
      When could they say (till now) that talked of Rome,
      That her wide walks encompassed but one man?   *155*
      Now is it Rome indeed, and room° enough,

129 **feeble temper** weak constitution   130 **get the start of** outdistance   131 **bear the palm** carry off the victor's prize   136 **Colossus** (an immense statue of Apollo, said to straddle the entrance to the harbor of Rhodes so that ships sailed under its legs)   138 **dishonorable** (because we are dominated by Caesar)   140 **stars** destinies (in Shakespeare's day one's temperament, and therefore one's actions and course of life, were thought to be largely determined by the position of the planets at one's birth)   143 **sounded** (1) spoken (2) proclaimed by trumpet   147 **start** raise   152 **great flood** (classical story told of the drowning of all mankind except Deucalion and his wife Pyrrha, spared by Zeus because of their virtue)   153 **But it was famed with** without the age being made famous by   156 **Rome ... room** (homonyms, hence a pun)

When there is in it but one only man.
O, you and I have heard our fathers say,
There was a Brutus° once that would have brooked°
160   Th' eternal devil to keep his state in Rome
As easily as a king.

Brutus. That you do love me, I am nothing jealous;°
What you would work me to,° I have some aim;°
How I have thought of this, and of these times,
165   I shall recount hereafter. For this present,
I would not so (with love I might entreat you)
Be any further moved. What you have said
I will consider; what you have to say
I will with patience hear, and find a time
170   Both meet° to hear and answer such high things.
Till then, my noble friend, chew° upon this:
Brutus had rather be a villager
Than to repute himself a son of Rome
Under these hard conditions as this time
Is like to lay upon us.

175 *Cassius.*   I am glad
That my weak words have struck but thus much show
Of fire from Brutus.

Enter Caesar and his Train.°

Brutus. The games are done, and Caesar is returning.

Cassius. As they pass by, pluck Casca by the sleeve,
180   And he will (after his sour fashion) tell you
What hath proceeded worthy note today.

Brutus. I will do so. But look you, Cassius,
The angry spot doth glow on Caesar's brow,
And all the rest look like a chidden train:
185   Calphurnia's cheek is pale, and Cicero

159 **a Brutus** (Lucius Junius Brutus helped expel the Tarquins and found
the Republic in 509 B.C.)   159 **brooked** tolerated   162 **nothing jealous**
not at all doubtful   163 **work me to** persuade me of   163 **aim** idea
170 **meet** suitable   171 **chew** reflect   177 s.d. **Train** retinue

Looks with such ferret° and such fiery eyes
As we have seen him in the Capitol,
Being crossed in conference° by some senators.

Cassius. Casca will tell us what the matter is.

Caesar. Antonius.   *190*

Antony. Caesar?

Caesar. Let me have men about me that are fat,
Sleek-headed men, and such as sleep a-nights.
Yond Cassius has a lean and hungry look;
He thinks too much: such men are dangerous.   *195*

Antony. Fear him not, Caesar, he's not dangerous;
He is a noble Roman, and well given.°

Caesar. Would he were fatter! But I fear him not.
Yet if my name were liable to fear,°
I do not know the man I should avoid   *200*
So soon as that spare Cassius. He reads much,
He is a great observer, and he looks
Quite through the deeds° of men. He loves no plays,
As thou dost, Antony; he hears no music;°
Seldom he smiles, and smiles in such a sort°   *205*
As if he mocked himself, and scorned his spirit
That could be moved to smile at anything.
Such men as he be never at heart's ease
Whiles they behold a greater than themselves,
And therefore are they very dangerous.   *210*
I rather tell thee what is to be feared
Than what I fear; for always I am Caesar.
Come on my right hand, for this ear is deaf,

186 **ferret** ferretlike (a ferret is a vicious, weasellike animal with red eyes) 188 **conference** debate 197 **given** disposed 199 **if my name ... to fear** i.e., if the idea of fear could ever be associated with me 203 **through the deeds** i.e., to the hidden motives of actions 204 **hears no music** (cf. *Merchant of Venice*, 5.1.83ff: "The man that hath no music in himself,/Nor is not moved with concord of sweet sounds,/Is fit for treasons. . . . Let no such man be trusted") 205 **sort** manner

    And tell me truly what thou think'st of him.
Sennet. Exeunt Caesar and his Train.

Casca. You pulled me by the cloak; would you speak
215   with me?

Brutus. Ay, Casca; tell us what hath chanced today,
  That Caesar looks so sad.°

Casca. Why, you were with him, were you not?

Brutus. I should not then ask Casca what had chanced.

220 *Casca.* Why, there was a crown offered him; and being
  offered him, he put it by° with the back of his hand,
  thus; and then the people fell a-shouting.

Brutus. What was the second noise for?

Casca. Why, for that too.

225 *Cassius.* They shouted thrice; what was the last cry for?

Casca. Why, for that too.

Brutus. Was the crown offered him thrice?

Casca. Ay, marry,° was't, and he put it by thrice, every
  time gentler than other; and at every putting-by mine
230   honest neighbors shouted.

Cassius. Who offered him the crown?

Casca. Why, Antony.

Brutus. Tell us the manner of it, gentle Casca.

Casca. I can as well be hanged as tell the manner of it:
235   it was mere foolery; I did not mark it. I saw Mark
  Antony offer him a crown—yet 'twas not a crown neither, 'twas one of these coronets°—and, as I told you,
  he put it by once; but for all that, to my thinking, he
  would fain° have had it. Then he offered it to him
240   again; then he put it by again; but to my thinking, he was very loath to lay his fingers off it. And

217 **sad** serious   221 **put it by** pushed it aside   228 **marry** truly (originally an oath, "By the Virgin Mary")   237 **coronets** small crowns
239 **fain** gladly

then he offered it the third time. He put it the third
time by; and still° as he refused it, the rabblement
hooted, and clapped their chopt° hands, and threw up
their sweaty nightcaps,° and uttered such a deal   245
of stinking breath because Caesar refused the crown,
that it had, almost, choked Caesar; for he swounded°
and fell down at it. And for mine own part, I durst not
laugh, for fear of opening my lips and receiving the
bad air.   250

Cassius. But, soft,° I pray you; what, did Caesar
swound?

Casca. He fell down in the market place, and foamed at
mouth, and was speechless.

Brutus. 'Tis very like he hath the falling-sickness.°

Cassius. No, Caesar hath it not; but you, and I,   255
And honest Casca, we have the falling-sickness.°

Casca. I know not what you mean by that, but I am sure
Caesar fell down. If the tag-rag people° did not clap
him and hiss him, according as he pleased and displeased them, as they use° to do the players in the   260
theater, I am no true man.

Brutus. What said he when he came unto himself?

Casca. Marry, before he fell down, when he perceived
the common herd was glad he refused the crown, he
plucked me ope his doublet° and offered them his   265
throat to cut. An I had been a man of any occupation,°
if I would not have taken him at a word, I would I
might go to hell among the rogues. And so he fell.
When he came to himself again, he said, if he had

---

243 **still** every time   244 **chopt** rough, chapped   245 **nightcaps** (contemptuous term for workingmen's caps)   247 **swounded** fainted
251 **soft** slowly, "wait a minute"   254 **falling-sickness** epilepsy   256 **we
have the falling-sickness** i.e., we are becoming powerless and are declin-
ing under Caesar's rule   258 **tag-rag people** ragged mob   260 **use** are
accustomed   265 **ope his doublet** open his jacket   266 **man of any occupation** (1) workingman, i.e., one of those to whom Caesar's speech was
addressed (2) "man of action"

270 done or said anything amiss, he desired their wor-
     ships to think it was his infirmity. Three or four
     wenches, where I stood, cried "Alas, good soul!" and
     forgave him with all their hearts; but there's no heed
     to be taken of them; if Caesar had stabbed their moth-
275 ers, they would have done no less.

Brutus. And after that, he came thus sad away?

Casca. Ay.

Cassius. Did Cicero say anything?

Casca. Ay, he spoke Greek.

280 *Cassius.* To what effect?

Casca. Nay, an I tell you that, I'll ne'er look you i' th'
     face again. But those that understood him smiled at
     one another and shook their heads; but for mine own
     part, it was Greek to me. I could tell you more news
285 too: Marullus and Flavius, for pulling scarfs off
     Caesar's images, are put to silence.° Fare you well.
     There was more foolery yet, if I could remember it.

Cassius. Will you sup with me tonight, Casca?

Casca. No, I am promised forth.°

290 *Cassius.* Will you dine with me tomorrow?

Casca. Ay, if I be alive, and your mind hold,° and your
     dinner worth the eating.

Cassius. Good; I will expect you.

Casca. Do so. Farewell, both.   *Exit.*

295 *Brutus.* What a blunt fellow is this grown to be!
     He was quick mettle° when he went to school.

Cassius. So is he now in execution
     Of any bold or noble enterprise,

286 **put to silence** silenced (by being stripped of their tribuneships, and
perhaps exiled or executed) 289 **am promised forth** have a previous
engagement 291 **hold** does not change 296 **quick mettle** of a lively
disposition

However he puts on this tardy form.°
This rudeness is a sauce to his good wit,°   300
Which gives men stomach° to disgest° his words
With better appetite.

Brutus. And so it is. For this time I will leave you.
Tomorrow, if you please to speak with me,
I will come home to you; or if you will,   305
Come home to me, and I will wait for you.

Cassius. I will do so. Till then, think of the world.°
                                        Exit Brutus.
Well, Brutus, thou art noble; yet I see
Thy honorable mettle° may be wrought
From that it is disposed;° therefore it is meet°   310
That noble minds keep ever with their likes;
For who so firm that cannot be seduced?
Caesar doth bear me hard,° but he loves Brutus.
If I were Brutus now, and he were Cassius,
He should not humor° me. I will this night,   315
In several hands,° in at his windows throw,
As if they came from several citizens,
Writings, all tending to° the great opinion
That Rome holds of his name; wherein obscurely
Caesar's ambition shall be glancèd at.°   320
And after this, let Caesar seat him sure;°
For we will shake him, or worse days endure.   *Exit.*

---

299 **tardy form** sluggish appearance   300 **wit** intelligence   301 **stomach** appetite   301 **disgest** digest   307 **the world** i.e., the current state of affairs   309 **mettle** (1) disposition (2) metal   309–10 **wrought ... disposed** shaped (like iron) contrary to its natural form   310 **meet** fitting   313 **bear me hard** hold a grudge against me   315 **humor** cajole, influence by flattery   316 **several hands** different handwritings   318 **tending to** bearing on   320 **glancèd at** indirectly touched upon   321 **seat him sure** make his position secure

[Scene 3. *A street.*]

Thunder and lightning. Enter [*from opposite sides,*]
Casca and Cicero.

Cicero. Good even, Casca; brought you Caesar home?
Why are you breathless? And why stare you so?

Casca. Are not you moved, when all the sway of earth°
Shakes like a thing unfirm? O Cicero,
5   I have seen tempests, when the scolding winds
Have rived° the knotty oaks, and I have seen
Th' ambitious ocean swell and rage and foam,
To be exalted with° the threat'ning clouds;
But never till tonight, never till now,
10   Did I go through a tempest dropping fire.
Either there is a civil strife in heaven,
Or else the world, too saucy° with the gods,
Incenses them to send destruction.

Cicero. Why, saw you anything more wonderful?

15   *Casca.* A common slave—you know him well by sight—
Held up his left hand, which did flame and burn
Like twenty torches joined, and yet his hand,
Not sensible of° fire, remained unscorched.
Besides—I ha' not since put up my sword—
20   Against° the Capitol I met a lion,
Who glazed° upon me and went surly by
Without annoying me. And there were drawn
Upon a heap° a hundred ghastly° women,

1.3.3 **all the sway of earth** i.e., the whole scheme of things (*sway*: ruling
principle)   6 **rived** split   8 **exalted with** elevated to   12 **saucy** pre-
sumptuous   18 **sensible of** sensitive to   20 **Against** directly opposite (?)
near (?)   21 **glazed** stared   22–23 **drawn/Upon a heap** huddled together   23 **ghastly** white as ghosts

Transformèd with their fear, who swore they saw
Men, all in fire, walk up and down the streets.   25
And yesterday the bird of night° did sit
Even at noonday upon the market place,
Hooting and shrieking. When these prodigies°
Do so conjointly meet,° let not men say,
"These are their reasons, they are natural,"   30
For I believe they are portentous things
Unto the climate° that they point upon.

Cicero. Indeed, it is a strange-disposèd° time:
But men may construe things after their fashion,°
Clean from the purpose° of the things themselves.   35
Comes Caesar to the Capitol tomorrow?

Casca. He doth; for he did bid Antonius
Send word to you he would be there tomorrow.

Cicero. Good night then, Casca; this disturbèd sky
Is not to walk in.

Casca.   Farewell, Cicero.   *Exit Cicero.*   40

                Enter Cassius.

Cassius. Who's there?

Casca.   A Roman.

Cassius.   Casca, by your voice.

Casca. Your ear is good. Cassius, what night is this?

Cassius. A very pleasing night to honest men.

Casca. Who ever knew the heavens menace so?

Cassius. Those that have known the earth so full of
    faults.   45
For my part, I have walked about the streets,
Submitting me unto the perilous night,

26 **bird of night** owl (a bird of ill omen)   28 **prodigies** unnatural
events   29 **conjointly meet** coincide   32 **climate** region   33 **strange-
disposèd** abnormal   34 **after their fashion** in their own way   35 **Clean
from the purpose** quite contrary to the real meaning

And thus unbracèd,° Casca, as you see,
Have bared my bosom to the thunder-stone;°
50   And when the cross° blue lightning seemed to open
The breast of heaven, I did present myself
Even in the aim and very flash of it.

Casca. But wherefore did you so much tempt the heavens?
It is the part° of men to fear and tremble
55   When the most mighty gods by tokens° send
Such dreadful heralds to astonish° us.

Cassius. You are dull, Casca, and those sparks of life
That should be in a Roman you do want,°
Or else you use not. You look pale, and gaze,
60   And put on° fear, and cast yourself in wonder,°
To see the strange impatience of the heavens;
But if you would consider the true cause
Why all these fires, why all these gliding ghosts,
Why birds and beasts from quality and kind,°
65   Why old men,° fools, and children calculate,°
Why all these things change from their ordinance,°
Their natures and preformèd faculties,°
To monstrous quality,° why, you shall find
That heaven hath infused them with these spirits°
70   To make them instruments of fear and warning
Unto some monstrous state.°
Now could I, Casca, name to thee a man
Most like this dreadful night,
That thunders, lightens, opens graves, and roars
75   As doth the lion in the Capitol;
A man no mightier than thyself, or me,

48 **unbracèd** with doublet unfastened   49 **thunder-stone** lightning
bolt   50 **cross** jagged   54 **part** role   55 **tokens** prophetic signs
56 **astonish** stun   58 **want** lack   60 **put on** display   60 **cast yourself in
wonder** are amazed   64 **from quality and kind** (act) against their
natures   65 **old men** i.e., the senile, in second childhood   65 **calculate**
make predictions (cf. proverb, "Fools and children often do prophesy")   66 **ordinance** natural order of behavior   67 **preformèd faculties**
innate qualities   68 **monstrous quality** unnatural condition   69 **spirits**
supernatural powers   71 **monstrous state** abnormal state of affairs

In personal action, yet prodigious° grown
And fearful,° as these strange eruptions° are.

Casca. 'Tis Caesar that you mean, is it not, Cassius?

Cassius. Let it be who it is; for Romans now   *80*
Have thews° and limbs like to their ancestors;
But, woe the while!° Our fathers' minds are dead,
And we are governed with our mothers' spirits;
Our yoke and sufferance° show us womanish.

Casca. Indeed, they say the senators tomorrow   *85*
Mean to establish Caesar as a king;
And he shall wear his crown by sea and land,
In every place save here in Italy.

Cassius. I know where I will wear this dagger then;
Cassius from bondage will deliver Cassius.   *90*
Therein,° ye gods, you make the weak most strong;
Therein, ye gods, you tyrants do defeat.
Nor stony tower, nor walls of beaten brass,
Nor airless dungeon, nor strong links of iron,
Can be retentive to° the strength of spirit;   *95*
But life, being weary of these worldly bars,
Never lacks power to dismiss itself.
If I know this, know all the world besides,
That part of tyranny that I do bear
I can shake off at pleasure.   *Thunder still.*

Casca.   So can I;   *100*
So every bondman in his own hand bears
The power to cancel his captivity.

Cassius. And why should Caesar be a tyrant then?
Poor man, I know he would not be a wolf
But that he sees the Romans are but sheep;   *105*
He were no lion, were not Romans hinds.°

---

77 **prodigious** ominous   78 **fearful** causing fear   78 **eruptions** distur-
bances of nature   81 **thews** sinews   82 **woe the while** alas for the
times   84 **yoke and sufferance** servitude and the meek endurance of
it   91 **Therein** i.e., in suicide   95 **be retentive to** hold in   106 **hinds** (1)
female deer (2) peasants (3) servants

Those that with haste will make a mighty fire
Begin it with weak straws. What trash is Rome,
What rubbish and what offal, when it serves
110 For the base matter to illuminate
So vile a thing as Caesar! But, O grief,
Where hast thou led me? I, perhaps, speak this
Before a willing bondman; then I know
My answer must be made.° But I am armed,
115 And dangers are to me indifferent.°

Casca. You speak to Casca, and to such a man
That is no fleering° tell-tale. Hold, my hand.
Be factious° for redress of all these griefs,
And I will set this foot of mine as far
As who goes farthest.   [*They clasp hands.*]

120 *Cassius.*   There's a bargain made.
Now know you, Casca, I have moved already
Some certain of the noblest-minded Romans
To undergo° with me an enterprise
Of honorable dangerous consequence;
125 And I do know, by this° they stay for me
In Pompey's porch;° for now, this fearful night,
There is no stir or walking in the streets,
And the complexion of the element°
In favor's like° the work we have in hand,
130 Most bloody, fiery, and most terrible.

Enter Cinna.

Casca. Stand close° awhile, for here comes one in haste.

Cassius. 'Tis Cinna; I do know him by his gait;
He is a friend. Cinna, where haste you so?

114 **My answer must be made** I shall have to answer for my
words   115 **indifferent** unimportant   117 **fleering** flattering   118 **fac-
tious** active in forming a political party   123 **undergo** undertake   125 **by
this** by this time   126 **Pompey's porch** portico of Pompey's Theater   128 **complexion of the element** condition of the sky   129 **In favor's like** in appearance is like   131 **close** hidden

Cinna. To find out you. Who's that? Metellus Cimber?

Cassius. No, it is Casca, one incorporate   *135*
  To° our attempts. Am I not stayed° for, Cinna?

Cinna. I am glad on't.° What a fearful night is this!
  There's two or three of us have seen strange sights.

Cassius. Am I not stayed for? Tell me.

Cinna.   Yes, you are.
  O Cassius, if you could   *140*
  But win the noble Brutus to our party—

Cassius. Be you content. Good Cinna, take this paper,
  And look you lay it in the praetor's chair,°
  Where Brutus may but find it;° and throw this
  In at his window; set this up with wax   *145*
  Upon old Brutus'° statue. All this done,
  Repair° to Pompey's porch, where you shall find us.
  Is Decius° Brutus and Trebonius there?

Cinna. All but Metellus Cimber, and he's gone
  To seek you at your house. Well, I will hie,°   *150*
  And so bestow these papers as you bade me.

Cassius. That done, repair to Pompey's Theater.
                          Exit Cinna.
  Come, Casca, you and I will yet ere day
  See Brutus at his house; three parts of him
  Is ours already, and the man entire   *155*
  Upon the next encounter yields him ours.

135–36 **incorporate/To** intimately bound up with   136 **stayed** waited
137 **on't** of it (i.e., that Casca has joined the conspiracy)   143 **praetor's
chair** official chair in which Brutus would sit as chief magistrate, an office
next in rank to consul   144 **Where Brutus may but find it** where only
Brutus may find it   146 **old Brutus** (Lucius Junius Brutus, founder of the
Roman Republic)   147 **Repair** go   148 **Decius** (actually Decimus, a
kinsman of Marcus Brutus; the error is found in North's Plutarch)
150 **hie** hurry

Casca. O, he sits high in all the people's hearts;
And that which would appear offense in us,
His countenance,° like richest alchemy,°
160 Will change to virtue and to worthiness.

Cassius. Him, and his worth, and our great need of him,
You have right well conceited.° Let us go,
For it is after midnight, and ere day
We will awake him and be sure of him.   *Exeunt.*

159 **countenance** support   159 **alchemy** (the "science" by which many
experimenters tried to turn base metals into gold)   162 **conceited** (1) understood (2) described in an elaborate simile

ACT 2

[Scene 1. *Rome*.]

Enter Brutus in his orchard.°

Brutus. What, Lucius, ho!
  I cannot, by the progress of the stars,
  Give guess how near to day. Lucius, I say!
  I would it were my fault to sleep so soundly.
  When, Lucius, when? Awake, I say! What, Lucius!   *5*

Enter Lucius.

Lucius. Called you, my lord?

Brutus. Get me a taper° in my study, Lucius.
  When it is lighted, come and call me here.

Lucius. I will, my lord.   *Exit.*

Brutus. It must be by his death; and for my part,   *10*
  I know no personal cause to spurn at° him,
  But for the general.° He would be crowned.
  How that might change his nature, there's the question.
  It is the bright day that brings forth the adder,
  And that craves° wary walking. Crown him that,   *15*
  And then I grant we put a sting in him

2.1.s.d. **orchard** garden 7 **taper** candle 11 **spurn at** rebel (literally "kick") against 12 **general** public welfare 15 **craves** demands

That at his will he may do danger° with.
Th' abuse of greatness is when it disjoins
Remorse° from power; and, to speak truth of Caesar,
20 I have not known when his affections swayed°
More than his reason. But 'tis a common proof°
That lowliness° is young ambition's ladder,
Whereto the climber upward turns his face;
But when he once attains the upmost round,°
25 He then unto the ladder turns his back,
Looks in the clouds, scorning the base degrees°
By which he did ascend. So Caesar may;
Then lest he may, prevent.° And, since the quarrel°
Will bear no color° for the thing he is,
30 Fashion it° thus: that what he is, augmented,
Would run to these and these extremities;°
And therefore think him as a serpent's egg
Which hatched, would as his kind° grow mischievous,
And kill him in the shell.

Enter Lucius.

35 *Lucius.* The taper burneth in your closet,° sir.
Searching the window for a flint, I found
This paper thus sealed up, and I am sure
It did not lie there when I went to bed.
Gives him the letter.

Brutus. Get you to bed again; it is not day.
40 Is not tomorrow, boy, the ides of March?

Lucius. I know not, sir.

Brutus. Look in the calendar and bring me word.

Lucius. I will, sir.   *Exit.*

17 **danger** harm   18–19 **disjoins/Remorse** separates mercy   20 **affections swayed** emotions ruled   21 **common proof** matter of common experience   22 **lowliness** humility   24 **round** rung   26 **base degrees** (1) low steps of the ladder (2) less important grades of office (3) common people   28 **prevent** take action to forestall   28 **quarrel** cause of complaint   29 **bear no color** have no excuse   30 **Fashion it** construct the case   31 **these and these extremities** such and such extremes (of tyranny)   33 **as his kind** according to its nature   35 **closet** study

Brutus. The exhalations° whizzing in the air
  Give so much light that I may read by them.   45
                        Opens the letter and reads.

     "Brutus, thou sleep'st; awake, and see thyself.
     Shall Rome, &c.° Speak, strike, redress.
     Brutus, thou sleep'st; awake."

  Such instigations have been often dropped
  Where I have took them up.   50
  "Shall Rome, &c." Thus must I piece it out:°
  Shall Rome stand under one man's awe?° What,
     Rome?
  My ancestors did from the streets of Rome
  The Tarquin drive, when he was called a king.
  "Speak, strike, redress." Am I entreated   55
  To speak and strike? O Rome, I make thee promise,
  If the redress will follow, thou receivest
  Thy full petition at the hand of° Brutus!

                        Enter Lucius.

Lucius. Sir, March is wasted fifteen days. *Knock within.*

Brutus. 'Tis good. Go to the gate; somebody knocks.   60
                        [*Exit Lucius.*]
  Since Cassius first did whet° me against Caesar,
  I have not slept.
  Between the acting of a dreadful thing
  And the first motion,° all the interim is
  Like a phantasma,° or a hideous dream.   65
  The genius° and the mortal instruments°
  Are then in council, and the state of a man,
  Like to a little kingdom, suffers then
  The nature of an insurrection.°

44 **exhalations** meteors   47, 51 **&c.** (read "et cetera")   51 **piece it out**
develop the meaning   52 **under one man's awe** in awe of one man
58 **Thy full ... hand of** all you ask from   61 **whet** incite   64 **motion**
prompting   65 **phantasma** hallucination   66 **genius** guardian spirit (?)
reasoning spirit (?)   66 **mortal instruments** the emotions and physical
powers (which should be ruled and guided by reason)   69 **nature of an
insurrection** a kind of insurrection

Enter Lucius.

70 *Lucius.* Sir, 'tis your brother° Cassius at the door,
    Who doth desire to see you.

Brutus.   Is he alone?

Lucius. No, sir, there are moe° with him.

Brutus.   Do you know them?

Lucius. No, sir; their hats are plucked about their ears,
    And half their faces buried in their cloaks,
75   That by no means I may discover° them
    By any mark of favor.°

Brutus.   Let 'em enter. [*Exit Lucius.*]
    They are the faction. O conspiracy,
    Sham'st thou to show thy dang'rous brow by night,
    When evils are most free?° O, then by day
80   Where wilt thou find a cavern dark enough
    To mask thy monstrous visage? Seek none, conspir-
        acy;
    Hide it in smiles and affability:
    For if thou path,° thy native semblance° on,
    Not Erebus° itself were dim enough
85   To hide thee from prevention.°

*Enter the conspirators, Cassius, Casca, Decius, Cinna,
    Metellus [Cimber], and Trebonius.*

Cassius. I think we are too bold upon° your rest.
    Good morrow, Brutus; do we trouble you?

Brutus. I have been up this hour, awake all night.
    Know I these men that come along with you?

90 *Cassius.* Yes, every man of them; and no man here
    But honors you; and every one doth wish

70 **brother** i.e., brother-in-law (Cassius was married to Brutus' sister) 72 **moe** more 75 **discover** recognize 76 **favor** appearance
79 **evils are most free** evil things roam most freely 83 **path** walk (verb)
83 **native semblance** true appearance 84 **Erebus** dark region between
earth and Hades 85 **from prevention** from being forestalled and hindered 86 **upon** in intruding on

You had but that opinion of yourself
Which every·noble Roman bears of you.
This is Trebonius.

Brutus.   He is welcome hither.

Cassius. This, Decius Brutus.

Brutus.   He is welcome too.   95

Cassius. This, Casca; this, Cinna; and this, Metellus
    Cimber.

Brutus. They are all welcome.
    What watchful cares° do interpose themselves
    Betwixt your eyes and night?

Cassius. Shall I entreat a word?   *They whisper.* 100

Decius. Here lies the east; doth not the day break here?

Casca. No.

Cinna. O, pardon, sir, it doth; and yon gray lines
    That fret° the clouds are messengers of day.

Casca. You shall confess that you are both deceived.   105
    Here, as I point my sword, the sun arises,
    Which is a great way growing on° the south,
    Weighing° the youthful season of the year.
    Some two months hence, up higher toward the north
    He first presents his fire; and the high° east   110
    Stands as the Capitol, directly here.

Brutus. Give me your hands all over, one by one.

Cassius. And lct us swear our resolution.

Brutus. No, not an oath. If not the face of men,°
    The sufferance° of our souls, the time's abuse°—   115

98 **watchful cares** cares that keep you awake   104 **fret** pattern, inter-
lace   107 **growing on** tending toward   108 **Weighing** considering   110 **high** due   114 **the face of men** i.e., the sincere and resolute
appearance of the conspirators, which should not be distrust-
ed   115 **sufferance** patient endurance   115 **time's abuse** corruption of
the age (i.e., Caesar's assumption of unconstitutional powers)

If these be motives weak, break off betimes,°
And every man hence to his idle bed:
So let high-sighted° tyranny range° on
Till each man drop by lottery.° But if these
120   (As I am sure they do) bear fire enough
To kindle cowards and to steel with valor
The melting spirits of women, then, countrymen,
What need we any spur but our own cause
To prick° us to redress? What other bond
125   Than secret Romans° that have spoke the word,
And will not palter?° And what other oath
Than honesty° to honesty engaged°
That this shall be, or we will fall for it?
Swear° priests and cowards and men cautelous,°
130   Old feeble carrions° and such suffering souls
That welcome wrongs; unto bad causes swear
Such creatures as men doubt; but do not stain
The even° virtue of our enterprise,
Nor th' insuppressive mettle° of our spirits,
135   To think that or our cause or° our performance
Did need an oath; when every drop of blood
That every Roman bears, and nobly bears,
Is guilty of a several bastardy°
If he do break the smallest particle
140   Of any promise that hath passed from him.

Cassius. But what of Cicero? Shall we sound him?
I think he will stand very strong with us.

Casca. Let us not leave him out.

Cinna.   No, by no means.

Metellus. O, let us have him, for his silver hairs

116 **betimes** immediately   118 **high-sighted** arrogant (viewing widely
from on high, like a falcon ready to swoop on prey)   118 **range** rove or fly
in search of prey   119 **by lottery** by chance, i.e., at the tyrant's
whim   124 **prick** urge   125 **secret Romans** the fact that we are Romans
capable of maintaining secrecy   126 **palter** equivocate   127 **honesty**
personal honor   127 **engaged** pledged   129 **Swear** bind by oath
129 **cautelous** deceitful   130 **carrions** wretches almost dead and rotting
133 **even** unblemished, perfect   134 **insuppressive mettle** indomitable
temper   135 **or ... or** either ... or   138 **guilty ... bastardy** i.e., guilty
of an act not truly Roman

Will purchase us a good opinion,°   *145*
And buy men's voices to commend our deeds.
It shall be said his judgment ruled our hands;
Our youths and wildness shall no whit° appear,
But all be buried in his gravity.°

Brutus. O, name him not! Let us not break with him;° *150*
For he will never follow anything
That other men begin.

Cassius.   Then leave him out.

Casca. Indeed, he is not fit.

Decius. Shall no man else be touched but only Caesar?

Cassius. Decius, well urged.° I think it is not meet   *155*
Mark Antony, so well beloved of Caesar,
Should outlive Caesar; we shall find of° him
A shrewd contriver;° and you know, his means;
If he improve° them, may well stretch so far
As to annoy° us all; which to prevent,°   *160*
Let Antony and Caesar fall together.

Brutus. Our course will seem too bloody, Caius Cassius,
To cut the head off and then hack the limbs,
Like wrath in death and envy° afterwards;
For Antony is but a limb of Caesar.   *165*
Let's be sacrificers, but not butchers, Caius.
We all stand up against the spirit of Caesar,°
And in the spirit of men there is no blood.
O, that we then could come by° Caesar's spirit,
And not dismember Caesar! But, alas,   *170*
Caesar must bleed for it. And, gentle° friends,
Let's kill him boldly, but not wrathfully;

145 **opinion** reputation   148 **no whit** not in the slightest   149 **gravity** sobriety and stability (Latin *gravitas*)   150 **break with him** divulge our plan to him   155 **urged** suggested   157 **of** in   158 **shrewd contriver** cunning and malicious plotter   159 **improve** make good use of   160 **annoy** harm   160 **prevent** forestall   164 **envy** malice, i.e., as though we were killing Caesar for personal spite and hatred   167 **the spirit of Caesar** the principles (of tyranny) for which Caesar stands   169 **come by** get possession of   171 **gentle** noble

Let's carve him as a dish fit for the gods,
Not hew him as a carcass fit for hounds.
175 And let our hearts, as subtle masters do,
Stir up their servants° to an act of rage,
And after seem to chide 'em. This shall make
Our purpose necessary, and not envious;°
Which so appearing to the common eyes,
180 We shall be called purgers,° not murderers.
And for Mark Antony, think not of him;
For he can do no more than Caesar's arm
When Caesar's head is off.

Cassius.   Yet I fear him;
For in the ingrafted° love he bears to Caesar——

185 *Brutus.* Alas, good Cassius, do not think of him.
If he love Caesar, all that he can do
Is to himself—take thought° and die for Caesar.
And that were much he should,° for he is given
To sports, to wildness, and much company.

190 *Trebonius.* There is no fear° in him; let him not die,
For he will live and laugh at this hereafter.
                                        Clock strikes.

Brutus. Peace! Count the clock.

Cassius.   The clock hath stricken three.

Trebonius. 'Tis time to part.

Cassius.   But it is doubtful yet
Whether Caesar will come forth today or no;
195 For he is superstitious grown of late,
Quite from the main° opinion he held once
Of fantasy, of dreams, and ceremonies.°
It may be these apparent prodigies,°
The unaccustomed terror of this night,

176 **servants** (1) the hands (2) the passions   178 **envious** malicious   180 **purgers** healers   184 **ingrafted** firmly rooted   187 **take
thought** grow melancholy with brooding   188 **that were much he should**
that would be too much to expect of him   190 **no fear** nothing to fear
196 **Quite from the main** at variance with the strong   197 **ceremonies**
omens   198 **apparent prodigies** obvious signs of disaster

And the persuasion of his augurers°   200
May hold him from the Capitol today.

Decius. Never fear that. If he be so resolved,
  I can o'ersway him;° for he loves to hear
  That unicorns may be betrayed with trees,°
  And bears with glasses,° elephants with holes,°   205
  Lions with toils,° and men with flatterers;
  But when I tell him he hates flatterers,
  He says he does, being then most flatterèd.
  Let me work;
  For I can give his humor° the true bent,°   210
  And I will bring him to the Capitol.

Cassius. Nay, we will all of us be there to fetch him.

Brutus. By the eighth hour; is that the uttermost?°

Cinna. Be that the uttermost, and fail not then.

Metellus. Caius Ligarius doth bear Caesar hard,°   215
  Who rated° him for speaking well of Pompey.
  I wonder none of you have thought of him.

Brutus. Now, good Metellus, go along by him.°
  He loves me well, and I have given him reasons;
  Send him but hither, and I'll fashion° him.   220

Cassius. The morning comes upon 's; we'll leave you,
    Brutus.
  And, friends, disperse yourselves; but all remember
  What you have said, and show yourselves true Romans.

Brutus. Good gentlemen, look fresh and merrily.
  Let not our looks put on° our purposes,   225

200 **augurers** augurs (priests who foretold, from omens, the future)
203 **o'ersway him** persuade him to change his mind   204 **betrayed
with trees** i.e., tricked into running at a tree (at the last moment its prey
steps aside so that the horn is deeply embedded and the unicorn is help-
less)   205 **glasses** mirrors   205 **holes** pitfalls   206 **toils** nets, snares
210 **humor** temperament   210 **bent** direction   213 **uttermost** latest
215 **bear Caesar hard** has a grudge against Caesar   216 **rated** berated
218 **him** his house   220 **fashion** shape (to our designs)   225 **put on** display

But bear it° as our Roman actors do,
With untired spirits and formal constancy.°
And so good morrow to you every one.
                              Exeunt. Manet° Brutus.
Boy! Lucius! Fast asleep? It is no matter;
230 Enjoy the honey-heavy dew° of slumber.
Thou hast no figures nor no fantasies°
Which busy care draws in the brains of men;
Therefore thou sleep'st so sound.

Enter Portia.

Portia.   Brutus, my lord.

Brutus. Portia, what mean you? Wherefore rise you now?
235 It is not for your health thus to commit
Your weak condition to the raw cold morning.

Portia. Nor for yours neither. Y'have ungently,° Brutus,
Stole from my bed; and yesternight at supper
You suddenly arose and walked about,
240 Musing and sighing, with your arms across;°
And when I asked you what the matter was,
You stared upon me with ungentle looks.
I urged you further; then you scratched your head,
And too impatiently stamped with your foot.
245 Yet I insisted, yet you answered not,
But with an angry wafter° of your hand
Gave sign for me to leave you. So I did,
Fearing to strengthen that impatience
Which seemed too much enkindled, and withal°
250 Hoping it was but an effect of humor,°
Which sometime hath his° hour with every man.
It will not let you eat, nor talk, nor sleep,
And could it work so much upon your shape

226 **bear it** play our parts 227 **formal constancy** consistent
decorum 228s.d. **Manet** remains 230 **dew** i.e., refreshment 231 **figures . . . fantasies** (both words specify figments of the imagination)
237 **ungently** discourteously 240 **across** folded (a sign of melancholy)
246 **wafter** waving 249 **withal** also 250 **effect of humor** i.e., sign of a
temporary mood 251 **his** its

As it hath much prevailed on your condition,°
I should not know you° Brutus. Dear my lord,　　　255
Make me acquainted with your cause of grief.

Brutus. I am not well in health, and that is all.

Portia. Brutus is wise and, were he not in health,
He would embrace the means to come by it.

Brutus. Why, so I do. Good Portia, go to bed.　　　260

Portia. Is Brutus sick, and is it physical°
To walk unbracèd° and suck up the humors°
Of the dank morning? What, is Brutus sick,
And will he steal out of his wholesome bed,
To dare the vile contagion of the night,°　　　265
And tempt the rheumy and unpurgèd air°
To add unto his sickness? No, my Brutus;
You have some sick offense° within your mind,
Which by the right and virtue of my place°
I ought to know of; and upon my knees　　　270
I charm° you, by my once commended beauty,
By all your vows of love, and that great vow
Which did incorporate° and make us one,
That you unfold to me, your self, your half,
Why you are heavy,° and what men tonight　　　275
Have had resort to you; for here have been
Some six or seven, who did hide their faces
Even from darkness.

Brutus.　　　　　　　　Kneel not, gentle Portia.

Portia. I should not need, if you were gentle Brutus.
Within the bond of marriage, tell me, Brutus,　　　280
Is it excepted° I should know no secrets
That appertain to you? Am I your self

254 **condition** disposition　255 **know you** recognize you as 261 **physical**
healthy　262 **unbracèd** with doublet unfastened　262 **humors** damp-
ness, mist　265 **night** (night air was thought to be harmful, even poison-
ous)　266 **tempt . . . air** risk the damp and unpurified (by the sun) air
268 **sick offense** sickness that harms　269 **place** situation (as wife)
271 **charm** entreat　273 **incorporate** make us one flesh (cf. Matthew 19:5,
"they twain shall be one flesh")　275 **heavy** dejected　281 **excepted**
made an exception that

But, as it were, in sort or limitation,°
To keep with you at meals, comfort your bed,
And talk to you sometimes? Dwell I but in the sub-
285   urbs°
Of your good pleasure? If it be no more,
Portia is Brutus' harlot, not his wife.

Brutus. You are my true and honorable wife,
As dear to me as are the ruddy drops
290   That visit my sad heart.

Portia. If this were true, then should I know this secret.
I grant I am a woman; but withal°
A woman that Lord Brutus took to wife.
I grant I am a woman; but withal
295   A woman well reputed; Cato's daughter.°
Think you I am no stronger than my sex,
Being so fathered and so husbanded?
Tell me your counsels,° I will not disclose 'em.
I have made strong proof of my constancy,°
300   Giving myself a voluntary wound
Here in the thigh; can I bear that with patience,
And not my husband's secrets?

Brutus.   O ye gods,
Render me worthy of this noble wife!   *Knock.*
Hark, hark! One knocks. Portia, go in a while,
305   And by and by thy bosom shall partake
The secrets of my heart.
All my engagements° I will construe° to thee,
All the charactery of° my sad brows.
Leave me with haste.   *Exit Portia.*

---

283 **in sort or limitation** after a fashion or within a certain restriction (legal terms)   285 **suburbs** outlying districts (where the brothels and least respectable taverns were found)   292 **withal** at the same time   295 **Cato's daughter** (Marcus Porcius Cato was famous for his integrity; he joined Pompey against Caesar and killed himself at Utica in 46 B.C. to avoid capture; he was Brutus' uncle as well as father-in-law)   298 **counsels** secrets   299 **proof of my constancy** trial of my resolution   307 **engagements** commitments   307 **construe** explain   308 **charactery of** writing upon, i.e., wrinkles of grief and worry

Enter Lucius and [Caius] Ligarius.

Lucius, who's that knocks?

Lucius. Here is a sick man that would speak with you.   310

Brutus. Caius Ligarius, that Metellus spake of.
  Boy, stand aside. Caius Ligarius! How?°

Caius. Vouchsafe° good morrow from a feeble tongue.

Brutus. O, what a time have you chose out, brave°
    Caius,
  To wear a kerchief!° Would you were not sick!   315

Caius. I am not sick, if Brutus have in hand
  Any exploit worthy the name of honor.

Brutus. Such an exploit have I in hand, Ligarius,
  Had you a healthful ear to hear of it.

Caius. By all the gods that Romans bow before,   320
  I here discard my sickness! Soul of Rome,
  Brave son, derived from honorable loins,°
  Thou, like an exorcist,° hast conjured up
  My mortifièd° spirit. Now bid me run,
  And I will strive with things impossible,   325
  Yea, get the better of them. What's to do?

Brutus. A piece of work that will make sick men whole.°

Caius. But are not some whole that we must make sick?

Brutus. That must we also. What it is, my Caius,
  I shall unfold to thee, as we are going   330
  To whom° it must be done.

Caius.   Set on° your foot,
  And with a heart new-fired I follow you,

312 **How** how are you   313 **Vouchsafe** please accept   314 **brave**
noble   315 **To wear a kerchief** (as a protection against drafts), i.e., to be
sick   322 **from honorable loins** i.e., descent from Lucius Junius Brutus,
founder of the Roman Republic   323 **exorcist** conjurer   324 **mortifièd**
deadened   327 **whole** healthy   331 **To whom** to the house of him to
whom   332 **Set on** advance

To do I know not what; but it sufficeth
That Brutus leads me on.   *Thunder.*

Brutus.   Follow me, then.   *Exeunt.*

[Scene 2. *Caesar's house.*]

*Thunder and lightning. Enter Julius Caesar in his
nightgown.°*

Caesar. Nor heaven nor earth have been at peace to-
night:
Thrice hath Calphurnia in her sleep cried out,
"Help, ho! They murder Caesar!" Who's within?

Enter a Servant.

Servant. My lord?

5   *Caesar.* Go bid the priests do present° sacrifice,
And bring me their opinions of success.°

Servant. I will, my lord.   *Exit.*

Enter Calphurnia.

Calphurnia. What mean you, Caesar? Think you to walk
forth?
You shall not stir out of your house today.

10   *Caesar.* Caesar shall forth. The things that threatened me
Ne'er looked but on my back; when they shall see
The face of Caesar, they are vanishèd.

Calphurnia. Caesar, I never stood on ceremonies,°
Yet now they fright me. There is one within,
15   Besides the things that we have heard and seen,
Recounts most horrid sights seen by the watch.°

2.2.s.d. **nightgown** dressing gown   5 **present** immediate   6 **opinions of
success** judgment as to the future course of events   13 **stood on ceremonies** paid attention to omens   16 **watch** nightwatchmen

A lioness hath whelpèd in the streets,
And graves have yawned, and yielded up their dead;
Fierce fiery warriors fought upon the clouds
In ranks and squadrons and right form° of war,   20
Which drizzled blood upon the Capitol;
The noise of battle hurtled° in the air,
Horses did neigh and dying men did groan,
And ghosts did shriek and squeal about the streets.
O Caesar, these things are beyond all use,°   25
And I do fear them.

Caesar.   What can be avoided
Whose end is purposed by the mighty gods?
Yet Caesar shall go forth; for these predictions
Are to° the world in general as to Caesar.

Calphurnia. When beggars die, there are no comets
seen;   30
The heavens themselves blaze forth° the death of
princes.

Caesar. Cowards die many times before their deaths;
The valiant never taste of death but once.
Of all the wonders that I yet have heard,
It seems to me most strange that men should fear,   35
Seeing that death, a necessary end,
Will come when it will come.

Enter a Servant.

                                What say the augurers?

Servant. They would not have you to stir forth today.
Plucking the entrails of an offering forth,
They could not find a heart within the beast.   40

Caesar. The gods do this in shame of cowardice:
Caesar should° be a beast without a heart°
If he should stay at home today for fear.
No, Caesar shall not; Danger knows full well
That Caesar is more dangerous than he.   45

20 **right form** proper military formation   22 **hurtled** clashed   25 **use**
normal experience   29 **Are to** apply to   31 **blaze forth** i.e., proclaim (by
comets and meteors)   42 **should** would   42 **heart** (the organ of courage)

We are two lions littered in one day,
And I the elder and more terrible,
And Caesar shall go forth.

Calphurnia.   Alas, my lord,
Your wisdom is consumed in confidence.°
50 Do not go forth today. Call it my fear
That keeps you in the house and not your own.
We'll send Mark Antony to the Senate House,
And he shall say you are not well today.
Let me, upon my knee, prevail in this.

55 *Caesar.* Mark Antony shall say I am not well,
And for thy humor,° I will stay at home.

Enter Decius.

Here's Decius Brutus, he shall tell them so.

Decius. Caesar, all hail! Good morrow, worthy Caesar;
I come to fetch° you to the Senate House.

60 *Caesar.* And you are come in very happy time°
To bear my greeting to the senators,
And tell them that I will not come today.
Cannot, is false; and that I dare not, falser:
I will not come today. Tell them so, Decius.

Calphurnia. Say he is sick.

65 *Caesar.*   Shall Caesar send a lie?
Have I in conquest stretched mine arm so far
To be afeard to tell graybeards the truth?
Decius, go tell them Caesar will not come.

Decius. Most mighty Caesar, let me know some cause,
70 Lest I be laughed at when I tell them so.

Caesar. The cause is in my will: I will not come.
That is enough to satisfy the Senate.
But for your private satisfaction,
Because I love you, I will let you know.

---

49 **consumed in confidence** destroyed by too much confidence   56 **humor** whim   59 **fetch** escort   60 **happy time** favorable time (i.e., just at the right moment)

Calphurnia here, my wife, stays° me at home.   75
She dreamt tonight° she saw my statue,°
Which, like a fountain with an hundred spouts,
Did run pure blood, and many lusty Romans
Came smiling and did bathe their hands in it.
And these does she apply for° warnings and portents°   80
And evils imminent, and on her knee
Hath begged that I will stay at home today.

Decius. This dream is all amiss interpreted;
It was a vision fair and fortunate:
Your statue spouting blood in many pipes,   85
In which so many smiling Romans bathed,
Signifies that from you great Rome shall suck
Reviving blood, and that great men shall press
For tinctures, stains, relics, and cognizance.°
This by Calphurnia's dream is signified.   90

Caesar. And this way have you well expounded it.

Decius. I have, when you have heard what I can say;
And know it now, the Senate have concluded
To give this day a crown to mighty Caesar.
If you shall send them word you will not come,   95
Their minds may change. Besides, it were a mock
Apt to be rendered,° for someone to say
"Break up the Senate till another time,
When Caesar's wife shall meet with better dreams."
If Caesar hide himself, shall they not whisper   100
"Lo, Caesar is afraid"?
Pardon me, Caesar, for my dear dear love
To your proceeding° bids me tell you this,
And reason to my love is liable.°

75 **stays** keeps   76 **tonight** i.e., last night   76 **statue** (trisyllabic; pronounced "stat-u-a")   80 **apply for** explain as   80 **portents** (accent on last syllable)   89 **tinctures . . . cognizance** (Samuel Johnson paraphrases the line: "The Romans, says Decius, all come to you, as to a saint, for relics; as to a prince, for honors")   **tinctures** (1) alchemical elixirs (2) colors, metals, etc. used in heraldry   **stains** colors in a coat of arms   **relics** venerated property of a martyr   **cognizance** mark of identification worn by a nobleman's followers   96–97 **mock . . . rendered** jeering remark likely to be made   103 **proceeding** advancement   104 **reason . . . liable** i.e., my affection proves stronger than my judgment (of impropriety) in telling you this (*liable* = subordinate)

Caesar. How foolish do your fears seem now,
105   Calphurnia!
    I am ashamèd I did yield to them.
    Give me my robe,° for I will go.

*Enter Brutus, Ligarius, Metellus [Cimber], Casca,
    Trebonius, Cinna, and Publius.*

And look where Publius is come to fetch me.

Publius. Good morrow, Caesar.

Caesar.   Welcome, Publius.
110   What, Brutus, are you stirred so early too?
    Good morrow, Casca. Caius Ligarius,
    Caesar was ne'er so much your enemy°
    As that same ague which hath made you lean.
    What is't o'clock?

Brutus.   Caesar, 'tis strucken eight.

115 *Caesar.* I thank you for your pains and courtesy.

Enter Antony.

    See! Antony, that revels long a-nights,
    Is notwithstanding up. Good morrow, Antony.

Antony. So to most noble Caesar.

Caesar.   Bid them prepare° within.
    I am to blame to be thus waited for.
120   Now, Cinna; now, Metellus; what, Trebonius,
    I have an hour's talk in store for you;
    Remember that you call on me today;
    Be near me, that I may remember you.

Trebonius. Caesar, I will [*aside*] and so near will I be,
125   That your best friends shall wish I had been further.

Caesar. Good friends, go in and taste some wine with
    me,

107 **robe** toga   112 **enemy** (Ligarius had supported Pompey against
Caesar in the Civil War and had recently been pardoned by Caesar)   118 **prepare** i.e., set out the wine mentioned in line 126

And we (like friends) will straightway go together.

Brutus. [*Aside*] That every like is not the same,° O Caesar,
The heart of Brutus earns° to think upon.   *Exeunt.*

[Scene 3. *A street near the Capitol, close to Brutus'
house.*]

Enter Artemidorus [*reading a paper*].

[*Artemidorus.*] "Caesar, beware of Brutus; take heed of
Cassius; come not near Casca; have an eye to Cinna;
trust not Trebonius; mark well Metellus Cimber;
Decius Brutus loves thee not; thou hast wronged
Caius Ligarius. There is but one mind in all these   5
men, and it is bent° against Caesar. If thou beest not
immortal, look about you: security gives way to con-
spiracy.° The mighty gods defend thee!
                        Thy lover,° ARTEMIDORUS."
Here will I stand till Caesar pass along,   10
And as a suitor° will I give him this.
My heart laments that virtue cannot live
Out of the teeth of emulation.°
If thou read this, O Caesar, thou mayest live;
If not, the Fates with traitors do contrive.°   *Exit.* 15

128 **That every like is not the same** i.e., what a pity that those who appear
like friends may actually be enemies   129 **earns** grieves
2.3.6 **bent** directed   7–8 **security gives way to conspiracy** overconfi-
dence gives conspiracy its opportunity   9 **lover** devoted friend   11 **as a
suitor** like a petitioner   13 **Out of the teeth of emulation** beyond the
reach of envious rivalry   15 **contrive** conspire

[Scene 4. *Another part of the street.*]

Enter Portia and Lucius.

Portia. I prithee, boy, run to the Senate House;
    Stay not to answer me, but get thee gone.
    Why dost thou stay?

Lucius.   To know my errand, madam.

Portia. I would have had thee there and here again
5   Ere I can tell thee what thou shouldst do there.
    O constancy,° be strong upon my side;
    Set a huge mountain 'tween my heart and tongue!
    I have a man's mind, but a woman's might.°
    How hard it is for women to keep counsel!°
    Art thou here yet?

10 *Lucius.*   Madam, what should I do?
    Run to the Capitol, and nothing else?
    And so return to you, and nothing else?

Portia. Yes, bring me word, boy, if thy lord look well,
    For he went sickly forth; and take good note
15   What Caesar doth, what suitors press to him.
    Hark, boy, what noise is that?

Lucius. I hear none, madam.

Portia.   Prithee, listen well.
    I heard a bustling rumor like a fray,°
    And the wind brings it from the Capitol.

20 *Lucius.* Sooth,° madam, I hear nothing.

2.4.6 **constancy** resolution   8 **might** physical strength   9 **counsel** secret
(Brutus has obviously told her of the conspiracy, though "stage time" has
allowed no opportunity for this; the inconsistency is not noticeable during
a performance)   18 **bustling rumor like a fray** confused noise as of
battle   20 **Sooth** truly

Enter the Soothsayer.

Portia. Come hither, fellow. Which way hast thou been?

Soothsayer. At mine own house, good lady.

Portia. What is't o'clock?

Soothsayer.   About the ninth hour, lady.

Portia. Is Caesar yet gone to the Capitol?

Soothsayer. Madam, not yet; I go to take my stand,   25
To see him pass on to the Capitol.

Portia. Thou hast some suit to Caesar, hast thou not?

Soothsayer. That I have, lady; if it will please Caesar
To be so good to Caesar as to hear me,
I shall beseech him to befriend himself.   30

Portia. Why, know'st thou any harm's intended towards
him?

Soothsayer. None that I know will be, much that I fear
may chance.°
Good morrow to you. Here the street is narrow;
The throng that follows Caesar at the heels,
Of senators, of praetors, common suitors,   35
Will crowd a feeble man almost to death.
I'll get me to a place more void,° and there
Speak to great Caesar as he comes along.   *Exit.*

Portia. I must go in. Ay me, how weak a thing
The heart of woman is! O Brutus,   40
The heavens speed° thee in thine enterprise!
Sure, the boy heard me—Brutus hath a suit
That Caesar will not grant—O, I grow faint.
Run, Lucius, and commend me° to my lord;
Say I am merry;° come to me again,   45
And bring me word what he doth say to thee.
                    Exeunt [*severally*].

---

32 **chance** happen   37 **more void** more empty (less crowded)   41 **speed**
prosper   44 **commend me** give my love   45 **merry** cheerful

ACT 3

[Scene 1. *Rome. Before the Capitol.*]

*Flourish. Enter Caesar, Brutus, Cassius, Casca, Decius,
Metellus [Cimber], Trebonius, Cinna, Antony, Lepidus,
Artemidorus, Publius, [Popilius,] and the Soothsayer.*

Caesar. The ides of March are come.

Soothsayer. Ay, Caesar, but not gone.

Artemidorus. Hail, Caesar! Read this schedule.°

Decius. Trebonius doth desire you to o'er-read,
5   At your best leisure, this his humble suit.

Artemidorus. O Caesar, read mine first; for mine's a suit
That touches° Caesar nearer. Read it, great Caesar.

Caesar. What touches us ourself shall be last served.

Artemidorus. Delay not, Caesar; read it instantly.

Caesar. What, is the fellow mad?

10 *Publius.*   Sirrah, give place.°

Cassius. What, urge you your petitions in the street?
Come to the Capitol.

3.1.3 **schedule** scroll   7 **touches** concerns   10 **Sirrah, give place** fellow, get out of the way

46

[*Caesar goes to the Capitol, the rest following.*]

Popilius. I wish your enterprise today may thrive.

Cassius. What enterprise, Popilius?

Popilius.   Fare you well.
                    [*Advances to Caesar.*]

Brutus. What said Popilius Lena?   *15*

Cassius. He wished today our enterprise might thrive.
  I fear our purpose is discovered.

Brutus. Look how he makes to° Caesar; mark him.

Cassius. Casca, be sudden,° for we fear prevention.°
  Brutus, what shall be done? If this be known,   *20*
  Cassius or Caesar never shall turn back,°
  For I will slay myself.

Brutus.   Cassius, be constant.°
  Popilius Lena speaks not of our purposes;
  For look, he smiles, and Caesar doth not change.°

Cassius. Trebonius knows his time; for look you, Brutus,   *25*
  He draws Mark Antony out of the way.
                    [*Exeunt Antony and Trebonius.*]

Decius. Where is Metellus Cimber? Let him go
  And presently prefer° his suit to Caesar.

Brutus. He is addressed.° Press near and second him.

Cinna. Casca, you are the first that rears your hand.   *30*

Caesar. Are we all ready? What is now amiss
  That Caesar and his Senate must redress?

Metellus. Most high, most mighty, and most puissant°
      Caesar,
  Metellus Cimber throws before thy seat
  An humble heart.   [*Kneeling.*]

18 **makes to** heads for   19 **sudden** swift   19 **prevention** being forestalled   21 **turn back** i.e., return alive   22 **constant** calm   24 **change**
change his expression   28 **presently prefer** immediately pres-
ent   29 **addressed** ready   33 **puissant** powerful

35 *Caesar.*   I must prevent thee, Cimber.
    These couchings° and these lowly courtesies°
    Might fire the blood of ordinary men,
    And turn preordinance and first decree°
    Into the law of children. Be not fond°
40 To think that Caesar bears such rebel blood°
    That will be thawed from the true quality°
    With that° which melteth fools—I mean sweet words,
    Low-crookèd curtsies, and base spaniel° fawning.
    Thy brother by decree is banishèd.
45 If thou dost bend and pray and fawn for him,
    I spurn thee like a cur out of my way.
    Know, Caesar doth not wrong, nor without cause
    Will he be satisfied.

    Metellus. Is there no voice more worthy than my own,
50 To sound more sweetly in great Caesar's ear
    For the repealing° of my banished brother?

    Brutus. I kiss thy hand, but not in flattery, Caesar,
    Desiring thee that Publius Cimber may
    Have an immediate freedom of repeal.°

    Caesar. What, Brutus?

55 *Cassius.*   Pardon, Caesar; Caesar, pardon!
    As low as to thy foot doth Cassius fall
    To beg enfranchisement° for Publius Cimber.

    Caesar. I could be well moved, if I were as you;
    If I could pray to move,° prayers would move me;
60 But I am constant as the Northern Star,°
    Of whose true-fixed and resting° quality

36 **couchings** low bowings   36 **lowly courtesies** humble obeisances
38 **preordinance and first decree** customs and laws established from
antiquity   39 **fond** so foolish as   40 **bears such rebel blood** has such
uncontrolled emotions   41 **true quality** proper quality (i.e., firmness)
42 **With that** by those things   43 **spaniel** doglike, cringing   51 **repeal-
ing** recalling   54 **freedom of repeal** permission to be recalled from exile   57 **enfranchisement** recall, freedom   59 **pray to move** i.e., beg
others to change their minds   60 **constant as the Northern Star** un-
changing as the polestar   61 **resting** changeless

There is no fellow° in the firmament.
The skies are painted with unnumb'red° sparks,
They are all fire and every one doth shine;
But there's but one in all doth hold° his place.   65
So in the world; 'tis furnished well with men,
And men are flesh and blood, and apprehensive;°
Yet in the number I do know but one
That unassailable holds on his rank,°
Unshaked of motion;° and that I am he,   70
Let me a little show it, even in this—
That I was constant° Cimber should be banished,
And constant do remain to keep him so.

Cinna. O Caesar——

Caesar.   Hence! Wilt thou lift up Olympus?°

Decius. Great Caesar——

Caesar.   Doth not Brutus bootless° kneel?   75

Casca. Speak hands for me!   *They stab Caesar.*

Caesar. Et tu, Brutè?° Then fall Caesar.   *Dies.*

Cinna. Liberty! Freedom! Tyranny is dead!
Run hence, proclaim, cry it about the streets.

Cassius. Some to the common pulpits,° and cry out   80
"Liberty, freedom, and enfranchisement!"

Brutus. People, and senators, be not affrighted.
Fly not; stand still; ambition's debt is paid.°

Casca. Go to the pulpit, Brutus.

Decius.   And Cassius too.

---

62 **fellow** equal   63 **unnumb'red** innumerable   65 **hold** keep   67 **apprehensive** capable of reason   69 **holds on his rank** maintains his position   70 **Unshaked of motion** i.e., unmoved by internal or external forces   72 **constant** firmly determined   74 **Olympus** a mountain in Greece where the gods lived and held court   75 **bootless** in vain   77 **Et tu, Brutè** and you (too), Brutus   80 **pulpits** platforms for public speakers   83 **ambition's debt is paid** ambition has received what was due to it

85   *Brutus.* Where's Publius?°

Cinna. Here, quite confounded with this mutiny.°

Metellus. Stand fast together, lest some friend of Caesar's
     Should chance——

Brutus. Talk not of standing.° Publius, good cheer;
90   There is no harm intended to your person,
     Nor to no Roman else. So tell them, Publius.

Cassius. And leave us, Publius, lest that the people
     Rushing on us should do your age some mischief.

Brutus. Do so; and let no man abide° this deed
95   But we the doers.

                    Enter Trebonius.

Cassius. Where is Antony?

Trebonius.   Fled to his house amazed.°
     Men, wives, and children stare, cry out and run,
     As° it were doomsday.

Brutus.   Fates, we will know your pleasures.
     That we shall die, we know; 'tis but the time,
100   And drawing days out, that men stand upon.°

Casca. Why, he that cuts off twenty years of life
     Cuts off so many years of fearing death.

Brutus. Grant that, and then is death a benefit.
     So are we Caesar's friends, that have abridged
105   His time of fearing death. Stoop, Romans, stoop,
     And let us bathe our hands in Caesar's blood
     Up to the elbows, and besmear our swords.
     Then walk we forth, even to the market place,°
     And waving our red weapons o'er our heads,

85 **Publius** an old senator, too infirm to flee   86 **confounded with this
mutiny** overwhelmed by this uproar   89 **Talk not of standing** i.e., don't
worry about making a stand, organizing resistance   94 **abide** bear the consequences of   96 **amazed** utterly confused   98 **As** as if   100 **drawing
. . . upon** (hope of) prolonging life, that men are concerned about   108 **the
market place** the Roman Forum, center of business and public affairs

Let's all cry "Peace, freedom, and liberty!"   *110*

Cassius. Stoop then, and wash. How many ages hence
Shall this our lofty scene be acted over
In states unborn and accents yet unknown!

Brutus. How many times shall Caesar bleed in sport,°
That now on Pompey's basis° lies along°   *115*
No worthier than the dust!

Cassius.   So oft as that shall be,
So often shall the knot° of us be called
The men that gave their country liberty.

Decius. What, shall we forth?

Cassius.   Ay, every man away.
Brutus shall lead, and we will grace° his heels   *120*
With the most boldest and best hearts of Rome.

Enter a Servant.

Brutus. Soft,° who comes here? A friend of Antony's.

Servant. Thus, Brutus, did my master bid me kneel;
Thus did Mark Antony bid me fall down;
And, being prostrate, thus he bade me say: *125*
Brutus is noble, wise, valiant, and honest;°
Caesar was mighty, bold, royal,° and loving.
Say I love Brutus and I honor him;
Say I feared Caesar, honored him, and loved him.
If Brutus will vouchsafe that Antony   *130*
May safely come to him and be resolved°
How Caesar hath deserved to lie in death,
Mark Antony shall not love Caesar dead
So well as Brutus living; but will follow
The fortunes and affairs of noble Brutus   *135*
Thorough° the hazards of this untrod state°

114 **in sport** for entertainment, i.e., as part of a play   115 **basis** pedestal
of statue   115 **along** stretched out   117 **knot** closely bound group
120 **grace** do honor to   122 **Soft** wait a moment   126 **honest** honorable   127 **royal** of princely generosity   131 **be resolved** have it explained to his satisfaction   136 **Thorough** through   136 **untrod state**
new and uncertain state of affairs

With all true faith. So says my master Antony.

Brutus. Thy master is a wise and valiant Roman;
I never thought him worse.
140   Tell him, so° please him come unto this place,
He shall be satisfied and, by my honor,
Depart untouched.

Servant.   I'll fetch him presently.°
                                        Exit Servant.

Brutus. I know that we shall have him well to friend.°

Cassius. I wish we may. But yet have I a mind
145   That fears him much; and my misgiving still
Falls shrewdly to the purpose.°

                    Enter Antony.

Brutus. But here comes Antony. Welcome, Mark
Antony.

Antony. O mighty Caesar! Dost thou lie so low?
Are all thy conquests, glories, triumphs, spoils,
150   Shrunk to this little measure? Fare thee well.
I know not, gentlemen, what you intend,
Who else must be let blood,° who else is rank.°
If I myself, there is no hour so fit
As Caesar's death's hour, nor no instrument
155   Of half that worth as those your swords, made rich
With the most noble blood of all this world.
I do beseech ye, if you bear me hard,°
Now, whilst your purpled° hands do reek and smoke,°
Fulfill your pleasure. Live° a thousand years,
160   I shall not find myself so apt° to die;

140 **so** if it should   142 **presently** immediately   143 **well to friend** as a
good friend   145–46 **misgiving . . . purpose** my forebodings always turn
out to be justified   152 **let blood** (1) bled, purged (common Elizabethan
practice of drawing blood to cure those swollen with disease) (2) put to
death   152 **rank** (1) swollen with disease (2) overgrown, i.e., too
powerful   157 **bear me hard** have a grudge against me   158 **purpled**
(1) made scarlet (with blood) (2) made royal (?)   158 **reek and smoke**
i.e., steam (with freshly shed warm blood)   159 **Live** though I live
160 **apt** prepared

No place will please me so, no mean° of death,
As here by Caesar, and by you cut off,
The choice and master spirits of this age.

Brutus. O Antony, beg not your death of us!
Though now we must appear bloody and cruel,   *165*
As by our hands and this our present act
You see we do, yet see you but our hands
And this the bleeding business they have done.
Our hearts you see not; they are pitiful;°
And pity to the general wrong of Rome—   *170*
As fire drives out fire, so pity pity°—
Hath done this deed on Caesar. For your part,
To you our swords have leaden° points, Mark An-
tony:
Our arms in strength of malice, and our hearts
Of brothers' temper,° do receive you in   *175*
With all kind love, good thoughts, and reverence.

Cassius. Your voice° shall be as strong as any man's
In the disposing of new dignities.°

Brutus. Only be patient till we have appeased
The multitude, beside themselves with fear,   *180*
And then we will deliver° you the cause
Why I, that did love Caesar when I struck him,
Have thus proceeded.

Antony.   I doubt not of your wisdom.
Let each man render me his bloody hand.
First, Marcus Brutus, will I shake with you;   *185*
Next, Caius Cassius, do I take your hand;
Now, Decius Brutus, yours; now yours, Metellus;
Yours, Cinna; and, my valiant Casca, yours;
Though last, not least in love, yours, good Trebonius.
Gentlemen all—alas, what shall I say?   *190*
My credit° now stands on such slippery ground

161 **mean** manner   169 **pitiful** full of pity   171 **pity pity** pity for Rome's
subjection drove out pity for Caesar   173 **leaden** blunt   174–75 **Our
arms ... temper** our arms, strong with the might inspired by enmity, and
our hearts, full of brotherly feeling   177 **voice** vote   178 **dignities**
offices   181 **deliver** communicate to   191 **credit** reputation

That one of two bad ways you must conceit° me,
Either a coward or a flatterer.
That I did love thee, Caesar, O, 'tis true!
195 If then thy spirit look upon us now,
Shall it not grieve thee dearer° than thy death
To see thy Antony making his peace,
Shaking the bloody fingers of thy foes,
Most noble, in the presence of thy corse?°
200 Had I as many eyes as thou hast wounds,
Weeping as fast as they stream forth thy blood,
It would become me better than to close°
In terms of friendship with thine enemies.
Pardon me, Julius! Here wast thou bayed,° brave
   hart;°
205 Here didst thou fall, and here thy hunters stand,
Signed in thy spoil° and crimsoned in thy lethe.°
O world, thou wast the forest to this hart;
And this indeed, O world, the heart of thee.
How like a deer, stroken° by many princes,
210 Dost thou here lie!

Cassius. Mark Antony——

Antony.   Pardon me, Caius Cassius.
The enemies of Caesar shall say this;
Then, in a friend, it is cold modesty.°

Cassius. I blame you not for praising Caesar so;
215 But what compact mean you to have with us?
Will you be pricked in number° of our friends,
Or shall we on,° and not depend on you?

---

192 **conceit** judge   196 **dearer** more deeply   199 **corse** corpse
202 **close** make an agreement   204 **bayed** brought to bay   204 **hart** (1)
deer (2) heart   206 **Signed in thy spoil** marked with the signs of your
slaughter   206 **lethe** (dissyllabic; the river of oblivion from which
the dead drank in Hades; here, by extension, "stream of death," or
"lifeblood")   209 **stroken** struck down   213 **modesty** moderation
216 **pricked in number** marked down (the modern "ticks off names"; the
Roman made small holes in his wax-covered tablets)   217 **on** proceed

Antony. Therefore I took your hands, but was indeed
　　Swayed from the point by looking down on Caesar.
　　Friends am I with you all, and love you all,   220
　　Upon this hope, that you shall give me reasons
　　Why, and wherein, Caesar was dangerous.

Brutus. Or else were this a savage spectacle.
　　Our reasons are so full of good regard°
　　That were you, Antony, the son of Caesar,   225
　　You should be satisfied.

Antony.   That's all I seek;
　　And am moreover suitor that I may
　　Produce° his body to the market place,
　　And in the pulpit, as becomes a friend,
　　Speak in the order° of his funeral.   230

Brutus. You shall, Mark Antony.

Cassius.   Brutus, a word with you.
　　[*Aside to Brutus*] You know not what you do; do not
　　　consent
　　That Antony speak in his funeral.
　　Know you how much the people may be moved
　　By that which he will utter?

Brutus.   By your pardon: 235
　　I will myself into the pulpit first,
　　And show the reason of our Caesar's death.
　　What Antony shall speak, I will protest°
　　He speaks by leave and by permission,
　　And that we are contented Caesar shall   240
　　Have all true° rites and lawful ceremonies.
　　It shall advantage° more than do us wrong.°

Cassius. I know not what may fall;° I like it not.

Brutus. Mark Antony, here, take you Caesar's body.
　　You shall not in your funeral speech blame us,   245
　　But speak all good you can devise of Caesar,
　　And say you do't by our permission;

224 **good regard** sound considerations   228 **Produce** bring forth
230 **order** course of ceremonies   238 **protest** declare   241 **true**
proper   242 **advantage** benefit   242 **wrong** harm   243 **fall** happen

Else shall you not have any hand at all
About his funeral. And you shall speak
250 In the same pulpit whereto I am going,
After my speech is ended.

Antony.   Be it so;
I do desire no more.

Brutus. Prepare the body then, and follow us.
Exeunt. Manet Antony.

Antony. O pardon me, thou bleeding piece of earth,
255 That I am meek and gentle with these butchers!
Thou art the ruins of the noblest man
That ever livèd in the tide of times.°
Woe to the hand that shed this costly blood!
Over thy wounds now do I prophesy
260 (Which like dumb mouths do ope their ruby lips
To beg the voice and utterance of my tongue),
A curse shall light upon the limbs of men;
Domestic fury and fierce civil strife
Shall cumber° all the parts of Italy;
265 Blood and destruction shall be so in use,°
And dreadful objects so familiar,
That mothers shall but smile when they behold
Their infants quartered with the hands of war,
All pity choked with custom of fell deeds;°
270 And Caesar's spirit, ranging° for revenge,
With Atè° by his side come hot from hell,
Shall in these confines° with a monarch's voice
Cry "Havoc,"° and let slip° the dogs of war,
That this foul deed shall smell above the earth
275 With carrion° men, groaning for burial.

Enter Octavius' Servant.

You serve Octavius Caesar, do you not?

---

257 **tide of times** course (ebb and flow) of history   264 **cumber** burden,
oppress   265 **in use** customary   269 **custom of fell deeds** habituation
to cruel acts   270 **ranging** roving widely in search of prey   271 **Atè**
Greek goddess of discord and vengeance   272 **confines** boundaries,
regions   273 **Cry "Havoc"** give the signal for unrestricted slaughter and
looting   273 **let slip** unleash   275 **carrion** dead and rotting

Servant. I do, Mark Antony.

Antony. Caesar did write for him to come to Rome.

Servant. He did receive his letters and is coming,
And bid me say to you by word of mouth—   280
O Caesar!   [*Seeing the body.*]

Antony. Thy heart is big;° get thee apart and weep.
Passion,° I see, is catching, for mine eyes,
Seeing those beads of sorrow stand in thine,
Began to water. Is thy master coming?   285

Servant. He lies tonight within seven leagues of Rome.

Antony. Post° back with speed, and tell him what hath
   chanced.°
Here is a mourning Rome, a dangerous Rome,
No Rome° of safety for Octavius yet.
Hie° hence and tell him so. Yet stay awhile;   290
Thou shalt not back till I have borne this corse
Into the market place; there shall I try°
In my oration how the people take
The cruel issue° of these bloody men;
According to the which, thou shalt discourse   295
To young Octavius of the state of things.
Lend me your hand.   *Exeunt.*

282 **big** swollen (with grief)   283 **Passion** intense emotion, grief
287 **Post** ride post (with relays of horses), hasten   287 **chanced**
happened   289 **Rome** (another play on the pronunciation "room"; cf.
1.2.156)   290 **Hie** hurry   292 **try** test   294 **cruel issue** outcome of the
cruelty

[Scene 2. *The Forum.*]

*Enter Brutus and goes into the pulpit, and Cassius, with
the Plebeians.*

Plebeians. We will be satisfied!° Let us be satisfied!

Brutus. Then follow me, and give me audience, friends.
Cassius, go you into the other street
And part the numbers.°
Those that will hear me speak, let 'em stay here;
Those that will follow Cassius, go with him;
And public reasons shall be renderèd
Of Caesar's death.

First Plebeian.   I will hear Brutus speak.

Second Plebeian. I will hear Cassius, and compare their
reasons,
When severally° we hear them renderèd.
          [*Exit Cassius, with some of the Plebeians.*]

Third Plebeian. The noble Brutus is ascended. Silence!

Brutus. Be patient till the last.°
Romans, countrymen, and lovers,° hear me for my
cause, and be silent, that you may hear. Believe me
for mine honor, and have respect° to mine honor,
that you may believe. Censure° me in your wisdom,
and awake your senses,° that you may the better
judge. If there be any in this assembly, any dear friend
of Caesar's, to him I say that Brutus' love to Caesar
was no less than his. If then that friend demand why

3.2.1 **will be satisfied** want a full explanation   4 **part the numbers** divide the crowd   10 **severally** separately   12 **last** conclusion (of my
speech)   13 **lovers** dear friends   15 **respect** regard   16 **Censure**
judge   17 **senses** powers of understanding, reason

Brutus rose against Caesar, this is my answer: Not that
I loved Caesar less, but that I loved Rome more. Had
you rather Caesar were living, and die all slaves, than
that Caesar were dead, to live all free men? As Caesar
loved me, I weep for him; as he was fortunate,   25
I rejoice at it; as he was valiant, I honor him; but, as
he was ambitious, I slew him. There is tears, for his
love; joy, for his fortune; honor, for his valor; and
death, for his ambition. Who is here so base, that
would be a bondman?° If any, speak; for him   30
have I offended. Who is here so rude,° that would not
be a Roman? If any, speak; for him have I offended.
Who is here so vile, that will not love his country? If
any, speak; for him have I offended. I pause for a
reply.   35

All. None, Brutus, none!

Brutus. Then none have I offended. I have done no more
to Caesar than you shall do° to Brutus. The question
of his death is enrolled° in the Capitol; his glory not
extenuated,° wherein he was worthy, nor his of-   40
fenses enforced,° for which he suffered death.

     Enter Mark Antony, with Caesar's body.

Here comes his body, mourned by Mark Antony, who,
though he had no hand in his death, shall receive the
benefit of his dying, a place° in the commonwealth,
as which of you shall not? With this I depart, that,   45
as I slew my best lover° for the good of Rome, I have
the same dagger for myself, when it shall please my
country to need my death.

All. Live, Brutus! Live, live!

First Plebeian. Bring him with triumph home unto his
house.   50

30 **bondman** slave   31 **rude** barbarous   38 **shall do** i.e., if I should
become equally tyrannical   38–39 **The question . . . enrolled** the considerations that made necessary his death are recorded   40 **extenuated** de-
preciated   41 **enforced** exaggerated   44 **place** i.e., as a free citizen
46 **lover** friend

Second Plebeian. Give him a statue with his ancestors.

Third Plebeian. Let him be Caesar.

Fourth Plebeian.   Càesar's better parts°
  Shall be crowned in Brutus.

First Plebeian. We'll bring him to his house with shouts
  and clamors.

Brutus. My countrymen——

55 *Second Plebeian.*   Peace! Silence! Brutus speaks.

First Plebeian. Peace, ho!

Brutus. Good countrymen, let me depart alone,
  And, for my sake, stay here with Antony.
  Do grace to Caesar's corpse, and grace his speech°
60 Tending° to Caesar's glories, which Mark Antony
  By our permission, is allowed to make.
  I do entreat you, not a man depart,
  Save I alone, till Antony have spoke.   *Exit.*

First Plebeian. Stay, ho! And let us hear Mark Antony.

65 *Third Plebeian.* Let him go up into the public chair;°
  We'll hear him. Noble Antony, go up.

Antony. For Brutus' sake, I am beholding° to you.

Fourth Plebeian. What does he say of Brutus?

Third Plebeian.   He says, for Brutus' sake,
  He finds himself beholding to us all.

Fourth Plebeian. 'Twere best he speak no harm of Bru-
70 tus here!

First Plebeian. This Caesar was a tyrant.

Third Plebeian.   Nay, that's certain.
  We are blest that Rome is rid of him.

52 **parts** qualities   59 **Do . . . speech** show respect to dead Caesar and listen respectfully to Antony's speech   60 **Tending** relating   65 **public
chair** pulpit, rostrum   67 **beholding** beholden, indebted

Second Plebeian. Peace! Let us hear what Antony can
    say.

Antony. You gentle Romans——

All.   Peace, ho! Let us hear him.

Antony. Friends, Romans, countrymen, lend me your
        ears;   75
    I come to bury Caesar, not to praise him.
    The evil that men do lives after them,
    The good is oft interrèd with their bones;
    So let it be with Caesar. The noble Brutus
    Hath told you Caesar was ambitious.   80
    If it were so, it was a grievous fault,
    And grievously hath Caesar answered° it.
    Here, under leave of Brutus and the rest
    (For Brutus is an honorable man,
    So are they all, all honorable men),   85
    Come I to speak in Caesar's funeral.
    He was my friend, faithful and just to me;
    But Brutus says he was ambitious,
    And Brutus is an honorable man.
    He hath brought many captives home to Rome,   90
    Whose ransoms did the general coffers° fill;
    Did this in Caesar seem ambitious?
    When that the poor have cried, Caesar hath wept;
    Ambition should be made of sterner stuff.
    Yet Brutus says he was ambitious;   95
    And Brutus is an honorable man.
    You all did see that on the Lupercal
    I thrice presented him a kingly crown,
    Which he did thrice refuse. Was this ambition?
    Yet Brutus says he was ambitious;   100
    And sure he is an honorable man.
    I speak not to disprove what Brutus spoke,
    But here I am to speak what I do know.
    You all did love him once, not without cause;
    What cause withholds you then to mourn for him?   105
    O judgment, thou art fled to brutish beasts,

82 **answered** paid the penalty for   91 **general coffers** public treasury

And men have lost their reason! Bear with me;
My heart is in the coffin there with Caesar,
And I must pause till it come back to me.

First Plebeian. Methinks there is much reason in his
110   sayings.

Second Plebeian. If thou consider rightly of the matter,
Caesar has had great wrong.

Third Plebeian.   Has he, masters?
I fear there will a worse come in his place.

Fourth Plebeian. Marked ye his words? He would not
take the crown,
115   Therefore 'tis certain he was not ambitious.

First Plebeian. If it be found so, some will dear abide it.°

Second Plebeian. Poor soul, his eyes are red as fire with
weeping.

Third Plebeian. There's not a nobler man in Rome than
Antony.

Fourth Plebeian. Now mark him, he begins again to
speak.

120 *Antony.* But yesterday the word of Caesar might
Have stood against the world; now lies he there,
And none so poor to° do him reverence.
O masters! If I were disposed to stir
Your hearts and minds to mutiny and rage,
125   I should do Brutus wrong and Cassius wrong,
Who, you all know, are honorable men.
I will not do them wrong; I rather choose
To wrong the dead, to wrong myself and you,
Than I will wrong such honorable men.
130   But here's a parchment with the seal of Caesar;
I found it in his closet;° 'tis his will.
Let but the commons° hear this testament,
Which, pardon me, I do not mean to read,

116 **dear abide it** pay dearly for it   122 **so poor to** so low in rank as
to   131 **closet** study (?) desk (?)   132 **commons** plebeians

And they would go and kiss dead Caesar's wounds,
And dip their napkins° in his sacred blood;   135
Yea, beg a hair of him for memory,
And dying, mention it within their wills,
Bequeathing it as a rich legacy
Unto their issue.°

Fourth Plebeian. We'll hear the will; read it, Mark
  Antony.   140

All. The will, the will! We will hear Caesar's will!

Antony. Have patience, gentle friends, I must not read it.
  It is not meet° you know how Caesar loved you.
  You are not wood, you are not stones, but men;
  And being men, hearing the will of Caesar,   145
  It will inflame you, it will make you mad.
  'Tis good you know not that you are his heirs;
  For if you should, O, what would come of it?

Fourth Plebeian. Read the will! We'll hear it, Antony!
  You shall read us the will, Caesar's will!   150

Antony. Will you be patient? Will you stay° awhile?
  I have o'ershot myself° to tell you of it.
  I fear I wrong the honorable men
  Whose daggers have stabbed Caesar; I do fear it.

Fourth Plebeian. They were traitors. Honorable men!   155

All. The will! The testament!

Second Plebeian. They were villains, murderers! The
  will! Read the will!

Antony. You will compel me then to read the will?
  Then make a ring about the corpse of Caesar,   160
  And let me show you him that made the will.
  Shall I descend? And will you give me leave?

All. Come down.

Second Plebeian. Descend.   [*Antony comes down.*]

135 **napkins** handkerchiefs   139 **issue** heirs   143 **meet** fitting
151 **stay** wait   152 **o'ershot myself** gone further than I intended

165   *Third Plebeian.* You shall have leave.

Fourth Plebeian. A ring! Stand round.

First Plebeian. Stand from the hearse, stand from the
      body!

Second Plebeian. Room for Antony, most noble Antony!

Antony. Nay, press not so upon me; stand far° off.

170   *All.* Stand back! Room! Bear back.

Antony. If you have tears, prepare to shed them now.
      You all do know this mantle;° I remember
      The first time ever Caesar put it on:
      'Twas on a summer's evening, in his tent,
175   That day he overcame the Nervii.°
      Look, in this place ran Cassius' dagger through;
      See what a rent the envious° Casca made;
      Through this the well-belovèd Brutus stabbed,
      And as he plucked his cursèd steel away,
180   Mark how the blood of Caesar followed it,
      As° rushing out of doors, to be resolved°
      If Brutus so unkindly° knocked, or no;
      For Brutus, as you know, was Caesar's angel.°
      Judge, O you gods, how dearly Caesar loved him!
185   This was the most unkindest° cut of all;
      For when the noble Caesar saw him stab,
      Ingratitude, more strong than traitors' arms,
      Quite vanquished him. Then burst his mighty heart;
      And, in his mantle muffling up his face,
190   Even at the base° of Pompey's statue°
      (Which all the while ran blood) great Caesar fell.
      O, what a fall was there, my countrymen!
      Then I, and you, and all of us fell down,
      Whilst bloody treason flourished° over us.

169 **far** farther   172 **mantle** cloak (here, the toga)   175 **Nervii** (a fierce
tribe decisively conquered by Caesar in 57 B.C.)   177 **envious** spite-
ful   181 **As** as though   181 **to be resolved** to learn for certain   182 **un-
kindly** (1) cruelly (2) unnaturally   183 **angel** favorite (i.e., considered
incapable of evil)   185 **most unkindest** most cruel and unnatural
190 **base** pedestal   190 **statue** (pronounced "stat-u-a")   194 **flourished**
(1) swaggered (2) brandished a sword in triumph

O, now you weep, and I perceive you feel   *195*
The dint° of pity; these are gracious drops.
Kind souls, what° weep you when you but behold
Our Caesar's vesture° wounded? Look you here,
Here is himself, marred° as you see with° traitors.

First Plebeian. O piteous spectacle!   *200*

Second Plebeian. O noble Caesar!

Third Plebeian. O woeful day!

Fourth Plebeian. O traitors, villains!

First Plebeian. O most bloody sight!

Second Plebeian. We will be revenged.   *205*

[*All.*] Revenge! About!° Seek! Burn! Fire! Kill! Slay!
Let not a traitor live!

Antony. Stay, countrymen.

First Plebeian. Peace there! Hear the noble Antony.

Second Plebeian. We'll hear him, we'll follow him,
we'll die with him!   *210*

Antony. Good friends, sweet friends, let me not stir you
up
To such a sudden flood of mutiny.
They that have done this deed are honorable.
What private griefs° they have, alas, I know not,   *215*
That made them do it. They are wise and honorable,
And will, no doubt, with reasons answer you.
I come not, friends, to steal away your hearts;
I am no orator, as Brutus is;
But (as you know me all) a plain blunt man   *220*
That love my friend, and that they know full well
That gave me public leave to speak° of him.
For I have neither writ, nor words, nor worth,

196 **dint** stroke   197 **what** why   198 **vesture** clothing   199 **marred** mangled   199 **with** by   206 **About** let's go   215 **private griefs** personal grievances   222 **public leave to speak** permission to speak in public

Action, nor utterance,° nor the power of speech
225 To stir men's blood; I only speak right on.°
I tell you that which you yourselves do know,
Show you sweet Caesar's wounds, poor poor dumb
    mouths,
And bid them speak for me. But were I Brutus,
And Brutus Antony, there were an Antony
230 Would ruffle up° your spirits, and put a tongue
In every wound of Caesar that should move
The stones of Rome to rise and mutiny.

All. We'll mutiny.

First Plebeian.   We'll burn the house of Brutus.

Third Plebeian. Away, then! Come, seek the conspirators.

235 *Antony.* Yet hear me, countrymen. Yet hear me speak.

All. Peace, ho! Hear Antony, most noble Antony!

Antony. Why, friends, you go to do you know not what:
Wherein hath Caesar thus deserved your loves?
Alas, you know not; I must tell you then:
240 You have forgot the will I told you of.

All. Most true, the will! Let's stay and hear the will.

Antony. Here is the will, and under Caesar's seal.
To every Roman citizen he gives,
To every several° man, seventy-five drachmas.

Second Plebeian. Most noble Caesar! We'll revenge his
245   death!

Third Plebeian. O royal° Caesar!

Antony. Hear me with patience.

All. Peace, ho!

223–24 **neither . . . utterance** neither a written speech, nor fluency, nor
reputation, nor (an orator's) gestures, nor good delivery (perhaps **writ**
should be emended to **wit,** "intellectual cleverness")   225 **right on** directly, without premeditation   230 **ruffle up** incite to rage   244 **several**
individual   246 **royal** nobly generous

Antony. Moreover, he hath left you all his walks,°
His private arbors, and new-planted orchards,°   250
On this side Tiber; he hath left them you,
And to your heirs forever: common pleasures,°
To walk abroad and recreate yourselves.
Here was a Caesar! When comes such another?

First Plebeian. Never, never! Come, away, away!   255
We'll burn his body in the holy place,
And with the brands fire the traitors' houses.
Take up the body.

Second Plebeian. Go fetch fire.

Third Plebeian. Pluck down benches.   260

Fourth Plebeian. Pluck down forms, windows,° any-
      thing!   *Exeunt Plebeians [with the body].*

Antony. Now let it work:° Mischief, thou art afoot,
Take thou what course thou wilt.

                    Enter Servant.

                                       How now, fellow?

Servant. Sir, Octavius is already come to Rome.   265

Antony. Where is he?

Servant. He and Lepidus are at Caesar's house.

Antony. And thither will I straight° to visit him;
He comes upon a wish.° Fortune is merry,
And in this mood will give us anything.   270

Servant. I heard him say, Brutus and Cassius
Are rid° like madmen through the gates of Rome.

Antony. Belike° they had some notice of° the people,
How I had moved them. Bring me to Octavius.
                                          Exeunt.

249 **walks** parks   250 **orchards** gardens   252 **common pleasures** public places of recreation   261 **forms, windows** long benches (and)
shutters   262 **work** (1) ferment (as yeast) (2) work itself out   268 **will I
straight** will I (go) at once   269 **upon a wish** just as I wished   272 **Are
rid** have ridden   273 **Belike** probably   273 **notice of** news about

[Scene 3. *A street.*]

Enter Cinna the Poet, and after him the Plebeians.

Cinna. I dreamt tonight° that I did feast with Caesar,
And things unluckily charge my fantasy.°
I have no will to wander forth° of doors,
Yet something leads me forth.

5 *First Plebeian.* What is your name?

Second Plebeian. Whither are you going?

Third Plebeian. Where do you dwell?

Fourth Plebeian. Are you a married man or a bachelor?

Second Plebeian. Answer every man directly.°

10 *First Plebeian.* Ay, and briefly.

Fourth Plebeian. Ay, and wisely.

Third Plebeian. Ay, and truly, you were best.

Cinna. What is my name? Whither am I going? Where
do I dwell? Am I a married man or a bachelor? Then,
15 to answer every man directly and briefly, wisely and
truly: wisely I say, I am a bachelor.

Second Plebeian. That's as much as to say, they are
fools that marry; you'll bear me a bang° for that, I
fear. Proceed directly.

20 *Cinna.* Directly, I am going to Caesar's funeral.

First Plebeian. As a friend or an enemy?

3.3.1 **tonight** last night 2 **things ... fantasy** events give ominous weight
to my imaginings 3 **forth** out 9 **directly** straightforwardly 18 **bear
me a bang** get a blow from me

Cinna. As a friend.

Second Plebeian. That matter is answered directly.

Fourth Plebeian. For your dwelling, briefly.

Cinna. Briefly, I dwell by the Capitol.   25

Third Plebeian. Your name, sir, truly.

Cinna. Truly, my name is Cinna.

First Plebeian. Tear him to pieces! He's a conspirator.

Cinna. I am Cinna the poet! I am Cinna the poet!

Fourth Plebeian. Tear him for his bad verses! Tear him   30
for his bad verses!

Cinna. I am not Cinna the conspirator.

Fourth Plebeian. It is no matter, his name's Cinna;
pluck but his name out of his heart, and turn him
going.°   35

Third Plebeian. Tear him, tear him! [*They attack him.*]
Come, brands, ho! Firebrands! To Brutus', to Cas-
sius'! Burn all! Some to Decius' house, and some to
Casca's; some to Ligarius'! Away, go!
        Exeunt all the Plebeians [with Cinna].

34–35 **turn him going** dispatch him

ACT 4

[Scene 1. *A house in Rome.*]

Enter Antony, Octavius, and Lepidus.

Antony. These many then shall die; their names are
    pricked.°

Octavius. Your brother too must die; consent you,
    Lepidus?

Lepidus. I do consent——

Octavius.   Prick him down, Antony.

Lepidus. Upon condition Publius shall not live,
5   Who is your sister's son, Mark Antony.

Antony. He shall not live; look, with a spot I damn him.°
    But, Lepidus, go you to Caesar's house;
    Fetch the will hither, and we shall determine
    How to cut off some charge° in legacies.

10 *Lepidus.* What, shall I find you here?

Octavius. Or° here or at the Capitol.   *Exit Lepidus.*

4.1.1 **pricked** ticked off, marked on the list   6 **with a spot I damn him**
with a dot (on the wax tablet) I condemn him   9 **cut off some charge** re-
duce expenses (by altering the amount left in bequests)   11 **Or** either

70

Antony. This is a slight unmeritable° man,
    Meet° to be sent on errands; is it fit,
    The threefold world° divided, he should stand
    One of the three to share it?

Octavius.   So you thought him,   *15*
    And took his voice° who should be pricked to die
    In our black sentence° and proscription.°

Antony. Octavius, I have seen more days° than you;
    And though we lay these honors on this man,
    To ease ourselves of divers sland'rous loads,°   *20*
    He shall but bear them as the ass bears gold,
    To groan and sweat under the business,°
    Either led or driven, as we point the way;
    And having brought our treasure where we will,
    Then take we down his load, and turn him off,°   *25*
    (Like to the empty° ass) to shake his ears
    And graze in commons.°

Octavius.   You may do your will;
    But he's a tried and valiant soldier.°

Antony. So is my horse, Octavius, and for that
    I do appoint him store° of provender.   *30*
    It is a creature that I teach to fight,
    To wind,° to stop, to run directly on,
    His corporal° motion governed by my spirit.°
    And, in some taste,° is Lepidus but so.°
    He must be taught, and trained, and bid go forth.   *35*
    A barren-spirited° fellow; one that feeds

12 **slight unmeritable** insignificant and undeserving   13 **Meet** fit
14 **threefold world** three areas of the Roman empire, Europe, Asia, and
Africa   16 **voice** vote   17 **black sentence** sentence of death   17 **proscription** condemnation to death or exile   18 **have seen more days** am
older (and more experienced)   20 **divers sland'rous loads** blame which
will be laid upon us for our various actions   22 **business** hard labor   25 **turn him off** drive him away   26 **empty** unburdened   27 **in
commons** on public pasture   28 **soldier** (trisyllabic)   30 **appoint him
store** allot him a supply   32 **wind** turn   33 **corporal** physical   33 **spirit**
mind   34 **taste** measure   34 **so** the same   36 **barren-spirited** lacking
initiative or ideas of his own

On objects, arts, and imitations,°
Which, out of use and staled° by other men,
Begin his fashion.° Do not talk of him
40 But as a property.° And now, Octavius,
Listen great things. Brutus and Cassius
Are levying powers;° we must straight make head.°
Therefore let our alliance be combined,
Our best friends made,° our means stretched;°
45 And let us presently° go sit in council
How covert matters may be best disclosed,
And open perils surest answerèd.°

Octavius. Let us do so; for we are at the stake,°
And bayed about with many enemies;
50 And some that smile have in their hearts, I fear,
Millions of mischiefs.°   *Exeunt.*

[Scene 2. *Camp near Sardis.*]

*Drum. Enter Brutus, Lucilius, [Lucius,] and the Army.
Titinius and Pindarus meet them.*

Brutus. Stand ho!

Lucilius. Give the word, ho! and stand.

Brutus. What now, Lucilius, is Cassius near?

37 **objects, arts, and imitations** curiosities, artifices, and fashions (or
styles)   38 **staled** made common   39 **Begin his fashion** i.e., he is always
far behind the times   40 **property** mere tool (a thing rather than a
person)   42 **powers** armed forces   42 **straight make head** immediately
gather troops   44 **Our best friends made** let our closest allies be
selected   44 **stretched** be used to the fullest advantage   45 **presently**
immediately   46–47 **How ... answerèd** to decide how hidden dangers
may best be discovered and open dangers most safely encountered   48 **at
the stake** (metaphor derived from Elizabethan sport of bearbaiting) i.e.,
like a bear tied to a stake and set upon by many dogs   51 **mischiefs** plans
to injure us

Lucilius. He is at hand, and Pindarus is come
    To do you salutation from his master.   5

Brutus. He greets me well.° Your master, Pindarus,
    In his own change, or by ill officers,°
    Hath given me some worthy° cause to wish
    Things done undone; but if he be at hand,
    I shall be satisfied.°

Pindarus.   I do not doubt   10
    But that my noble master will appear
    Such as he is, full of regard° and honor.

Brutus. He is not doubted. A word, Lucilius,
    How he received you; let me be resolved.°

Lucilius. With courtesy and with respect enough,   15
    But not with such familiar instances,°
    Nor with such free and friendly conference°
    As he hath used of old.

Brutus.   Thou hast described
    A hot friend cooling. Ever note, Lucilius,
    When love begins to sicken and decay   20
    It useth an enforcèd ceremony.°
    There are no tricks in plain and simple faith;
    But hollow° men, like horses hot at hand,°
    Make gallant show and promise of their mettle;°
                         Low march within.
    But when they should endure the bloody spur,   25
    They fall their crests,° and like deceitful jades°
    Sink in the trial.° Comes his army on?

Lucilius. They mean this night in Sardis to be quartered;

4.2.6 **He greets me well** he sends greetings by a very good man   7 **In his
. . . officers** either from a change in his feelings toward me or through the
actions of bad subordinates   8 **worthy** substantial   10 **be satisfied**
receive a satisfactory explanation   12 **full of regard** worthy of respect   14 **resolved** fully informed   16 **familiar instances** marks of
friendship   17 **conference** conversation   21 **enforcèd ceremony** strained
formality   23 **hollow** insincere   23 **hot at hand** overspirited at the
start   24 **mettle** quality, courage   26 **fall their crests** let fall the ridges of
their necks   26 **jades** nags   27 **Sink in the trial** fail when put to the test

The greater part, the horse in general,°
Are come with Cassius.

Enter Cassius and his Powers.

30 *Brutus.*   Hark! He is arrived.
    March gently° on to meet him.

Cassius. Stand, ho!

Brutus. Stand, ho! Speak the word along.

[*First Soldier.*] Stand!

35 [*Second Soldier.*] Stand!

[*Third Soldier.*] Stand!

Cassius. Most noble brother, you have done me wrong.

Brutus. Judge me, you gods! Wrong I mine enemies?
    And if not so, how should I wrong a brother.

40 *Cassius.* Brutus, this sober form° of yours hides wrongs;
    And when you do them——

Brutus.   Cassius, be content.°
    Speak your griefs° softly; I do know you well.
    Before the eyes of both our armies here
    (Which should perceive nothing but love from us)
45 Let us not wrangle. Bid them move away;
    Then in my tent, Cassius, enlarge° your griefs,
    And I will give you audience.

Cassius.   Pindarus,
    Bid our commanders lead their charges° off
    A little from this ground.

50 *Brutus.* Lucilius, do you the like, and let no man
    Come to our tent till we have done our conference.
    Let Lucius and Titinius guard our door.
                    Exeunt. Mane[n]t Brutus and Cassius.

29 **the horse in general** all the cavalry   31 **gently** slowly   40 **sober
form** staid manner   41 **be content** keep calm   42 **griefs** grievances   46 **enlarge** freely express   48 **charges** troops

[Scene 3. *Brutus' tent.*]

Cassius. That you have wronged me doth appear in this:
  You have condemned and noted° Lucius Pella
  For taking bribes here of the Sardians;
  Wherein my letters, praying on his side,°
  Because I knew the man, was slighted off.°   5

Brutus. You wronged yourself to write in such a case.

Cassius. In such a time as this it is not meet
  That every nice offense should bear his comment.°

Brutus. Let me tell you, Cassius, you yourself
  Are much condemned to have an itching palm,°   10
  To sell and mart° your offices for gold
  To undeservers.

Cassius.   I an itching palm?
  You know that you are Brutus that speaks this,
  Or, by the gods, this speech were else your last.

Brutus. The name of Cassius honors° this corruption,   15
  And chastisement doth therefore hide his head.

Cassius. Chastisement!

Brutus. Remember March, the ides of March remember.
  Did not great Julius bleed for justice' sake?
  What villain touched his body, that did stab,   20
  And not° for justice? What, shall one of us,
  That struck the foremost man of all this world

4.3.2. **noted** publicly disgraced   4 **praying on his side** appealing on his
behalf   5 **was slighted off** was contemptuously disregarded ("letters"
takes a singular verb because of its singular meaning)   8 **nice . . . comment** trivial fault should receive criticism (*his* = its)   10 **condemned . . .
palm** accused of being mercenary   11 **mart** traffic in   15 **honors** lends
an air of respectability   21 **And not** except

But for supporting robbers,° shall we now
Contaminate our fingers with base bribes,
25 And sell the mighty space of our large honors°
For so much trash° as may be graspèd thus?°
I had rather be a dog, and bay° the moon,
Than such a Roman.

Cassius.   Brutus, bait° not me;
I'll not endure it. You forget yourself
30 To hedge me in.° I am a soldier, I,
Older in practice, abler than yourself
To make conditions.°

Brutus.   Go to! You are not, Cassius.

Cassius. I am.

Brutus. I say you are not.

35 *Cassius.* Urge° me no more, I shall forget myself;
Have mind upon your health;° tempt° me no farther.

Brutus. Away, slight° man!

Cassius. Is't possible?

Brutus.   Hear me, for I will speak.
Must I give way and room to your rash choler?°
40 Shall I be frighted when a madman stares?°

Cassius. O ye gods, ye gods! Must I endure all this?

23 **supporting robbers** i.e., protecting dishonest officials (a point made by Plutarch but mentioned only now by Shakespeare)   25 **mighty . . . honors** vast capacity to be honorable and magnanimous (with suggestion of potentiality for making other men free, and honorable in office)   26 **trash** rubbish, i.e., money   26 **graspèd thus** (the small confined area of the closed fist contrasts with the "mighty space" gained by their honorable deeds in abolishing injustice and corruption)   27 **bay** howl at   28 **bait** harass and worry (as a bear tied to a stake is baited by dogs)   30 **hedge me in** limit my freedom of action   32 **make conditions** manage practical matters   35 **Urge** drive, bully   36 **health** safety   36 **tempt** provoke   37 **slight** insignificant   39 **give . . . choler** let your hasty temper have free vent and run its course unchecked   40 **stares** glares

Brutus. All this? Ay, more: fret till your proud heart
   break.
  Go show your slaves how choleric you are,
  And make your bondmen tremble. Must I budge?°
  Must I observe° you? Must I stand and crouch°   *45*
  Under your testy humor?° By the gods,
  You shall digest the venom° of your spleen,°
  Though it do split you; for, from this day forth,
  I'll use you for my mirth, yea, for my laughter,
  When you are waspish.

Cassius.   Is it come to this?   *50*

Brutus. You say you are a better soldier:
  Let it appear so; make your vaunting° true,
  And it shall please me well. For mine own part,
  I shall be glad to learn of° noble men.

Cassius. You wrong me every way; you wrong me,
    Brutus;   *55*
  I said, an elder soldier, not a better.
  Did I say, better?

Brutus.   If you did, I care not.

Cassius. When Caesar lived, he durst not thus have
  moved° me.

Brutus. Peace, peace, you durst not so have tempted°
  him.

Cassius. I durst not?   *60*

Brutus. No.

Cassius. What? Durst not tempt him?

Brutus.   For your life you durst not.

44 **budge** defer to it 45 **observe** wait on 45 **crouch** bow 46 **testy humor** irritability 47 **digest the venom** swallow the poison 47 **spleen** (considered the source of sudden passions) i.e., fiery temper 52 **vaunting** boasting 54 **learn of** (1) hear about the exploits of (2) take lessons from 58 **moved** exasperated 59 **tempted** provoked

Cassius. Do not presume too much upon my love;
I may do that I shall be sorry for.

65 *Brutus.* You have done that you should be sorry for.
There is no terror, Cassius, in your threats;
For I am armed so strong in honesty°
That they pass by me as the idle wind,
Which I respect° not. I did send to you
70 For certain sums of gold, which you denied me;
For I can raise no money by vile means.
By heaven, I had rather coin my heart
And drop my blood for drachmas than to wring
From the hard hands of peasants their vile trash
75 By any indirection.° I did send
To you for gold to pay my legions,
Which you denied me. Was that done like Cassius?
Should I have answered Caius Cassius so?
When Marcus Brutus grows so covetous
80 To lock such rascal counters° from his friends,
Be ready, gods, with all your thunderbolts,
Dash him to pieces!

Cassius.   I denied you not.

Brutus. You did.

Cassius.   I did not. He was but a fool
That brought my answer back. Brutus hath rived°
   my heart.
85 A friend should bear his friend's infirmities;
But Brutus makes mine greater than they are.

Brutus. I do not, till you practice them on me.

Cassius. You love me not.

Brutus.   I do not like your faults.

Cassius. A friendly eye could never see such faults.

67 **honesty** integrity   69 **respect** heed   75 **indirection** irregular methods   80 **rascal counters** base (and worthless) coins   84 **rived** broken

Brutus. A flatterer's would not, though they do appear   90
  As huge as high Olympus.

Cassius. Come, Antony, and young Octavius, come,
  Revenge yourselves alone° on Cassius,
  For Cassius is aweary of the world:
  Hated by one he loves; braved° by his brother;   95
  Checked° like a bondman; all his faults observed,
  Set in a notebook, learned and conned by rote°
  To cast into my teeth.° O, I could weep
  My spirit from mine eyes! There is my dagger,
  And here my naked breast; within, a heart   100
  Dearer than Pluto's mine,° richer than gold;
  If that thou be'st a Roman, take it forth.
  I, that denied thee gold, will give my heart.
  Strike as thou didst at Caesar; for I know,
  When thou didst hate him worst, thou lovedst him
    better   105
  Than ever thou lovedst Cassius.

Brutus.   Sheathe your dagger.
  Be angry when you will, it shall have scope.°
  Do what you will, dishonor shall be humor.°
  O Cassius, you are yokèd with a lamb
  That carries anger as the flint bears fire,   110
  Who, much enforcèd,° shows a hasty spark,
  And straight° is cold again.

Cassius.   Hath Cassius lived
  To be but mirth and laughter to his Brutus
  When grief and blood ill-tempered° vexeth him?

Brutus. When I spoke that, I was ill-tempered too.   115

93 **alone** only   95 **braved** defied   96 **Checked** rebuked   97 **conned by rote** learned by heart   98 **cast into my teeth** i.e., throw in my face   101 **Dearer than Pluto's mine** more precious than all the riches in the earth (Pluto, god of the underworld, and Plutus, god of riches, were frequently confused)   107 **shall have scope** (your anger) shall have free play   108 **dishonor shall be humor** insults shall be regarded as quirks of temperament   111 **much enforcèd** greatly provoked   112 **straight** immediately   114 **blood ill-tempered** i.e., a "black mood"

Cassius. Do you confess so much? Give me your hand.

Brutus. And my heart too.

Cassius.   O Brutus!

Brutus.   What's the matter?

Cassius. Have not you love enough to bear with me
 When that rash humor° which my mother gave me
 Makes me forgetful?

120 *Brutus.*   Yes, Cassius, and from henceforth,
 When you are over-earnest with your Brutus,
 He'll think your mother° chides, and leave you so.°

Enter a Poet, [followed by Lucilius, Titinius, and Lucius].

Poet. Let me go in to see the generals;
 There is some grudge° between 'em; 'tis not meet
125 They be alone.

Lucilius. You shall not come to them.

Poet. Nothing but death shall stay me.

Cassius. How now. What's the matter?

Poet. For shame, you generals! What do you mean?
130 Love, and be friends, as two such men should be;
 For I have seen more years, I'm sure, than ye.

Cassius. Ha, ha! How vilely doth this cynic° rhyme!

Brutus. Get you hence, sirrah! Saucy° fellow, hence!

Cassius. Bear with him, Brutus, 'tis his fashion.

135 *Brutus.* I'll know his humor when he knows his time.°
 What should the wars do with these jigging° fools?
 Companion,° hence!

119 **rash humor** hasty temperament   122 **your mother** i.e., your inherited temperament   122 **leave you so** leave it at that   124 **grudge** bad
feeling   132 **cynic** rude fellow   133 **Saucy** impertinent   135 **I'll . . .
time** I'll accept his eccentricity when he can judge the suitable time for
it   136 **jigging** doggerel-writing, rhyming   137 **Companion** base fellow

Cassius.   Away, away, be gone!
                                             Exit Poet.

Brutus. Lucilius and Titinius, bid the commanders
Prepare to lodge their companies tonight.

Cassius. And come yourselves, and bring Messala with
  you   *140*
Immediately to us.   [*Exeunt Lucilius and Titinius.*]

Brutus.   Lucius, a bowl of wine.
                                             [*Exit Lucius.*]

Cassius. I did not think you could have been so angry.

Brutus. O Cassius, I am sick of many griefs.

Cassius. Of your philosophy you make no use,
If you give place° to accidental evils.°   *145*

Brutus. No man bears sorrow better. Portia is dead.

Cassius. Ha? Portia?

Brutus. She is dead.

Cassius. How scaped I killing when I crossed° you so?
O insupportable and touching° loss!   *150*
Upon° what sickness?

Brutus.   Impatient of° my absence,
And grief that young Octavius with Mark Antony
Have made themselves so strong—for with her death
That tidings came°—with this she fell distract,°
And (her attendants absent) swallowed fire.°   *155*

Cassius. And died so?

Brutus.   Even so.

145 **place** way   145 **accidental evils** misfortunes brought on by chance (Brutus seems not to be behaving as a Stoic philosopher should)   149 **crossed** contradicted   150 **touching** wounding, grievous   151 **Upon** as a result of   151 **Impatient of** unable to endure   153–54 **for . . . came** i.e., news of her death came at the same time as news of their strength   154 **fell distract** became distraught   155 **swallowed fire** (according to Plutarch she choked herself by putting hot coals into her mouth)

Cassius.   O ye immortal gods!

Enter Boy [Lucius], with wine and tapers.

Brutus. Speak no more of her. Give me a bowl of wine.
   In this I bury all unkindness, Cassius.   *Drinks.*

Cassius. My heart is thirsty for that noble pledge.
160   Fill, Lucius, till the wine o'erswell the cup;
   I cannot drink too much of Brutus' love.
                    [*Drinks. Exit Lucius.*]

Enter Titinius and Messala.

Brutus. Come in, Titinius! Welcome, good Messala.
   Now sit we close about this taper here,
   And call in question° our necessities.

Cassius. Portia, art thou gone?

165 *Brutus.*   No more, I pray you.
   Messala, I have here receivèd letters
   That young Octavius and Mark Antony
   Come down upon us with a mighty power,°
   Bending their expedition° toward Philippi.

170 *Messala.* Myself have letters of the selfsame tenure.°

Brutus. With what addition?

Messala. That by proscription° and bills of outlawry°
   Octavius, Antony, and Lepidus
   Have put to death an hundred senators.

175 *Brutus.* Therein our letters do not well agree.
   Mine speak of seventy senators that died
   By their proscriptions, Cicero being one.

Cassius. Cicero one?

Messala.   Cicero is dead,
   And by that order of proscription.
180   Had you your letters from your wife, my lord?

---

164 **call in question** consider   168 **power** army   169 **Bending their ex-
pedition** directing their rapid march   170 **tenure** tenor, general meaning   172 **proscription** proclamation of the death sentence   172 **bills of
outlawry** lists of those proscribed

Brutus. No, Messala.

Messala. Nor nothing in your letters writ of her?

Brutus. Nothing, Messala.

Messala.   That methinks is strange.

Brutus. Why ask you? Hear you aught of her in yours?

Messala. No, my lord.   *185*

Brutus. Now as you are a Roman, tell me true.

Messala. Then like a Roman bear the truth I tell,
For certain she is dead, and by strange manner.

Brutus. Why, farewell, Portia. We must die, Messala.
With meditating that she must die once,°   *190*
I have the patience to endure it now.

Messala. Even so great men great losses should endure.

Cassius. I have as much of this in art° as you,
But yet my nature could not bear it so.°

Brutus. Well, to our work alive.° What do you think   *195*
Of marching to Philippi presently?°

Cassius. I do not think it good.

Brutus.   Your reason?

Cassius.   This it is:
'Tis better that the enemy seek us;
So shall he waste his means, weary his soldiers,
Doing himself offense,° whilst we, lying still,   *200*
Are full of rest, defense, and nimbleness.

Brutus. Good reasons must of force° give place to better.
The people 'twixt Philippi and this ground

190 **once** at some time   193 **this in art** i.e., this Stoicism in theory   180–
94 **Had . . . so** (some editors suggest that this was the original version of
Shakespeare's account of Portia's death and that he later deleted this and
wrote in lines 142–57, preferring to demonstrate Brutus' humanity rather
than his Stoicism; the Folio printer then set up both versions by mistake.
Line 158 would follow 141—as 195 would follow 179—neatly enough to
make this an attractive theory)   195 **alive** as men still living   196 **presently** immediately   200 **offense** harm   202 **force** necessity

Do stand but in a forced affection;°
205 For they have grudged us contribution.
The enemy, marching along by them,
By them shall make a fuller number up,
Come on refreshed, new-added° and encouraged;
From which advantage shall we cut him off
210 If at Philippi we do face him there,
These people at our back.

Cassius.   Hear me, good brother.

Brutus. Under your pardon.° You must note beside
That we have tried the utmost of our friends,
Our legions are brimful, our cause is ripe.
215 The enemy increaseth every day;
We, at the height, are ready to decline.
There is a tide in the affairs of men
Which, taken at the flood, leads on to fortune;
Omitted,° all the voyage of their life
220 Is bound in° shallows and in miseries.
On such a full sea are we now afloat,
And we must take the current when it serves,
Or lose our ventures.°

Cassius.   Then, with your will,° go on;
We'll along ourselves and meet them at Philippi.

225 *Brutus.* The deep of night is crept upon our talk,
And nature must obey necessity,
Which we will niggard with a little rest.°
There is no more to say?

Cassius.   No more. Good night.
Early tomorrow will we rise and hence.°

Enter Lucius.

204 **Do . . . affection** i.e., support us only under compulsion 208 **new-
added** reinforced 212 **Under your pardon** excuse me 219 **Omitted**
neglected 220 **bound in** limited to 223 **ventures** shipping trade,
i.e., risks 223 **with your will** as you wish 227 **niggard with a little
rest** i.e., put off with the shortest possible sleep 229 **hence** leave this
place

Brutus. Lucius, my gown.°   *Exit Lucius.*
                Farewell, good Messala.   230
   Good night, Titinius. Noble, noble Cassius,
   Good night, and good repose.

Cassius.   O my dear brother,
   This was an ill beginning of the night.
   Never come° such division 'tween our souls!
   Let it not, Brutus.

         Enter Lucius, with the gown.

Brutus.   Everything is well.   235

Cassius. Good night, my lord.

Brutus.   Good night, good brother.

Titinius, Messala. Good night, Lord Brutus.

Brutus.   Farewell, every one.
                       Exeunt.
  Give me the gown. Where is thy instrument?°

Lucius. Here in the tent.

Brutus.   What, thou speak'st drowsily?
   Poor knave,° I blame thee not; thou art o'erwatched.°   240
   Call Claudius and some other of my men;
   I'll have them sleep on cushions in my tent.

Lucius. Varro and Claudius!

         Enter Varro and Claudius.

Varro. Calls my lord?

Brutus. I pray you, sirs, lie in my tent and sleep.   245
   It may be I shall raise° you by and by
   On business to my brother Cassius.

Varro. So please you, we will stand and watch your
     pleasure.°

230 **gown** dressing gown   234 **Never come** may there never again
come   238 **instrument** (probably a lute)   240 **knave** boy   240 **o'erwatched** tired out from lack of sleep   246 **raise** rouse   248 **watch your
pleasure** be on the watch for your command

Brutus. I will not have it so; lie down, good sirs;
250   It may be I shall otherwise bethink me.°

                       [*Varro and Claudius lie down.*]
   Look, Lucius, here's the book I sought for so;
   I put it in the pocket of my gown.

Lucius. I was sure your lordship did not give it me.

Brutus. Bear with me, good boy, I am much forgetful.
255   Canst thou hold up thy heavy eyes awhile,
   And touch° thy instrument a strain° or two?

Lucius. Ay, my lord, an't° please you.

Brutus.   It does, my boy.
   I trouble thee too much, but thou art willing.

Lucius. It is my duty, sir.

260 *Brutus.* I should not urge thy duty past thy might;
   I know young bloods° look for a time of rest.

Lucius. I have slept, my lord, already.

Brutus. It was well done, and thou shalt sleep again;
   I will not hold thee long. If I do live,
265   I will be good to thee.

               Music, and a song.

   This is a sleepy tune. O murd'rous° slumber!
   Layest thou thy leaden° mace° upon my boy,
   That plays thee music? Gentle knave, good night;
   I will not do thee so much wrong to wake thee.
270   If thou dost nod, thou break'st thy instrument;
   I'll take it from thee; and, good boy, good night.
   Let me see, let me see; is not the leaf turned down
   Where I left reading? Here it is, I think.

         Enter the Ghost of Caesar.

250 **otherwise bethink me** change my mind   256 **touch** play on
256 **strain** tune   257 **an't** if it   261 **young bloods** youthful constitu-
tions   266 **murd'rous** deathlike   267 **leaden** heavy (association also
with death, for lead was used in coffinmaking)   267 **mace** staff of office
(with which a man was touched on the shoulder when arrested)

How ill this taper burns.° Ha! Who comes here?
I think it is the weakness of mine eyes   275
That shapes this monstrous apparition.
It comes upon° me. Art thou anything?
Art thou some god, some angel, or some devil,
That mak'st my blood cold, and my hair to stare?°
Speak to me what thou art.   280

Ghost. Thy evil spirit, Brutus.

Brutus.   Why com'st thou?

Ghost. To tell thee thou shalt see me at Philippi.

Brutus. Well; then I shall see thee again?

Ghost. Ay, at Philippi.

Brutus. Why, I will see thee at Philippi then.   285
                              [*Exit Ghost.*]

Now I have taken heart thou vanishest.
Ill spirit, I would hold more talk with thee.
Boy! Lucius! Varro! Claudius! Sirs, awake!
Claudius!

Lucius. The strings, my lord, are false.°   290

Brutus. He thinks he still is at his instrument.
Lucius, awake!

Lucius. My lord?

Brutus. Didst thou dream, Lucius, that thou so criedst
out?

Lucius. My lord, I do not know that I did cry.   295

Brutus. Yes, that thou didst. Didst thou see anything?

Lucius. Nothing, my lord.

Brutus. Sleep again, Lucius. Sirrah Claudius!
[*To Varro*] Fellow thou, awake!

274 **How . . . burns** (lights allegedly burned dimly or blue in the presence
of a supernatural being) 277 **upon** toward 279 **stare** stand on
end 290 **false** out of tune

300 *Varro.* My lord?

    Claudius. My lord?

    Brutus. Why did you so cry out, sirs, in your sleep?

    Both. Did we, my lord?

    Brutus.   Ay. Saw you anything?

    Varro. No, my lord, I saw nothing.

    Claudius.   Nor I, my lord.

305 *Brutus.* Go and commend me° to my brother Cassius;
    Bid him set on his pow'rs betimes before,°
    And we will follow.

    Both.   It shall be done, my lord.

                               Exeunt.

305 **commend me** give my greetings   306 **set . . . before** advance his
forces early in the morning before me

ACT 5

[Scene 1. *The plains of Philippi.*]

Enter Octavius, Antony, and their Army.

Octavius. Now, Antony, our hopes are answerèd;
You said the enemy would not come down,
But keep the hills and upper regions.
It proves not so; their battles° are at hand;
They mean to warn° us at Philippi here,   5
Answering before we do demand° of them.

Antony. Tut, I am in their bosoms,° and I know
Wherefore they do it. They could be content
To visit other places,° and come down
With fearful° bravery,° thinking by this face°   10
To fasten in our thoughts° that they have courage;
But 'tis not so.

Enter a Messenger.

Messenger.   Prepare you, generals,
The enemy comes on in gallant show;
Their bloody sign° of battle is hung out,

5.1.4 **battles** armies   5 **warn** challenge   6 **Answering . . . demand** appearing in opposition before we force a meeting   7 **I am in their bosoms** I understand their inmost thoughts   8–9 **They could . . . places** they would prefer to be somewhere else   10 **fearful** (1) frightened (2) awe-inspiring   10 **bravery** bravado (and show of splendor)   10 **face** appearance   11 **fasten in our thoughts** persuade us   14 **bloody sign** red flag

89

15   And something to be done immediately.

Antony. Octavius, lead your battle softly° on
      Upon the left hand of the even° field.

Octavius. Upon the right hand I; keep thou the left.

Antony. Why do you cross° me in this exigent?°

20   *Octavius.* I do not cross you; but I will do so. *March.*

Drum. Enter Brutus, Cassius, and their Army; [Lucilius,
      Titinius, Messala, and others].

Brutus. They stand, and would have parley.

Cassius. Stand fast, Titinius, we must out and talk.

Octavius. Mark Antony, shall we give sign of battle?

25   *Antony.* No, Caesar, we will answer on their charge.°
      Make forth;° the generals would have some words.

Octavius. Stir not until the signal.

Brutus. Words before blows; is it so, countrymen?

Octavius. Not that we love words better, as you do.

Brutus. Good words are better than bad strokes, Octa-
      vius.

Antony. In your bad strokes, Brutus, you give good
30   words;
      Witness the hole you made in Caesar's heart,
      Crying "Long live! Hail, Caesar!"

Cassius.   Antony,
      The posture° of your blows are yet unknown;
      But for your words, they rob the Hybla° bees,
      And leave them honeyless.

35   *Antony.*   Not stingless too.

16 **battle softly** army slowly   17 **even** level   19 **cross** oppose, contra-
dict   19 **exigent** crisis   24 **answer on their charge** meet them when
they attack   25 **Make forth** go forward   33 **posture** nature, quality   34 **Hybla** a Sicilian town famous for its sweet honey

Brutus. O, yes, and soundless too;
　　For you have stol'n their buzzing, Antony,
　　And very wisely threat before you sting.

Antony. Villains! You did not so, when your vile daggers
　　Hacked one another in the sides of Caesar.
　　You showed your teeth° like apes, and fawned like 　　40
　　　　hounds,
　　And bowed like bondmen, kissing Caesar's feet;
　　Whilst damnèd Casca, like a cur, behind
　　Struck Caesar on the neck. O you flatterers!

Cassius. Flatterers! Now, Brutus, thank yourself;　　　45
　　This tongue had not offended so today,
　　If Cassius might have ruled.°

Octavius. Come, come, the cause.° If arguing make us
　　　　sweat,
　　The proof° of it will turn to redder drops.
　　Look,　　　　　　　　　　　　　　　　　　　　50
　　I draw a sword against conspirators.
　　When think you that the sword goes up° again?
　　Never, till Caesar's three and thirty wounds
　　Be well avenged; or till another Caesar°
　　Have added slaughter to° the sword of traitors.　　55

Brutus. Caesar, thou canst not die by traitors' hands,
　　Unless thou bring'st them with thee.

Octavius.　　　　　　　　　　　　　So I hope.
　　I was not born to die on Brutus' sword.

Brutus. O, if thou wert the noblest of thy strain,°
　　Young man, thou couldst not die more honorable.　60

41 **showed your teeth** grinned   47 **ruled** had his way (i.e., in urging that
Antony be slain)   48 **cause** business at hand   49 **proof** test   52 **up** into
the sheath   54 **another Caesar** i.e., Octavius himself   55 **Have added
slaughter to** has also been killed by   59 **strain** family, line of descent

Cassius. A peevish° schoolboy, worthless° of such honor,
    Joined with a masker and a reveler.°

Antony. Old Cassius still!

Octavius.   Come, Antony; away!
    Defiance, traitors, hurl we in your teeth.
65   If you dare fight today, come to the field;
    If not, when you have stomachs.°
                  Exit Octavius, Antony, and Army.

Cassius. Why, now blow wind, swell billow, and swim
    bark!
    The storm is up, and all is on the hazard.°

Brutus. Ho, Lucilius, hark, a word with you.
             Lucilius and Messala stand forth.

Lucilius.   My lord?
        [Brutus and Lucilius converse apart.]

Cassius. Messala.

Messala.   What says my general?

70 *Cassius.*   Messala,
    This is my birthday; as this very day
    Was Cassius born. Give me thy hand, Messala:
    Be thou my witness that against my will
    (As Pompey was)° am I compelled to set°
75   Upon one battle all our liberties.
    You know that I held Epicurus strong,°
    And his opinion; now I change my mind,
    And partly credit things that do presage.°
    Coming from Sardis, on our former° ensign

61 **peevish** childish (Octavius was 21) 61 **worthless** unworthy
62 **masker and a reveler** i.e., that dissipated Antony, who loved par-
ticipating in masques and wild parties (cf. 1.2.203–04, 2.1.189, 2.2.116)
66 **stomachs** inclination, appetite   68 **on the hazard** at stake   74 **As
Pompey was** (at Pharsalus where, having been persuaded to give battle
against his will, he was decisively defeated and later murdered)   74 **set**
stake   76 **held Epicurus strong** believed strongly in the philosophy of
Epicurus (a materialist who believed that because the gods were not interested in human affairs omens were to be discounted)   78 **presage** foretell
the future   79 **former** foremost

Two mighty eagles fell,° and there they perched, 80
Gorging and feeding from our soldiers' hands,
Who to Philippi here consorted° us.
This morning are they fled away and gone,
And in their steads do ravens, crows, and kites°
Fly o'er our heads and downward look on us 85
As we were sickly° prey; their shadows seem
A canopy most fatal,° under which
Our army lies, ready to give up the ghost.

Messala. Believe not so.

Cassius.   I but believe it partly,
For I am fresh of spirit and resolved 90
To meet all perils very constantly.°

Brutus. Even so, Lucilius.

Cassius.   Now, most noble Brutus,
The gods today stand friendly, that we may,
Lovers° in peace, lead on our days to age!
But since the affairs of men rests still incertain,° 95
Let's reason with the worst that may befall.°
If we do lose this battle, then is this
The very last time we shall speak together.
What are you then determinèd to do?

Brutus. Even by the rule of that philosophy° 100
By which I did blame Cato for the death
Which he did give himself; I know not how,
But I do find it cowardly and vile,
For fear of what might fall,° so to prevent°
The time° of life, arming myself with patience 105
To stay the providence° of some high powers
That govern us below.

80 **fell** swooped down   82 **consorted** accompanied   84 **ravens, crows, and kites** (scavengers; traditionally, they know when a battle is pending and accompany the armies)   86 **sickly** ready for death   87 **fatal** presaging death   91 **constantly** resolutely   94 **Lovers** devoted friends   95 **rests still incertain** always stand in doubt   96 **reason . . . befall** consider what must be done if the worst happens   100 **that philosophy** i.e., Stoicism   104 **fall** befall   104 **prevent** anticipate   105 **time** term, natural end   106 **stay the providence** await the ordained fate

Cassius.   Then, if we lose this battle,
         You are contented to be led in triumph°
         Thorough the streets of Rome?

110 *Brutus.* No, Cassius, no; think not, thou noble Roman,
         That ever Brutus will go bound to Rome;
         He bears too great a mind. But this same day
         Must end that work the ides of March begun;
         And whether we shall meet again I know not.
115   Therefore our everlasting farewell take.
         Forever, and forever, farewell, Cassius!
         If we do meet again, why, we shall smile;
         If not, why then this parting was well made.

     Cassius. Forever, and forever, farewell, Brutus!
120   If we do meet again, we'll smile indeed;
         If not, 'tis true this parting was well made.

     Brutus. Why then, lead on. O, that a man might know
         The end of this day's business ere it come!
         But it sufficeth that the day will end,
125   And then the end is known. Come, ho! Away! *Exeunt.*

                    [Scene 2. *The field of battle.*]

              Alarum.° Enter Brutus and Messala.

     Brutus. Ride, ride, Messala, ride, and give these bills°
         Unto the legions on the other side.°   *Loud alarum.*
         Let them set on at once; for I perceive
         But cold demeanor° in Octavius' wing,
5   And sudden push° gives them the overthrow.
         Ride, ride, Messala! Let them all come down. *Exeunt.*

108 **in triumph** (as a captive) in the victor's procession   5.2.1s.d. **Ala-rum** call to arms (drums or trumpets)   1 **bills** written orders   2 **side wing** (commanded by Cassius)   4 **But cold demeanor** marked lack of spirit in fighting   5 **push** attack

[Scene 3. *The field of battle.*]

Alarums. Enter Cassius and Titinius.

Cassius. O, look, Titinius, look, the villains° fly!
　Myself have to mine own° turned enemy.
　This ensign° here of mine was turning back;
　I slew the coward, and did take it° from him.

Titinius. O Cassius, Brutus gave the word too early,　　5
　Who, having some advantage on Octavius,
　Took it too eagerly; his soldiers fell to spoil,°
　Whilst we by Antony are all enclosed.

Enter Pindarus.

Pindarus. Fly further off, my lord, fly further off!
　Mark Antony is in your tents, my lord.　　　　　10
　Fly, therefore, noble Cassius, fly far° off!

Cassius. This hill is far enough. Look, look, Titinius!
　Are those my tents where I perceive the fire?

Titinius. They are, my lord.

Cassius.　　　　　　Titinius, if thou lovest me,
　Mount thou my horse and hide thy spurs in him　　15
　Till he have brought thee up to yonder troops
　And here again, that I may rest assured
　Whether yond troops are friend or enemy.

Titinius. I will be here again even with a thought.°
　　　　　　　　　　　　　　　　　Exit.

Cassius. Go, Pindarus, get higher on that hill;　　　20

5.3.1 **villains** i.e., cowardly soldiers of his own side　2 **mine own** my own
men　3 **ensign** standard-bearer　4 **it** i.e., the standard　7 **spoil** looting　11 **far** farther　19 **even with a thought** as quickly as thought

My sight was ever thick.° Regard Titinius,
And tell me what thou not'st about the field.
                              [*Exit Pindarus.*]
This day I breathèd first. Time is come round,
And where I did begin, there shall I end.
25 My life is run his compass.° Sirrah, what news?

Pindarus. (*Above*)° O my lord!

Cassius. What news?

Pindarus. [*Above*] Titinius is enclosèd round about
With horsemen that make to him on the spur;°
30 Yet he spurs on. Now they are almost on him.
Now, Titinius! Now some light.° O, he lights too!
He's ta'en!° (*Shout.*) And, hark! They shout for joy.

Cassius. Come down; behold no more.
O, coward that I am, to live so long,
35 To see my best friend ta'en before my face!

                    Enter Pindarus.

Come hither, sirrah.
In Parthia did I take thee prisoner;
And then I swore thee, saving of° thy life,
That whatsoever I did bid thee do,
40 Thou shouldst attempt it. Come now, keep thine oath.
Now be a freeman, and with this good sword,
That ran through Caesar's bowels, search° this bosom.
Stand° not to answer. Here, take thou the hilts,
And when my face is covered, as 'tis now,
45 Guide thou the sword—Caesar, thou art revenged,
Even with the sword that killed thee.   [*Dies.*]

Pindarus. So, I am free; yet would not so have been,
Durst I have done my will. O Cassius!
Far from this country Pindarus shall run,
50 Where never Roman shall take note of him.   [*Exit.*]

21 **My . . . thick** I have always been nearsighted   25 **is run his compass** has completed its circuit   26 s.d. **Above** on the upper stage   29 **make . . . spur** ride toward him at top speed   31 **light** dismount   32 **ta'en** taken, captured   38 **swore . . . of** made you swear, when I spared   42 **search** penetrate   43 **Stand** delay

Enter Titinius and Messala.

Messala. It is but change,° Titinius; for Octavius
    Is overthrown by noble Brutus' power,
    As Cassius' legions are by Antony.

Titinius. These tidings will well comfort Cassius.

Messala. Where did you leave him?

Titinius.   All disconsolate,   55
    With Pindarus his bondman, on this hill.

Messala. Is not that he that lies upon the ground?

Titinius. He lies not like the living. O my heart!

Messala. Is not that he?

Titinius.   No, this was he, Messala,
    But Cassius is no more. O setting sun,   60
    As in thy red rays thou dost sink to night,
    So in his red blood Cassius' day is set.
    The sun of Rome is set. Our day is gone;
    Clouds, dews,° and dangers come; our deeds are done!
    Mistrust of° my success hath done this deed.   65

Messala. Mistrust of good success hath done this deed.
    O hateful Error, Melancholy's child,°
    Why dost thou show to the apt° thoughts of men
    The things that are not? O Error, soon conceived,
    Thou never com'st unto a happy birth,   70
    But kill'st the mother° that engend'red thee!

Titinius. What, Pindarus! Where art thou, Pindarus?

Messala. Seek him, Titinius, whilst I go to meet
    The noble Brutus, thrusting this report
    Into his ears. I may say "thrusting" it;   75

51 **change** exchange (of fortune)   64 **dews** (considered unwhole-
some)   65 **Mistrust of** lack of confidence in   67 **Melancholy's child**
(i.e., those of despondent temperament are liable to be introspective and full
of imaginary fears)   68 **apt** easily impressed   71 **mother** i.e., the melancholy person, Cassius, who conceived the error

For piercing steel and darts envenomèd
Shall be as welcome to the ears of Brutus
As tidings of this sight.

Titinius.   Hie° you, Messala,
And I will seek for Pindarus the while.

                              [*Exit Messala.*]

80 Why didst thou send me forth, brave° Cassius?
Did I not meet thy friends, and did not they
Put on my brows this wreath of victory,
And bid me give it thee? Didst thou not hear their
    shouts?
Alas, thou hast misconstrued everything!
85 But hold thee,° take this garland on thy brow;
Thy Brutus bid me give it thee, and I
Will do his bidding. Brutus, come apace,°
And see how I regarded° Caius Cassius.
By your leave,° gods. This is a Roman's part:°
90 Come, Cassius' sword, and find Titinius' heart. *Dies.*

*Alarum. Enter Brutus, Messala, young Cato, Strato,
Volumnius, and Lucilius.*

Brutus. Where, where, Messala, doth his body lie?

Messala. Lo, yonder, and Titinius mourning it.

Brutus. Titinius' face is upward.

Cato.   He is slain.

Brutus. O Julius Caesar, thou art mighty yet!
95 Thy spirit walks abroad, and turns our swords
In our own proper° entrails.   *Low alarums.*

Cato.   Brave° Titinius!
Look, whe'r° he have not crowned dead Cassius.

Brutus. Are yet two Romans living such as these?
The last of all the Romans, fare thee well!

78 **Hie** hasten   80 **brave** noble   85 **hold thee** wait a moment   87 **apace**
quickly   88 **regarded** honored   89 **By your leave** with your permission
(because he is ending his life before the time appointed by the gods)
89 **part** role, duty   96 **own proper** (emphatic) very own   96 **Brave**
noble   97 **whe'r** whether

It is impossible that ever Rome   100
Should breed thy fellow.° Friends, I owe moe° tears
To this dead man than you shall see me pay.
I shall find time, Cassius; I shall find time.
Come, therefore, and to Thasos° send his body;
His funerals shall not be in our camp,   105
Lest it discomfort us.° Lucilius, come,
And come, young Cato; let us to the field.
Labeo and Flavius set our battles° on.
'Tis three o'clock; and, Romans, yet ere night
We shall try fortune in a second fight.   *Exeunt.*   110

[Scene 4. *The field of battle.*]

Alarum. Enter Brutus, Messala, [young] Cato, Lucilius,
and Flavius.

Brutus. Yet, countrymen, O, yet hold up your heads!
                    [*Exit, with followers.*]

Cato. What bastard° doth not? Who will go with me?
I will proclaim my name about the field.
I am the son of Marcus Cato,° ho!
A foe to tyrants, and my country's friend.   5
I am the son of Marcus Cato, ho!

                Enter Soldiers and fight.

Lucilius.° And I am Brutus, Marcus Brutus, I;
Brutus, my country's friend; know me for Brutus!
                    [*Young Cato falls.*]

101 **fellow** equal   101 **moe** more   104 **Thasos** an island near Philippi   106 **discomfort us** dishearten our troops   108 **battles** armies
5.4.2 **What bastard** who is such a low fellow that he   4 **son of Marcus Cato** son of Cato of Utica, hence, brother of Brutus' wife   7 **Lucilius** (the Folio fails to provide a speech prefix for lines 7–8, but because it is clear from Plutarch and from line 14 that Lucilius impersonates Brutus it is plausible to attribute 7–8 to Lucilius)

O young and noble Cato, art thou down?
10   Why, now thou diest as bravely as Titinius,
And mayst be honored, being Cato's son.

[*First*] *Soldier.* Yield, or thou diest.

Lucilius.   Only I yield to die°.
There is so much° that thou wilt kill me straight;°
Kill Brutus, and be honored in his death.

15   [*First*] *Soldier.* We must not. A noble prisoner!

Enter Antony.

Second Soldier. Room, ho! Tell Antony, Brutus is ta'en.

First Soldier. I'll tell thee news. Here comes the general.
Brutus is ta'en, Brutus is ta'en, my lord.

Antony. Where is he?

20   *Lucilius.* Safe, Antony; Brutus is safe enough.
I dare assure thee that no enemy
Shall ever take alive the noble Brutus.
The gods defend him from so great a shame!
When you do find him, or alive or dead,
25   He will be found like Brutus, like himself.°

Antony. This is not Brutus, friend, but, I assure you,
A prize no less in worth. Keep this man safe;
Give him all kindness. I had rather have
Such men my friends than enemies. Go on,
30   And see whe'r Brutus be alive or dead,
And bring us word unto Octavius' tent
How everything is chanced.°   *Exeunt.*

12 **Only I yield to die** I yield only to die   13 **so much** so great an induce-
ment, i.e., gaining great honor by killing Brutus (?), so much to be blamed
for (?), a sum of money (offered to the soldier) (?)   13 **straight**
immediately   25 **like himself** i.e., behaving in accordance with his noble
nature   32 **is chanced** has turned out

[Scene 5. *The field of battle.*]

Enter Brutus, Dardanius, Clitus, Strato, and Volumnius.

Brutus. Come, poor remains° of friends, rest on this
      rock.

Clitus. Statilius showed the torchlight,° but, my lord,
      He came not back; he is or ta'en or slain.

Brutus. Sit thee down, Clitus. Slaying is the word;
      It is a deed in fashion. Hark thee, Clitus.   5
                                        [*Whispers.*]

Clitus. What, I, my lord? No, not for all the world!

Brutus. Peace then, no words.

Clitus.   I'll rather kill myself.

Brutus. Hark thee, Dardanius.   [*Whispers.*]

Dardanius.   Shall I do such a deed?

Clitus. O Dardanius!

Dardanius. O Clitus!   10

Clitus. What ill request did Brutus make to thee?

Dardanius. To kill him, Clitus. Look, he meditates.

Clitus. Now is that noble vessel° full of grief,
      That it runs over even at his eyes.

5.5.1 **poor remains** wretched survivors   2 **showed the torchlight** (Statilius had volunteered to see if Cassius' camp was occupied by the enemy;
he signaled on arrival there but was obviously captured thereafter)
13 **vessel** (figurative for "human being." Also an allusion to the small jars
of tears offered to the dead)

15　*Brutus.* Come hither, good Volumnius; list° a word.

Volumnius. What says my lord?

Brutus.　　　　　　　　　　Why, this, Volumnius:
　　The ghost of Caesar hath appeared to me
　　Two several° times by night; at Sardis once,
　　And this last night here in Philippi fields.
　　I know my hour is come.

20　*Volumnius.*　　　　　　　　Not so, my lord.

Brutus. Nay, I am sure it is, Volumnius.
　　Thou seest the world, Volumnius, how it goes;
　　Our enemies have beat us to the pit.°　*Low alarums.*
　　It is more worthy to leap in ourselves
25　Than tarry till they push us. Good Volumnius,
　　Thou know'st that we two went to school together;
　　Even for that our love of old, I prithee
　　Hold thou my sword-hilts whilst I run on it.

Volumnius. That's not an office for a friend, my lord.
　　　　　　　　　　　　　　Alarum still.°

30　*Clitus.* Fly, fly, my lord, there is no tarrying here.

Brutus. Farewell to you; and you; and you, Volumnius.
　　Strato, thou hast been all this while asleep;
　　Farewell to thee too, Strato. Countrymen,
　　My heart doth joy that yet in all my life
35　I found no man but he was true to me.
　　I shall have glory by this losing day
　　More than Octavius and Mark Antony
　　By this vile conquest° shall attain unto.
　　So fare you well at once,° for Brutus' tongue
40　Hath almost ended his life's history.
　　Night hangs upon mine eyes; my bones would rest,

---

15 **list** hear　18 **several** separate　23 **pit** (1) trap for capturing wild animals (2) grave　29 s.d. **still** continuing　38 **vile conquest** i.e., overthrow of the revolution against tyranny　39 **at once** without further delay

That have but labored to attain this hour.°
          Alarum. Cry within, "Fly, fly, fly!"

Clitus. Fly, my lord, fly!

Brutus.   Hence! I will follow.
          [*Exeunt Clitus, Dardanius, and Volumnius.*]
I prithee, Strato, stay thou by thy lord,
Thou art a fellow of a good respect.°   45
Thy life hath had some smatch° of honor in it;
Hold then my sword, and turn away thy face,
While I do run upon it. Wilt thou, Strato?

Strato. Give me your hand first. Fare you well, my lord.

Brutus. Farewell, good Strato—Caesar, now be still;   50
     I killed not thee with half so good a will.   *Dies.*

     *Alarum. Retreat. Enter Antony, Octavius, Messala,
          Lucilius, and the Army.*

Octavius. What man is that?

Messala. My master's man.° Strato, where is thy master?

Strato. Free from the bondage you are in, Messala;
     The conquerors can but make a fire of him.   55
     For Brutus only overcame himself,°
     And no man else hath honor by his death.

Lucilius. So Brutus should be found. I thank thee,
          Brutus,
     That thou hast proved Lucilius' saying° true.

Octavius. All that served Brutus, I will entertain° them.   60
     Fellow, wilt thou bestow° thy time with me?

Strato. Ay, if Messala will prefer° me to you.

Octavius. Do so, good Messala.

42 **but . . . hour** i.e., worked hard only to reach this goal of death (which
brings, for a Stoic, rest from life's trials)   45 **respect** reputation
46 **smatch** smack, taste   53 **man** servant   56 **Brutus only overcame
himself** only Brutus overcame Brutus   59 **saying** (see 5.4.21–25)
60 **entertain** take into service   61 **bestow** spend   62 **prefer** recommend

Messala. How died my master, Strato?

65 *Strato.* I held the sword, and he did run on it.

Messala. Octavius, then take him to follow thee,
   That did the latest° service to my master.

Antony. This was the noblest Roman of them all.
   All the conspirators save only he
70   Did that they did in envy of great Caesar;
   He, only in a general honest thought
   And common good to all, made one of them.°
   His life was gentle,° and the elements°
   So mixed° in him that Nature might stand up
75   And say to all the world, "This was a man!"

Octavius. According to his virtue,° let us use° him
   With all respect and rites of burial.
   Within my tent his bones tonight shall lie,
   Most like a soldier ordered honorably.°
80   So call the field° to rest, and let's away
   To part° the glories of this happy day. *Exeunt omnes.*

FINIS

67 **latest** last   71–72 **He only . . . them** he, moved only by impersonal
motives directed to the good of the community, joined the conspirators   73 **gentle** noble   73 **elements** (the four opposed elements, of which
all nature was thought to be composed, were represented in the human
body by the four liquids, bile, phlegm, blood, and choler; the dominance of
one of these determined a man's temperament—melancholic, phlegmatic,
sanguine, or choleric)   74 **So mixed** i.e., so well-balanced   76 **virtue**
excellence   76 **use** treat   79 **ordered honorably** arrayed (and treated)
with all honor   80 **field** army   81 **part** divide

Textual Note

The First Folio of 1623 provides us with the text for *Julius Caesar*; there are no early quarto editions. In setting this play for the press, the printer's compositors probably worked from the playhouse promptbook, for the Folio text contains remarkably few misprints, serious errors in punctuation, or misattribution of speeches. The stage directions, unusually numerous and detailed, also suggest a stage manager's prompt copy; stage directions like "Alarum still" and "Enter Boy with wine and tapers" are obviously closely connected with actual performance.

In the present edition, the names of characters have been normalized so that *Marullus* appears for the Folio Murellus (and Murrellus), *Casca* for Caska, *Lucilius* for Lucillius. Occasionally the Folio uses the forms "Antonio" (1.2.3, 4, 6, 190; 1.3.37), "Claudio" (4.3.241, 243, 243 s.d., 288), "Flavio," "Labio" (5.3.108), "Octavio" (3.1.275 s.d., 5.2.4), "Varrus" (4.3.243, 243 s.d., 288); these are standardized, appearing as *Antonius*, *Claudius*, *Flavius*, *Labeo*, *Octavius*, and *Varro*. The present edition modernizes spelling and punctuation, corrects a few obvious misprints, translates the act divisions from Latin into English, expands the speech prefixes, and alters the lineation of a few passages. The only other substantial departures from the Folio are listed below, the present reading in italics and then the Folio's reading in roman.

1.3.129 *In favor's* Is Fauors
2.1.40 *ides* first   213 *eighth* eight

2.2.19 *fought* fight   23 *did neigh* do neigh   46 *are* heare
3.1.39 *law* lane   113 *states* State   115 *lies* lye   283 *for* from
3.2.106 *art* are
4.3.253 *not* it not
5.1.41 *teeth* teethes
5.3.104 *Thasos* Tharsus
5.4.7 *Lucilius* [F omits, and prints "Lucilius" as the prefix to line 9]

The Source of *Julius Caesar*

Shakespeare's main source for *Julius Caesar* was Sir Thomas North's translation of Plutarch's *The Lives of the Noble Grecians and Romans*, printed in 1579 and again in 1595. A classicist might be somewhat alarmed to learn that North translated not from the Greek of Plutarch but the French translation of Jacques Amyot. A student, unaware of the practice of Elizabethan dramatists, might be taken aback by Shakespeare's close adherence to various sources in writing his plays. Indeed, Shakespeare's use of Plutarch is detailed, literal, and incontrovertible. Sometimes he seems to versify directly from the book; at other times he selects, cuts, compresses, and amalgamates events from the full range of Plutarch's material dealing with the history of Julius Caesar. A complete understanding of his skill can be gained only by reading through Plutarch's comparisons of Demetrius and Antony, Dion and Brutus, and more particularly, the chapters on Julius Caesar, Brutus, and Antony, where we sometimes find three variant accounts of the same event, from each of which Shakespeare has taken some details to construct his own version.

Since it was impossible to give a complete selection of versions for each event of the play, let alone indicate all the historical events that Shakespeare does not use, we present one version of each happening—the one that seems closest to Shakespeare's own dramatization—and arrange these to read as a connected story. In addition, we add some brief selections to give a fuller view of each main character in the story. This use of extracts has inevitably led to some omis-

sions and overlapping; however, we hope that readers will be
stimulated to go to the sources themselves.

A number of other sources, besides Plutarch, have been
suggested for this play, and those who are interested will find
comprehensive discussions of this subject in the introduction to the New Arden edition of *Julius Caesar,* edited by
T. S. Dorsch, and in Kenneth Muir's book *Shakespeare's
Sources* (Vol. I). Although Shakespeare must of course have
used a sixteenth-century edition of North's Plutarch, because
the 1612 edition—reprinted in modernized spelling by Walter
W. Skeat, *Shakespeare's Plutarch* (Macmillan, 1875)—is the
only one readily available to most readers, the selections below have been drawn from Skeat, and Skeat's page numbers
have been given. In these selections the 1612 edition has no
additions or subtractions in matters of substance; the only
differences are trivial ones (e.g., "O Ligarius" vs. "Ligarius")
that do not affect the study of Shakespeare's use of Plutarch.

PLUTARCH

Selections from The Lives of the Noble
Grecians and Romans

Caesar Overcomes the Sons of Pompey

After all these things were ended, he was chosen Consul
the fourth time, and went into Spain to make war with the
sons of Pompey: who were yet but very young, but had notwithstanding raised a marvelous great army together and
showed they had manhood and courage worthy to command
such an army, insomuch as they put Caesar himself in great
danger of his life. The greatest battle that was fought between them in all this war was by the city of Munda. For
then Caesar, seeing his men sorely distressed, and having
their hands full of their enemies, he ran into the press among

his men that fought, and cried out unto them: "What, are ye
not ashamed to be beaten and taken prisoners, yielding yourselves with your own hands to these young boys?" And so,
with all the force he could make, having with much ado put
his enemies to flight, he slew above thirty thousand of them
in the field, and lost of his own men a thousand of the best
he had. After this battle he went into his tent and told his
friends that he had often before fought for victory, but, this
last time now, that he had fought for the safety of his own
life. He won this battle on the very feast day of the Baccha-
nalians, in the which men say that Pompey the Great went
out of Rome, about four years before, to begin this civil war.
For his sons, the younger scaped from the battle; but, within
few days after, Didius brought the head of the elder. This
was the last war that Caesar made. But the triumph he made
into Rome for the same did as much offend the Romans, and
more, than anything that ever he had done before: because he
had not overcome captains that were strangers, nor barbarous
kings, but had destroyed the sons of the noblest man of
Rome, whom fortune had overthrown. And because he had
plucked up his race by the roots, men did not think it meet
for him to triumph so for the calamities of his country, rejoicing at a thing for the which he had but one excuse to al-
lege in his defense unto the gods and men, that he was
compelled to do that he did. And the rather they thought it
not meet, because he had never before sent letters nor mes-
sengers unto the commonwealth at Rome, for any victory
that he had ever won in all the civil wars: but did always for
shame refuse the glory of it. [*The Life of Julius Caesar*, pp.
91–92.]

Caesar Is Given Dictatorial Powers

This notwithstanding, the Romans, inclining to Caesar's
prosperity and taking the bit in the mouth, supposing that to
be ruled by one man alone, it would be a good mean for
them to take breath a little, after so many troubles and miseries as they had abidden in these civil wars, they chose him
perpetual Dictator. This was a plain tyranny: for to this abso-

lute power of Dictator, they added this, never to be afraid to
be deposed. Cicero pronounced before the Senate, that they
should give him such honors as were meet for a man: howbeit others afterwards added too honors beyond all reason.
For men striving who should most honor him, they made him
hateful and troublesome to themselves that most favored
him, by reason of the unmeasurable greatness and honors
which they gave him. Thereupon it is reported, that even
they that most hated him were no less favorers and furtherers
of his honors than they that most flattered him, because they
might have greater occasions to rise, and that it might appear
they had just cause and color to attempt that they did against
him. And now for himself, after he had ended his civil wars,
he did so honorably behave himself, that there was no fault
to be found in him: and therefore methinks, amongst other
honors they gave him, he rightly deserved this, that they
should build him a temple of Clemency, to thank him for his
courtesy he had used unto them in his victory. For he pardoned many of them that had borne arms against him, and
furthermore, did prefer some of them to honor and office in
the commonwealth: as, amongst others, Cassius and Brutus,
both the which were made Praetors. And, where Pompey's
images had been thrown down, he caused them to be set up
again: whereupon Cicero said then, that, Caesar setting up
Pompey's images again, he made his own to stand the surer.
And when some of his friends did counsel him to have a
guard for the safety of his person, and some also did offer
themselves to serve him, he would never consent to it, but
said: "It was better to die once than always to be afraid of
death." [*The Life of Julius Caesar*, p. 92.]

Caesar's Ambition

But the chiefest cause that made him mortally hated was
the covetous desire he had to be called king: which first gave
the people just cause, and next his secret enemies honest
color, to bear him ill will. This notwithstanding, they that
procured him this honor and dignity gave it out among the
people that it was written in the Sibylline prophecies, "how

the Romans might overcome the Parthians, if they made war
with them and were led by a king, but otherwise that they
were unconquerable." And furthermore they were so bold besides, that, Caesar returning to Rome from the city of Alba,
when they came to salute him, they called him king. But the
people being offended, and Caesar also angry, he said he was
not called king, but Caesar. Then every man keeping silence,
he went his way heavy and sorrowful. When they had decreed divers honors for him in the Senate, the Consuls and
Praetors, accompanied with the whole assembly of the Senate, went unto him in the market place, where he was set by
the pulpit for orations, to tell him what honors they had decreed for him in his absence. But he, sitting still in his majesty, disdaining to rise up unto them when they came in, as
if they had been private men, answered them: "that his honors had more need to be cut off than enlarged." This did not
only offend the Senate but the common people also, to see
that he should so lightly esteem of the magistrates of the
commonwealth: insomuch as every man that might lawfully
go his way departed thence very sorrowfully. Thereupon also
Caesar rising departed home to his house, and tearing open
his doublet collar, making his neck bare, he cried out aloud
to his friends, "that his throat was ready to offer to any man
that would come and cut it." Notwithstanding it is reported
that afterwards, to excuse his folly, he imputed it to his disease, saying, "that their wits are not perfect which have this
disease of the falling evil, when standing on their feet they
speak to the common people, but are soon troubled with a
trembling of their body, and a sudden dimness and giddi-
ness." But that was not true, for he would have risen up to
the Senate, but Cornelius Balbus one of his friends (or rather
a flatterer) would not let him, saying: "What, do you not remember that you are Caesar, and will you not let them reverence you and do their duties?" [*The Life of Julius Caesar*,
pp. 94–95.]

Caesar Refuses the Crown

Besides these occasions and offenses, there followed also his shame and reproach, abusing the Tribunes of the people in this sort. At that time the feast *Lupercalia* was celebrated, the which in old time men say was the feast of shepherds or herdmen, and is much like unto the feast of the Lycaeans in Arcadia. But howsoever it is, that day there are divers noblemen's sons, young men (and some of them magistrates themselves that govern them), which run naked through the city, striking in sport them they meet in their way with leather thongs, hair and all on, to make them give place. And many noblewomen and gentlewomen also go of purpose to stand in their way, and do put forth their hands to be stricken, as scholars hold them out to their schoolmaster to be stricken with the ferula: persuading themselves that, being with child, they shall have good delivery; and so, being barren, that it will make them to conceive with child. Caesar sat to behold that sport upon the pulpit for orations, in a chair of gold, appareled in triumphant manner. Antonius, who was Consul at that time, was one of them that ran this holy course. So when he came into the market place, the people made a lane for him to run at liberty, and he came to Caesar, and presented him a diadem wreathed about with laurel. Whereupon there rose a certain cry of rejoicing, not very great, done only by a few appointed for the purpose. But when Caesar refused the diadem, then all the people together made an outcry of joy. [*The Life of Julius Caesar*, pp. 95–96.]

Antonius again did put it on his head: Caesar again refused it: and thus they were striving off and on a great while together. As oft as Antonius did put this laurel crown unto him, a few of his followers rejoiced at it: and as oft also as Caesar refused it, all the people together clapped their hands. And this was a wonderful thing, that they suffered all things subjects should do by commandment of their kings: and yet they could not abide the name of a king, detesting it as the utter destruction of their liberty. Caesar, in a rage, arose out of his seat, and plucking down the collar of his gown from his neck, he showed it naked, bidding any man strike off his

head that would. This laurel crown was afterwards put upon
the head of one of Caesar's statues or images, the which one
of the tribunes plucked off. The people liked his doing
therein so well that they waited on him home to his house,
with great clapping of hands. Howbeit Caesar did turn them
out of their offices for it. [*The Life of Marcus Antonius*,
p. 164.]

Attempts to Turn Brutus Against Caesar

Hereupon the people went straight unto Marcus Brutus,
who from his father came of the first Brutus, and by his
mother of the house of the Servilians, a noble house as any
was in Rome, and was also nephew and son-in-law of
Marcus Cato. Notwithstanding, the great honors and favor
Caesar showed unto him kept him back that of himself alone
he did not conspire nor consent to depose him of his kingdom. For Caesar did not only save his life after the battle of
Pharsalia, when Pompey fled, and did at his request also save
many mo of his friends besides: but furthermore, he put a
marvelous confidence in him. For he had already preferred
him to the Praetorship for that year, and furthermore was appointed to be Consul the fourth year after that, having
through Caesar's friendship obtained it before Cassius, who
likewise made suit for the same: and Caesar also, as it is reported, said in this contention, "Indeed Cassius hath alleged
best reason, but yet shall he not be chosen before Brutus."
Some one day accusing Brutus while he practiced this conspiracy, Caesar would not hear of it, but, clapping his hand
on his body, told them, "Brutus will look for this skin":
meaning thereby, that Brutus for his virtue deserved to rule
after him, but yet that, for ambition's sake, he would not
show himself unthankful or dishonorable. Now they that desired change, and wished Brutus only their prince and governor above all other, they durst not come to him themselves
to tell him what they would have him to do, but in the night
did cast sundry papers into the Praetor's seat, where he gave
audience, and the most of them to this effect: "Thou sleepest,
Brutus, and art not Brutus indeed." Cassius, finding Brutus'

ambition stirred up the more by these seditious bills, did prick him forward and egg him on the more, for a private quarrel he had conceived against Caesar: the circumstance whereof we have set down more at large in Brutus' life. Caesar also had Cassius in great jealousy, and suspected him much: whereupon he said on a time to his friends, "What will Cassius do, think ye? I like not his pale looks." Another time when Caesar's friends complained unto him of Antonius and Dolabella, that they pretended some mischief towards him: he answered them again, "As for those fat men and smooth-combed heads," quoth he, "I never reckon of them; but these pale-visaged and carrion-lean people, I fear them most," meaning Brutus and Cassius. [*The Life of Julius Caesar*, pp. 96–97.]

The Conspiracy Is Formed

Now when Cassius felt his friends, and did stir them up against Caesar: they all agreed, and promised to take part with him, so Brutus were the chief of their conspiracy. For they told him that so high an enterprise and attempt as that, did not so much require men of manhood and courage to draw their swords, as it stood them upon to have a man of such estimation as Brutus, to make every man boldly think, that by his only presence the fact were holy and just. If he took not this course, then that they should go to it with fainter hearts; and when they had done it, they should be more fearful: because every man would think that Brutus would not have refused to have made one with them, if the cause had been good and honest. Therefore Cassius, considering this matter with himself, did first of all speak to Brutus, since they grew strange together for the suit they had for the praetorship. So when he was reconciled to him again, and that they had embraced one another, Cassius asked him if he were determined to be in the Senate House the first day of the month of March, because he heard say that Caesar's friends should move the council that day, that Caesar should be called king by the Senate. Brutus answered him, he would not be there. "But if we be sent for," said Cassius, "how then?" "For myself then," said Brutus, "I mean not to hold my peace, but to withstand it, and rather die than lose my liberty."

Cassius being bold, and taking hold of this word: "Why," quoth he, "what Roman is he alive that will suffer thee to die for thy liberty? What? Knowest thou not that thou art Brutus? Thinkest thou that they be cobblers, tapsters, or suchlike base mechanical people, that write these bills and scrolls which are found daily in thy Praetor's chair, and not the noblest men and best citizens that do it? No; be thou well assured that of other Praetors they look for gifts, common distributions amongst the people, and for common plays, and to see fencers fight at the sharp, to show the people pastime: but at thy hands they specially require (as a due debt unto them) the taking away of the tyranny, being fully bent to suffer any extremity for thy sake, so that thou wilt show thyself to be the man thou art taken for, and that they hope thou art." Thereupon he kissed Brutus and embraced him: and so each taking leave of other, they went both to speak with their friends about it. Now amongst Pompey's friends, there was one called Caius Ligarius, who had been accused unto Caesar for taking part with Pompey, and Caesar discharged him. But Ligarius thanked not Caesar so much for his discharge, as he was offended with him for that he was brought in danger by his tyrannical power; and therefore in his heart he was always his mortal enemy, and was besides very familiar with Brutus, who went to see him being sick in his bed, and said unto him: "Ligarius, in what a time art thou sick?" Ligarius rising up in his bed, and taking him by the right hand, said unto him: "Brutus," said he, "if thou hast any great enterprise in hand worthy of thyself, I am whole."

After that time they began to feel all their acquaintance whom they trusted, and laid their heads together, consulting upon it, and did not only pick out their friends, but all those also whom they thought stout enough to attempt any desperate matter, and that were not afraid to lose their lives. For this cause they durst not acquaint Cicero with their conspiracy, although he was a man whom they loved dearly, and trusted best: for they were afraid that he being a coward by nature, and age also having increased his fear, he would quite turn and alter all their purpose, and quench the heat of their enterprise (the which specially required hot and earnest execution), seeking by persuasion to bring all things to such safety, as there should be no peril. Brutus also did let other of his friends alone, as Statilius Epicurian, and Faonius, that made profession to follow Marcus Cato: because that, having cast out words afar off, disputing together in philosophy to feel their minds, Faonius answered, "that civil war was worse than tyrannical government usurped against the law." [*The Life of Marcus Brutus*, pp. 112–14.]

Brutus and Porcia Are Troubled

Furthermore, the only name and great calling of Brutus did bring on the most of them to give consent to this conspiracy: who having never taken oaths together, nor taken or given any caution or assurance, nor binding themselves one to another by any religious oaths, they all kept the matter so secret to themselves, and could so cunningly handle it, that notwithstanding the gods did reveal it by manifest signs and tokens from above, and by predictions of sacrifices, yet all this would not be believed. Now Brutus, who knew very well that for his sake all the noblest, valiantest, and most courageous men of Rome did venture their lives, weighing with himself the greatness of the danger: when he was out of his house, he did so frame and fashion his countenance and looks that no man could discern he had anything to trouble his mind. But when night came that he was in his own house, then he was clean changed: for either care did wake him against his will when he would have slept, or else oftentimes of himself he fell into such deep thoughts of this enterprise, casting in his mind all the dangers that might happen: that his wife, lying by him, found that there was some marvelous great matter that troubled his mind, not being wont to be in that taking, and that he could not well determine with himself.

His wife Porcia (as we have told you before) was the daughter of Cato, whom Brutus married being his cousin, not a maiden, but a young widow after the death of her first husband Bibulus, by whom she had also a young son called Bibulus, who afterwards wrote a book of the acts and gests of Brutus, extant at this present day. This young lady, being excellently well seen in philosophy, loving her husband well, and being of a noble courage, as she was also wise: because she would not ask her husband what he ailed before she had made some proof by herself: she took a little razor, such as barbers occupy to pare men's nails, and, causing her maids and women to go out of her chamber, gave herself a great gash withal in her thigh, that she was straight all of a gore blood: and incontinently after a vehement fever took her, by reason of the pain of her wound. Then perceiving her husband was marvelously out of quiet, and that he could take no rest, even in her greatest pain of all she spoke in this sort unto him: "I being, O Brutus," said she, "the daughter of Cato, was married unto thee; not to be thy bedfellow and companion in bed and at board only, like a harlot, but to be partaker also with thee of thy good and evil fortune. Now for thyself, I can find no cause of fault in thee touching our match: but for my part, how may I show my duty towards thee and how much I would do for thy sake, if I cannot constantly bear a secret mischance or grief with thee, which requireth secrecy and fidelity? I confess that a woman's wit commonly is too weak to keep a secret safely: but yet, Brutus, good education and the company of virtuous men have some power to reform the defect of nature. And for myself, I have this benefit moreover, that I am the daughter of Cato, and wife of Brutus. This notwithstanding, I did not trust to any of these things before, until that now I have found by experience that no pain or grief whatsoever can overcome me." With those words she showed him her wound on her thigh, and told him what she had done to prove herself. Brutus was amazed to hear what she said unto him, and lifting up his hands to heaven, he besought the gods to give him the grace he might bring his enterprise to so good pass, that he might be found a husband worthy of so noble a wife as Porcia: so he then did comfort her the best he could. [*The Life of Marcus Brutus*, pp. 114–16.]

Omens and Events Preceding the Murder

Certainly destiny may easier be foreseen than avoided, considering the strange and wonderful signs that were said to be seen before Caesar's death. For, touching the fires in the element, and spirits running up and down in the night, and also the solitary birds to be seen at noondays sitting in the great market place, are not all these signs perhaps worth the noting, in such a wonderful chance as happened? But Strabo the philosopher writeth, that divers men were seen going up and down in fire: and furthermore, that there was a slave of the soldiers that did cast a marvelous burning flame out of his hand, insomuch as they that saw it thought he had been burnt; but when the fire was out, it was found he had no hurt. Caesar self also doing sacrifice unto the gods, found that one of the beasts which was sacrificed had no heart: and that was a strange thing in nature, how a beast could live without a heart. Furthermore there was a certain soothsayer that had given Caesar warning long time afore, to take heed of the day of the Ides of March (which is the fifteenth of the month), for on that day he should be in great danger. That day being come, Caesar going unto the Senate House, and speaking merrily unto the soothsayer, told him, "The Ides of March be come": "So they be," softly answered the soothsayer, "but yet are they not past." And the very day before, Caesar, supping with Marcus Lepidus, sealed certain letters, as he was wont to do, at the board: so, talk falling out amongst them, reasoning what death was best, he, preventing their opinions, cried out aloud, "Death unlooked for." Then going to bed the same night, as his manner was, and lying with his wife Calpurnia, all the windows and doors of his chamber flying open, the noise awoke him, and made him afraid when he saw such light: but more, when he heard his wife Calpurnia, being fast asleep, weep and sigh, and put forth many fumbling lamentable speeches: for she dreamed that Caesar was slain, and that she had him in her arms. Others also do deny that she had any such dream, as, amongst other, Titus Livius writeth that it was in this sort: the Senate having set upon the top of Caesar's house, for an ornament and setting forth of the same, a certain pinnacle, Calpurnia dreamed that she saw it broken down, and that she thought she lamented and wept for it. Insomuch that, Caesar rising in the morning, she prayed him, if it were possible, not to go out of the doors that day, but to adjourn the session of the Senate until another day. And if that he made no reckoning of her dream, yet that he would search further of the sooth-sayers by their sacrifices, to know what should happen him that day. Thereby it seemed that Caesar likewise did fear or suspect somewhat, because his wife Calpurnia until that time was never given to any fear and superstition: and that then he saw her so troubled in mind with this dream she had. But much more afterwards, when the soothsayers having sacri-ficed many beasts one after another, told him that none did like them: then he determined to send Antonius to adjourn the session of the Senate.

But in the meantime came Decius Brutus, surnamed Al-binus, in whom Caesar put such confidence, that in his last will and testament he had appointed him to be his next heir, and yet was of the conspiracy with Cassius and Brutus: he, fearing that if Caesar did adjourn the session that day, the conspiracy would be betrayed, laughed at the soothsayers, and reproved Caesar, saying, "that he gave the Senate occa-sion to mislike with him, and that they might think he mocked them, considering that by his commandment they were assembled, and that they were ready willingly to grant him all things, and to proclaim him king of all his provinces of the Empire of Rome out of Italy, and that he should wear his diadem in all other places both by sea and land. And fur-thermore, that if any man should tell them from him they should depart for that present time, and return again when Calpurnia should have better dreams, what would his ene-mies and ill-willers say, and how could they like of his friends' words? And who could persuade them otherwise, but that they would think his dominion a slavery unto them and tyrannical in himself? And yet if it be so," said he, "that you utterly mislike of this day, it is better that you go yourself in person, and, saluting the Senate, to dismiss them till another time." Therewithal he took Caesar by the hand, and brought him out of his house. Caesar was not gone far from his house, but a bondman, a stranger, did what he could to speak with him: and when he saw he was put back by the great press and multitude of people that followed him, he went straight into his house, and put himself into Calpurnia's hands, to be kept till Caesar came back again, telling her that he had greater matters to impart unto him. And one Artemidorus also, born in the isle of Gnidos, a doctor of rhetoric in the Greek tongue, who by means of his profession was very familiar with certain of Brutus' confederates, and therefore knew the most part of all their practices against Caesar, came and brought him a little bill, written with his own hand, of all that he meant to tell him. He, marking how Caesar received all the supplications that were offered him, and that he gave them straight to his men that were about him, pressed nearer to him, and said: "Caesar, read this memorial to yourself, and that quickly, for they be matters of great weight, and touch you nearly." Caesar took it of him, but could never read it, though he many times attempted it, for the number of people that did salute him: but holding it still in his hand, keeping it to himself, went on withal into the Senate House. Howbeit others are of opinion, that it was some man else that gave him that memorial, and not Artemidorus, who did what he could all the way as he went to give it Caesar, but he was always repulsed by the people. For these things, they may seem to come by chance; but the place where the murder was prepared, and where the Senate were assembled, and where also there stood up an image of Pompey dedicated by himself amongst other ornaments which he gave unto the theater, all these were manifest proofs that it was the ordinance of some god that made this treason to be executed, specially in that very place. It is also reported that Cassius (though otherwise he did favor the doctrine of Epicurus) beholding the image of Pompey, before they entered into the action of their traitorous enterprise, he did softly call upon it to aid him: but the instant danger of the present time, taking away his former reason, did suddenly put him into a furious passion, and made him like a man half beside himself. [*The Life of Julius Caesar*, pp. 97–100.]

. . . One came unto Casca being a conspirator, and taking him by the hand, said unto him: "O Casca, thou keptest it

close from me, but Brutus hath told me all." Casca being
amazed at it, the other went on with his tale, and said: "Why,
how now, how cometh it to pass thou art thus rich, that thou
dost sue to be Aedilis?" Thus Casca being deceived by the
other's doubtful words, he told them it was a thousand to
one, he blabbed not out all the conspiracy. Another Senator,
called Popilius Laena, after he had saluted Brutus and Cassius more friendly than he was wont to do, he rounded softly
in their ears, and told them: "I pray the gods you may go
through with that you have taken in hand; but withal, dispatch, I read you, for your enterprise is betrayed." When he
had said, he presently departed from them, and left them
both afraid that their conspiracy would out.

Now in the meantime, there came one of Brutus' men
posthaste unto him, and told him his wife was a-dying. For
Porcia, being very careful and pensive for that which was to
come, and being too weak to away with so great and inward
grief of mind, she could hardly keep within, but was frighted
with every little noise and cry she heard, as those that are
taken and possessed with the fury of the Bacchantes; asking
every man that came from the market place what Brutus did,
and still sent messenger after messenger, to know what news.
At length Caesar's coming being prolonged (as you have
heard), Porcia's weakness was not able to hold out any
longer, and thereupon she suddenly swooned, that she had no
leisure to go to her chamber, but was taken in the midst of
her house, where her speech and senses failed her. Howbeit
she soon came to herself again, and so was laid in her bed
and attended by her women. When Brutus heard these news,
it grieved him, as it is to be presupposed: yet he left not off
the care of his country and commonwealth, neither went
home to his house for any news he heard. [*The Life of
Marcus Brutus*, p. 117.]

When Caesar came out of his litter, Popilius Laena (that
had talked before with Brutus and Cassius, and had prayed
the gods they might bring this enterprise to pass) went unto
Caesar and kept him a long time with a talk. Caesar gave
good ear unto him: wherefore the conspirators (if so they
should be called) not hearing what he said to Caesar, but

conjecturing by that he had told them a little before that his talk was none other but the very discovery of their conspiracy, they were afraid, every man of them; and, one looking in another's face, it was easy to see that they all were of a mind, that it was no tarrying for them till they were apprehended, but rather that they should kill themselves with their own hands. And when Cassius and certain other clapped their hands on their swords under their gowns to draw them, Brutus, marking the countenance and gesture of Laena, and considering that he did use himself rather like an humble and earnest suitor than like an accuser, he said nothing to his companions (because there were many amongst them that were not of the conspiracy) but with a pleasant countenance encouraged Cassius. And immediately after Laena went from Caesar, and kissed his hand; which showed plainly that it was for some matter concerning himself that he had held him so long in talk. [*The Life of Marcus Brutus*, p. 118.]

The Assassination

Now Antonius, that was a faithful friend to Caesar, and a valiant man besides of his hands, him Decius Brutus Albinus entertained out of the Senate House, having begun a long tale of set purpose. So Caesar coming into the house, all the Senate stood up on their feet to do him honor. Then part of Brutus' company and confederates stood round about Caesar's chair, and part of them also came towards him, as though they made suit with Metellus Cimber, to call home his brother again from banishment: and thus prosecuting still their suit, they followed Caesar till he was set in his chair. Who denying their petitions, and being offended with them one after another, because the more they were denied the more they pressed upon him and were the earnester with him, Metellus at length, taking his gown with both his hands, pulled it over his neck, which was the sign given the confederates to set upon him. Then Casca, behind him, struck him in the neck with his sword; howbeit the wound was not great nor mortal, because it seemed the fear of such a devilish attempt did amaze him and take his strength from him, that he

killed him not at the first blow. But Caesar, turning straight
unto him, caught hold of his sword and held it hard; and they
both cried out, Caesar in Latin: "O vile traitor Casca, what
doest thou?" and Casca, in Greek, to his brother: "Brother,
help me." At the beginning of this stir, they that were present, not knowing of the conspiracy, were so amazed with the
horrible sight they saw, they had no power to fly, neither to
help him, nor so much as once to make an outcry. They on
the other side that had conspired his death compassed him in
on every side with their swords drawn in their hands, that
Caesar turned him nowhere but he was stricken at by some,
and still had naked swords in his face, and was hackled and
mangled among them, as a wild beast taken of hunters. For
it was agreed among them that every man should give him a
wound, because all their parts should be in this murder: and
then Brutus himself gave him one wound about his privities.
Men report also, that Caesar did still defend himself against
the rest, running every way with his body: but when he saw
Brutus with his sword drawn in his hand, then he pulled his
gown over his head, and made no more resistance, and was
driven either casually or purposedly, by the counsel of the
conspirators, against the base whereupon Pompey's image
stood, which ran all of a gore blood till he was slain. Thus
it seemed that the image took just revenge of Pompey's enemy, being thrown down on the ground at his feet, and yielding up the ghost there, for the number of wounds he had
upon him. For it is reported, that he had three-and-twenty
wounds upon his body: and divers of the conspirators did
hurt themselves, striking one body with so many blows. [*The
Life of Julius Caesar*, pp. 100–01.]

Caesar being slain in this manner, Brutus, standing in the
midst of the house, would have spoken and stayed the other
Senators that were not of the conspiracy, to have told them
the reason why they had done this fact. But they, as men both
afraid and amazed, fled one upon another's neck in haste to
get out at the door, and no man followed them. For it was set
down and agreed between them that they should kill no man
but Caesar only, and should entreat all the rest to look to defend their liberty. All the conspirators, but Brutus, determin-

ing upon this matter, thought it good also to kill Antonius, because he was a wicked man, and that in nature favored tyranny: besides also, for that he was in great estimation with soldiers, having been conversant of long time amongst them: and especially having a mind bent to great enterprise, he was also of great authority at that time, being Consul with Caesar. But Brutus would not agree to it. First, for that he said it was not honest: secondly, because he told them there was hope to change in him. For he did not mistrust but that Antonius, being a noble-minded and courageous man (when he should know that Caesar was dead), would willingly help his country to recover her liberty, having them an example unto him to follow their courage and virtue. So Brutus by this means saved Antonius' life, who at that present time disguised himself and stole away: but Brutus and his consorts, having their swords bloody in their hands, went straight to the Capitol, persuading the Romans as they went to take their liberty again. Now at the first time, when the murder was newly done, there were sudden outcries of people that ran up and down the city, the which indeed did the more increase the fear and tumult. But when they saw they slew no man, neither did spoil or make havoc of anything, then certain of the Senators and many of the people, emboldening themselves, went to the Capitol unto them. [*The Life of Marcus Brutus*, pp. 119–20.]

Public Reaction; Antony Gains Control

There, a great number of men being assembled together one after another, Brutus made an oration unto them, to win the favor of the people, and to justify that they had done. All those that were by said they had done well, and cried unto them that they should boldly come down from the Capitol: whereupon Brutus and his companions came boldly down into the market place. The rest followed in troupe, but Brutus went foremost, very honorably compassed in round about with the noblest men of the city, which brought him from the Capitol, through the market place, to the pulpit for orations. When the people saw him in the pulpit, although they were a multitude of rakehells of all sorts, and had a good will to make some stir; yet, being ashamed to do it, for the reverence they bore unto Brutus, they kept silence to hear what he would say. When Brutus began to speak, they gave him quiet audience: howbeit, immediately after, they showed that they were not all contented with the murder. For when another, called Cinna, would have spoken, and began to accuse Caesar, they fell into a great uproar among them, and marvelously reviled him; insomuch that the conspirators returned again into the Capitol. There Brutus, being afraid to be besieged, sent back again the noblemen that came thither with him, thinking it no reason that they, which were no partakers of the murder, should be partakers of the danger. Then the next morning, the Senate being assembled, and held within the temple of the goddess Tellus, to wit, the Earth: and Antonius, Plancus, and Cicero, having made a motion to the Senate in that assembly that they should take an order to pardon and forget all that was past, and to establish friendship and peace again: it was decreed, that they should not only be pardoned, but also that the Consuls should refer it to the Senate, what honors should be appointed unto them. This being agreed upon, the Senate broke up; and Antonius the Consul, to put them in heart that were in the Capitol, sent them his son for a pledge. Upon this assurance, Brutus and his companions came down from the Capitol, where every man saluted and embraced each other; among the which Antonius himself did bid Cassius to supper to him, and Lepidus also bade Brutus; and so one bade another, as they had friendship and acquaintance together.

The next day following, the Senate, being called again to council, did first of all commend Antonius, for that he had wisely stayed and quenched the beginning of a civil war: then they also gave Brutus and his consorts great praises; and lastly they appointed them several governments of provinces. For unto Brutus they appointed Crete; Africa unto Cassius; Asia unto Trebonius; Bithynia unto Cimber; and unto the other, Decius Brutus Albinus, Gaul on this side of the Alps. When this was done, they came to talk of Caesar's will and testament and of his funerals and tomb. Then Antonius, thinking good his testament should be read openly, and also that his body should be honorably buried, and not in hugger-mugger, lest the people might thereby take occasion to be worse offended if they did otherwise: Cassius stoutly spoke against it. But Brutus went with the motion, and agreed unto it; wherein it seemeth he committed a second fault. For the first fault he did, was when he would not consent to his fellow conspirators, that Antonius should be slain; and therefore he was justly accused that thereby he had saved and strengthened a strong and grievous enemy of their conspiracy. The second fault was when he agreed that Caesar's funerals should be as Antonius would have them, the which indeed marred all. For first of all, when Caesar's testament was openly read among them, whereby it appeared that he bequeathed unto every citizen of Rome 75 drachmas a man; and that he left his gardens and arbors unto the people, which he had on this side of the river Tiber, in the place where now the temple of Fortune is built: the people then loved him, and were marvelous sorry for him. Afterwards, when Caesar's body was brought into the market place, Antonius making his funeral oration in praise of the dead, according to the ancient custom of Rome, and perceiving that his words moved the common people to compassion, he framed his eloquence to make their hearts yearn the more; and taking Caesar's gown all bloody in his hand, he laid it open to the sight of them all, showing what a number of cuts and holes it had upon it. Therewithal the people fell presently into such a rage and mutiny, that there was no more order kept amongst the common people. For some of them cried out, "Kill the murderers": others plucked up forms, tables, and stalls about the market place, as they had done before at the funerals of Clodius, and having laid them all on a heap together, they set them on fire, and thereupon did put the body of Caesar, and burnt it in the midst of the most holy places. And furthermore, when the fire was throughly kindled, some here, some there, took burning firebrands, and ran with them to the murderers' houses that killed him, to set them on fire. Howbeit the conspirators, foreseeing the danger before, had wisely provided for themselves and fled.

But there was a poet called Cinna, who had been no partaker of the conspiracy, but was always one of Caesar's chiefest friends: he dreamed, the night before, that Caesar bade him to supper with him, and that, he refusing to go, Caesar was very importunate with him, and compelled him; so that at length he led him by the hand into a great dark place, where, being marvelously afraid, he was driven to follow him in spite of his heart. This dream put him all night into a fever; and yet notwithstanding, the next morning, when he heard that they carried Caesar's body to burial, being ashamed not to accompany his funerals, he went out of his house, and thrust himself into the press of the common people that were in a great uproar. And because someone called him by his name Cinna, the people, thinking he had been that Cinna who in an oration he made had spoken very evil of Caesar, they, falling upon him in their rage, slew him outright in the market place. This made Brutus and his companions more afraid than any other thing, next unto the change of Antonius. Wherefore they got them out of Rome, and kept at the first in the city of Antium, hoping to return again to Rome, when the fury of the people was a little assuaged. The which they hoped would be quickly, considering that they had to deal with a fickle and inconstant multitude, easy to be carried, and that the Senate stood for them: who notwithstanding made no enquiry for them that had torn poor Cinna the poet in pieces, but caused them to be sought for and apprehended that went with firebrands to set fire on the conspirators' houses. [*The Life of Marcus Brutus*, pp. 120–22.]

Supernatural Events Follow Caesar's Death

But his great prosperity and good fortune that favored him all his lifetime, did continue afterwards in the revenge of his death, pursuing the murderers both by sea and land, till they had not left a man more to be executed, of all them that were actors or counselers in the conspiracy of his death. Furthermore, of all the chances that happen unto men upon the earth, that which came to Cassius above all other, is most to be wondered at: for he, being overcome in battle at the journey of Philippi, slew himself with the same sword with the which he struck Caesar. Again, of signs in the element, the great comet, which seven nights together was seen very bright after Caesar's death, the eighth night after was never seen more. Also the brightness of the sun was darkened, the which all that year through rose very pale and shined not out, whereby it gave but small heat: therefore the air being very cloudy and dark, by the weakness of the heat that could not come forth, did cause the earth to bring forth but raw and unripe fruit, which rotted before it could ripe. [*The Life of Julius Caesar*, p. 103.]

The Triumvirate

Now the state of Rome standing in these terms, there fell out another change and alteration, when the young man Octavius Caesar came to Rome. He was the son of Julius Caesar's niece, whom he had adopted for his son, and made his heir, by his last will and testament. But when Julius Caesar, his adopted father, was slain, he was in the city of Apollonia (where he studied) tarrying for him, because he was determined to make war with the Parthians: but when he heard the news of his death, he returned again to Rome. Where, to begin to curry favor with the common people, he first of all took upon him his adopted father's name, and made distribution among them of the money which his father had bequeathed unto them. By this means he troubled Antonius sorely, and by force of money got a great number of his father's soldiers together, that had served in the wars with him. [*The Life of Marcus Brutus*, p. 123.]

[After much political and military maneuvering, Octavius Caesar, Antonius, and Lepidus met] in an island environed round about with a little river, and there remained three days together. Now as touching all other matters they were easily agreed, and did divide all the Empire of Rome between them, as if it had been their own inheritance. But yet they could hardly agree whom they would put to death: for every one of them would kill their enemies, and save their kinsmen and friends. Yet at length, giving place to their greedy desire

to be revenged of their enemies, they spurned all reverence
of blood and holiness of friendship at their feet. For Caesar
left Cicero to Antonius' will, Antonius also forsook Lucius
Caesar, who was his uncle by his mother: and both of them
together suffered Lepidus to kill his own brother Paulus. Yet
some writers affirm, that Caesar and Antonius requested
Paulus might be slain, and that Lepidus was contented with
it. In my opinion there was never a more horrible, unnatural,
and crueler change than this was. For thus changing murder
for murder, they did as well kill those whom they did forsake
and leave unto others, as those also which others left unto
them to kill: but so much more was their wickedness and
cruelty great unto their friends, for that they put them to
death being innocents, and having no cause to hate them.
[*The Life of Marcus Antonius*, p. 169.]

Disagreements Between Brutus and Cassius

Now whilst Brutus and Cassius were together in the city
of Smyrna, Brutus prayed Cassius to let him have some part
of his money whereof he had great store; because all that he
could rap and rend of his side, he had bestowed it in making
so great a number of ships, that by means of them they
should keep all the sea at their commandment. Cassius'
friends hindered this request and earnestly dissuaded him
from it, persuading him, that it was no reason that Brutus
should have the money which Cassius had gotten together by
sparing and levied with great evil will of the people their
subjects, for him to bestow liberally upon his soldiers, and
by this means to win their good wills, by Cassius' charge.
This notwithstanding, Cassius gave him the third part of this
total sum. [*The Life of Marcus Brutus*, pp. 130–31.]

. . . [Later] Brutus sent to pray Cassius to come to the city
of Sardis, and so he did. Brutus, understanding of his coming, went to meet him with all his friends. There both their
armies being armed, they called them both *Emperors*. Now
as it commonly happened in great affairs between two persons, both of them having many friends and so many cap-

tains under them, there ran tales and complaints betwixt
them. Therefore, before they fell in hand with any other matter, they went into a little chamber together, and bade every
man avoid, and did shut the doors to them. Then they began
to pour out their complaints one to the other, and grew hot
and loud, earnestly accusing one another, and at length fell
both a-weeping. Their friends that were without the chamber,
hearing them loud within, and angry between themselves,
they were both amazed and afraid also, lest it would grow to
further matter: but yet they were commanded that no man
should come to them. Notwithstanding, one Marcus Faonius,
that had been a friend and a follower of Cato while he lived,
and took upon him to counterfeit a philosopher, not with wisdom and discretion, but with a certain bedlam and frantic
motion: he would needs come into the chamber, though the
men offered to keep him out. But it was no boot to let
Faonius, when a mad mood or toy took him in the head: for
he was a hot, hasty man, and sudden in all his doings, and
cared for never a Senator of them all. Now, though he used
this bold manner of speech after the profession of the Cynic
philosophers (as who would say, *Dogs*), yet his boldness did
no hurt many times, because they did but laugh at him to see
him so mad. This Faonius at that time, in despite of the door-
keepers, came into the chamber, and with a certain scoffing
and mocking gesture, which he counterfeited of purpose, he
rehearsed the verses which old Nestor said in Homer:

> My lords, I pray you hearken both to me,
> For I have seen moe years than suchie three.

Cassius fell a-laughing at him: but Brutus thrust him out of
the chamber, and called him dog, and counterfeit Cynic.
Howbeit his coming in broke their strife at that time, and so
they left each other. . . . The next day after, Brutus, upon
complaint of the Sardians, did condemn and note Lucius
Pella for a defamed person, that had been a praetor of the
Romans, and whom Brutus had given charge unto: for that
he was accused and convicted of robbery and pilfery in his
office. This judgment much misliked Cassius, because he
himself had secretly (not many days before) warned two of

his friends, attainted and convicted of the like offenses, and openly had cleared them: but yet he did not therefore leave to employ them in any manner of service as he did before. And therefore he greatly reproved Brutus, for that he would show himself so straight and severe, in such a time as was meeter to bear a little than to take things at the worst. Brutus in contrary manner answered, that he should remember the Ides of March, at which time they slew Julius Caesar, who neither pilled nor polled the country, but only was a favorer and suborner of all them that did rob and spoil, by his countenance and authority. And if there were any occasion whereby they might honestly set aside justice and equity, they should have had more reason to have suffered Caesar's friends to have robbed and done what wrong and injury they had would than to bear with their own men. "For then," said he, "they could but have said we had been cowards, but now they may accuse us of injustice, beside the pains we take, and the danger we put ourselves into." And thus may we see what Brutus' intent and purpose was. [*The Life of Marcus Brutus*, pp. 134–35.]

The Ghost of Caesar; Omens of Defeat and Decisions of War

But as they both prepared to pass over again out of Asia into Europe, there went a rumor that there appeared a wonderful sign unto him. Brutus was a careful man, and slept very little, both for that his diet was moderate, as also because he was continually occupied. He never slept in the daytime, and in the night no longer than the time he was driven to be alone, and when everybody else took their rest. But now whilst he was in war, and his head ever busily occupied to think of his affairs and what would happen, after he had slumbered a little after supper, he spent all the rest of the night in dispatching of his weightiest causes; and after he had taken order for them, if he had any leisure left him, he would read some book till the third watch of the night, at what time the captains, petty captains, and colonels, did use to come to him. So, being ready to go into Europe, one night very late (when all the camp took quiet rest) as he was in his tent with a little light, thinking of weighty matters, he thought he heard one come in to him, and casting his eye towards the door of his tent, that he saw a wonderful strange and monstrous shape of a body coming towards him, and said never a word. So Brutus boldly asked what he was, a god or a man, and what cause brought him thither? The spirit answered him, "I am thy evil spirit, Brutus: and thou shalt see me by the city of Philippi." Brutus, being no otherwise afraid, replied again unto it: "Well, then I shall see thee again." The spirit presently vanished away: and Brutus called his men unto him, who told him that they heard no noise, nor saw anything at all. Thereupon Brutus returned again to think on his matters as he did before: and when the day broke, he went unto Cassius, to tell him what vision had appeared unto him in the night. Cassius being in opinion an Epicurean, and reasoning thereon with Brutus, spoke to him touching the vision thus. "In our sect, Brutus, we have an opinion, that we do not always feel or see that which we suppose we do both see and feel, but that our senses being credulous and therefore easily abused (when they are idle and unoccupied in their own objects) are induced to imagine they see and conjecture that which in truth they do not. . . ." With these words Cassius did somewhat comfort and quiet Brutus. When they raised their camp, there came two eagles that, flying with a marvelous force, lighted upon two of the foremost ensigns, and always followed the soldiers, which gave them meat and fed them, until they came near to the city of Philippi: and there, one day only before the battle, they both flew away. . . . The Romans called the valley between both camps, the Philippian fields: and there were never seen two so great armies of the Romans, one before the other, ready to fight. In truth, Brutus' army was inferior to Octavius Caesar's in number of men; but for bravery and rich furniture, Brutus' army far excelled Caesar's. For the most part of their armors were silver and gilt, which Brutus had bountifully given them: although, in all other things, he taught his captains to live in order without excess. . . . [*The Life of Marcus Brutus*, pp. 135–37.]

Brutus . . . mustered his army, and did purify it in the

fields, according to the manner of the Romans. . . . Notwithstanding, being busily occupied about the ceremonies of this
purification, it is reported that there chanced certain unlucky
signs unto Cassius. For one of his sergeants that carried the
rods before him, brought him the garland of flowers turned
backward, the which he should have worn on his head in the
time of sacrificing. Moreover it is reported also, that another
time before, in certain sports and triumph where they carried
an image of Cassius' victory, of clean gold, it fell by chance,
the man stumbling that carried it. And yet further, there was
seen a marvelous number of fowls of prey, that feed upon
dead carcasses: and beehives also were found, where bees
were gathered together in a certain place within the trenches
of the camp: the which place the soothsayers thought good to
shut out of the precinct of the camp, for to take away the superstitious fear and mistrust men would have of it. The
which began somewhat to alter Cassius' mind from Epicurus' opinions, and had put the soldiers also in a marvelous
fear. Thereupon Cassius was of opinion not to try this war at
one battle, but rather to delay time, and to draw it out in
length, considering that they were the stronger in money, and
the weaker in men and armor. But Brutus, in contrary manner, did alway before, and at that time also, desire nothing
more than to put all to the hazard of battle, as soon as might
be possible: to the end he might either quickly restore his
country to her former liberty, or rid him forthwith of this
miserable world, being still troubled in following and maintaining of such great armies together. But perceiving that, in
the daily skirmishes and bickerings they made, his men were
always the stronger and ever had the better, that yet quick-
ened his spirits again, and did put him in better heart. And
furthermore, because that some of their own men had already
yielded themselves to their enemies, and that it was suspected moreover divers others would do the like, that made
many of Cassius' friends which were of his mind before
(when it came to be debated in council, whether the battle
should be fought or not) that they were then of Brutus'
mind. . . . Thereupon it was presently determined they should
fight battle the next day. So Brutus, all supper time, looked
with a cheerful countenance, like a man that had good hope,

and talked very wisely of philosophy, and after supper went to bed. But touching Cassius, Messala reporteth that he supped by himself in his tent with a few of his friends, and that all supper time he looked very sadly, and was full of thoughts, although it was against his nature: and that after supper he took him by the hand, and holding him fast (in token of kindness, as his manner was) told him in Greek: "Messala, I protest unto thee, and make thee my witness, that I am compelled against my mind and will (as Pompey the Great was) to jeopard the liberty of our country to the hazard of a battle. And yet we must be lively, and of good courage, considering our good fortune, whom we should wrong too much to mistrust her, although we follow evil counsel." Messala writeth, that Cassius having spoken these last words unto him, he bade him farewell, and willed him to come to supper to him the next night following, because it was his birthday. The next morning, by break of day, the signal of battle was set out in Brutus' and Cassius' camp, which was an arming scarlet coat: and both the chieftains spoke together in the midst of their armies. There Cassius began to speak first, and said: "The gods grant us, O Brutus, that this day we may win the field, and ever after to live all the rest of our life quietly one with another. But sith the gods have so ordained it, that the greatest and chiefest things amongst men are most uncertain, and that if the battle fall out otherwise today than we wish or look for, we shall hardly meet again, what art thou then determined to do, to fly or die?" Brutus answered him, being yet but a young man and not over greatly experienced in the world: "I trust (I know not how) a certain rule of philosophy, by the which I did greatly blame and reprove Cato for killing himself, as being no lawful nor godly act, touching the gods: nor concerning men, valiant; not to give place and yield to divine providence, and not constantly and patiently to take whatsoever it pleaseth him to send us, but to draw back and fly: but being now in the midst of the danger, I am of a contrary mind. For if it be not the will of God that this battle fall out fortunate for us, I will look no more for hope, neither seek to make any new supply for war again, but will rid me of this miserable world, and content me with my fortune. For I gave up my life for

my country in the Ides of March, for the which I shall live
in another more glorious world." Cassius fell a-laughing to
hear what he said, and embracing him, "Come on then," said
he, "let us go and charge our enemies with this mind. For either we shall conquer, or we shall not need to fear the conquerors." After this talk, they fell to consultation among their
friends for the ordering of the battle. Then Brutus prayed
Cassius he might have the leading of the right wing, the
which men thought was far meeter for Cassius, both because
he was the elder man, and also for that he had the better experience. But yet Cassius gave it him, and willed that
Messala (who had charge of one of the warlikest legions they
had) should be also in that wing with Brutus. So Brutus presently sent out his horsemen, who were excellently well appointed, and his footmen also were as willing and ready to
give charge. [*The Life of Marcus Brutus*, pp. 138–40.]

The Battle

In the meantime Brutus, that led the right wing, sent little
bills to the colonels and captains of private bands, in the
which he wrote the word of the battle; and he himself, riding
a-horseback by all the troops, did speak to them, and encouraged them to stick to it like men. So by this means very few
of them understood what was the word of the battle, and besides, the most part of them never tarried to have it told
them, but ran with great fury to assail the enemies; whereby,
through this disorder, the legions were marvelously scattered
and dispersed one from the other. For first of all Messala's
legion, and then the next unto them, went beyond the left
wing of the enemies and did nothing, but glancing by them
overthrew some as they went; and so going on further, fell
right upon Caesar's camp, out of the which (as himself
writeth in his commentaries) he had been conveyed away a
little before, through the counsel and advice of one of his
friends called Marcus Artorius: who, dreaming in the night,
had a vision appeared unto him, that commanded Octavius
Caesar should be carried out of his camp. Insomuch as it was
thought he was slain, because his litter (which had nothing in

it) was thrust through and through with pikes and darts. There was great slaughter in this camp. For amongst others, there were slain 2,000 Lacedaemonians, who were arrived but even a little before, coming to aid Caesar. The other also that had not glanced by, but had given a charge full upon Caesar's battle, they easily made them fly, because they were greatly troubled for the loss of their camp; and of them there were slain by hand three legions. Then, being very earnest to follow the chase of them that fled, they ran in amongst them hand over head into their camp, and Brutus among them. But that which the conquerors thought not of, occasion showed it unto them that were overcome; and that was, the left wing of their enemies left naked and unguarded of them of the right wing, who were strayed too far off, in following of them that were overthrown. So they gave a hot charge upon them. But, notwithstanding all the force they made, they could not break into the midst of their battle, where they found them that received them and valiantly made head against them. Howbeit they broke and overthrew the left wing where Cassius was, by reason of the great disorder among them, and also because they had no intelligence how the right wing had sped. So they chased them, beating them into their camp, the which they spoiled, none of both the chieftains being present there. For Antonius, as it is reported, to fly the fury of the first charge, was gotten into the next marsh: and no man could tell what became of Octavius Caesar after he was carried out of his camp. Insomuch that there were certain soldiers that showed their swords bloodied, and said that they had slain him, and did describe his face, and showed what age he was of. Furthermore, the voward and the midst of Brutus' battle had already put all their enemies to flight that withstood them, with great slaughter: so that Brutus had conquered all on his side and Cassius had lost all on the other side. For nothing undid them but that Brutus went not to help Cassius, thinking he had overcome them as himself had done; and Cassius on the other side tarried not for Brutus, thinking he had been overthrown as himself was. And to prove that the victory fell on Brutus' side, Messala confirmeth that they won three eagles and divers other ensigns of the enemies, and their enemies won never a one of theirs.

Now Brutus returning from the chase, after he had slain and sacked Caesar's men, he wondered much that he could not see Cassius' tent standing up high as it was wont, neither the other tents of his camp standing as they were before, because all the whole camp had been spoiled, and the tents thrown down, at the first coming of their enemies. But they that were about Brutus, whose sight served them better, told him that they saw a great glistering of harness, and a number of silvered targets that went and came into Cassius' camp, and were not (as they took it) the armors nor the number of men that they had left there to guard the camp; and yet that they saw not such a number of dead bodies and great overthrow as there should have been, if so many legions had been slain. This made Brutus at the first mistrust that which had happened. So he appointed a number of men to keep the camp of his enemy which he had taken, and caused his men to be sent for that yet followed the chase, and gathered them together, thinking to lead them to aid Cassius, who was in this state as you shall hear. [*The Life of Marcus Brutus*, pp. 140–42.]

The Death of Cassius

First of all, he was marvelous angry to see how Brutus' men ran to give charge upon their enemies, and tarried not for the word of the battle, nor commandment to give charge: and it grieved him beside that after he had overcome them, his men fell straight to spoil and were not careful to compass in the rest of the enemies behind: but with tarrying too long also, more than through the valiantness or foresight of the captains his enemies, Cassius found himself compassed in with the right wing of his enemies' army. Whereupon his horsemen broke immediately, and fled for life towards the sea. Furthermore perceiving his footmen to give ground, he did what he could to keep them from flying, and took an ensign from one of the ensign-bearers that fled, and stuck it fast at his feet: although with much ado he could scant keep his own guard together.

So Cassius himself was at length compelled to fly, with a

few about him, unto a little hill, from whence they might easily see what was done in all the plain: howbeit Cassius himself saw nothing, for his sight was very bad, saving that he saw (and yet with much ado) how the enemies spoiled his camp before his eyes. He saw also a great troop of horsemen, whom Brutus sent to aid him, and thought that they were his enemies that followed him: but yet he sent Titinius, one of them that was with him, to go and know what they were. Brutus' horsemen saw him coming afar off, whom when they knew that he was one of Cassius' chiefest friends, they shouted out for joy; and they that were familiarly acquainted with him lighted from their horses, and went and embraced him. The rest compassed him in round about on horseback, with songs of victory and great rushing of their harness, so that they made all the field ring again for joy. But this marred all. For Cassius, thinking indeed that Titinius was taken of the enemies, he then spoke these words: "Desiring too much to live, I have lived to see one of my best friends taken, for my sake, before my face." After that, he got into a tent where nobody was, and took Pindarus with him, one of his bondsmen whom he reserved ever for such a pinch, since the cursed battle of the Parthians, where Crassus was slain, though he notwithstanding scaped from that over-throw: but then, casting his cloak over his head, and holding out his bare neck unto Pindarus, he gave him his head to be stricken off. So the head was found severed from the body: but after that time Pindarus was never seen more. Where-upon some took occasion to say that he had slain his master without his commandment. By and by they knew the horse-men that came towards them, and might see Titinius crowned with a garland of triumph, who came before with great speed unto Cassius. But when he perceived, by the cries and tears of his friends which tormented themselves, the misfortune that had chanced to his captain Cassius by mistaking, he drew out his sword, cursing himself a thousand times that he had tarried so long, and so slew himself presently in the field. Brutus in the meantime came forward still, and under-stood also that Cassius had been overthrown: but he knew nothing of his death till he came very near to his camp. So when he was come thither, after he had lamented the death of Cassius, calling him the last of all the Romans, being impossible that Rome should ever breed again so noble and valiant a man as he, he caused his body to be buried, and sent it to the city of Thasos, fearing lest his funerals within his camp should cause great disorder. [*The Life of Marcus Brutus*, pp. 142–44.]

The Exploits of Young Cato and Lucilius

There was the son of Marcus Cato slain, valiantly fighting among the lusty youths. For notwithstanding that he was very weary and overharried, yet would he not therefore fly; but manfully fighting and laying about him, telling aloud his name and also his father's name, at length he was beaten down amongst many other dead bodies of his enemies, which he had slain round about him. So there were slain in the field all the chiefest gentlemen and nobility that were in his army, who valiantly ran into any danger to save Brutus' life: amongst whom there was one of Brutus' friends called Lucilius, who seeing a troop of barbarous men making no reckoning of all men else they met in their way, but going all together right against Brutus, he determined to stay them with the hazard of his life; and being left behind, told them that he was Brutus: and because they should believe him, he prayed them to bring him to Antonius, for he said he was afraid of Caesar, and that he did trust Antonius better. These barbarous men, being very glad of this good hap, and thinking themselves happy men, they carried him in the night, and sent some before unto Antonius, to tell him of their coming. He was marvelous glad of it, and went out to meet them that brought him. Others also understanding of it that they had brought Brutus prisoner, they came out of all parts of the camp to see him, some pitying his hard fortune and others saying that it was not done like himself, so cowardly to be taken alive of the barbarous people for fear of death. When they came near together, Antonius stayed a while bethinking himself how he should use Brutus. In the meantime Lucilius was brought to him, who stoutly with a bold countenance said: "Antonius, I dare assure thee, that no enemy hath taken nor shall take Marcus Brutus alive, and I beseech God keep him from that fortune: for wheresoever he be found, alive or dead, he will be found like himself. And now for myself, I am come unto thee, having deceived these men of arms here, bearing them down that I was Brutus, and do not refuse to suffer any torment thou wilt put me to." Lucilius' words made them all amazed that heard him. Antonius on the other side, looking upon all them that had brought him, said unto them: "My companions, I think ye are sorry you have failed of your purpose, and that you think this man hath done you great wrong: but I assure you, you have taken a better booty than that you followed. For instead of an enemy you have brought me a friend: and for my part, if you had brought me Brutus alive, truly I cannot tell what I should have done to him. For I had rather have such men my friends, as this man here, than mine enemies." Then he embraced Lucilius, and at that time delivered him to one of his friends in custody; and Lucilius ever after served him faithfully, even to his death. [*The Life of Marcus Brutus*, pp. 148–49.]

The Death of Brutus

Now Brutus having passed a little river, walled in on every side with high rocks and shadowed with great trees, being then dark night, he went no further, but stayed at the foot of a rock with certain of his captains and friends that followed him: and looking up to the firmament that was full of stars, sighing, he rehearsed two verses, of the which Volumnius wrote the one, to this effect:

Let not the wight from whom this mischief went,
O Jove, escape without due punishment:

and saith that he had forgotten the other. Within a little while after, naming his friends that he had seen slain in battle before his eyes, he fetched a greater sigh than before, specially when he came to name Labeo and Flavius, of whom the one was his lieutenant, and the other captain of the pioneers of his camp. In the meantime one of the company being athirst, and seeing Brutus athirst also, he ran to the river for water and brought it in his sallet. At the same time they heard a noise on the other side of the river: whereupon Volumnius took Dardanus, Brutus' servant, with him, to see what it was: and returning straight again, asked if there were any water left. Brutus smiling, gently told him, "All is drunk, but they shall bring you some more." Thereupon he sent him again that went for water before, who was in great danger of being taken by the enemies, and hardly escaped, being sore hurt.

Furthermore, Brutus thought that there was no great number of men slain in battle: and to know the truth of it, there was one called Statilius that promised to go through his enemies, for otherwise it was impossible to go see their camp: and from thence, if all were well, that he would lift up a torchlight in the air and then return again with speed to him. The torchlight was lift up as he had promised, for Statilius went thither. Now Brutus seeing Statilius tarry long after that, and that he came not again, he said: "If Statilius be alive, he will come again." But his evil fortune was such that, as he came back, he lighted in his enemies' hands and was slain. Now the night being far spent, Brutus, as he sat, bowed towards Clitus, one of his men, and told him somewhat in his ear: the other answered him not, but fell a-weeping. Thereupon he proved Dardanus, and said somewhat also to him: at length he came to Volumnius himself, and speaking to him in Greek, prayed him for the studies' sake which brought them acquainted together that he would help him to put his hand to his sword, to thrust it in him to kill him. Volumnius denied his request, and so did many others: and amongst the rest, one of them said, there was no tarrying for them there, but that they must needs fly. Then Brutus, rising up, "We must fly indeed," said he, "but it must be with our hands, not with our feet." Then taking every man by the hand, he said these words unto them with a cheerful countenance: "It rejoiceth my heart, that not one of my friends hath failed me at my need, and I do not complain of my fortune, but only for my country's sake: for as for me, I think myself happier than they that have overcome, considering that I leave a perpetual fame of virtue and honesty, the which our enemies the conquerors shall never attain unto by force or money; neither can let their posterity to say that they, being naughty and unjust men, have slain good men, to usurp tyrannical power not pertaining to them." Having so said, he prayed every man to shift for himself, and then he went a little aside with two or three only, among the which Strato was one, with whom he came first acquainted by the study of rhetoric. He came as near to him as he could, and taking his sword by the hilt with both his hands, and falling down upon the point of it, ran himself through. Others say that not he, but Strato (at his request) held the sword in his hand, and turned his head aside, and that Brutus fell down upon it, and so ran himself through, and died presently. Messala, that had been Brutus' great friend, became afterwards Octavius Caesar's friend: so, shortly after, Caesar being at good leisure, he brought Strato, Brutus' friend, unto him, and weeping said: "Caesar, behold, here is he that did the last service to my Brutus." Caesar welcomed him at that time, and afterwards he did him as faithful service in all his affairs as any Grecian else he had about him, until the battle of Actium. It is reported also that this Messala himself answered Caesar one day, when he gave him great praise before his face, that he had fought valiantly and with great affection for him at the battle of Actium (notwithstanding that he had been his cruel enemy before, at the battle of Philippi, for Brutus' sake): "I ever loved," said he, "to take the best and justest part." [*The Life of Marcus Brutus*, pp. 149–51.]

Antonius having found Brutus' body after this battle, blaming him much for the murder of his brother Caius, whom he had put to death in Macedon for revenge of Cicero's cruel death, and yet laying the fault more in Hortensius than in him, he made Hortensius to be slain on his brother's tomb. Furthermore he cast his coat-armor (which was wonderful rich and sumptuous) upon Brutus' body, and gave commandment to one of his slaves enfranchised, to defray the charge of his burial. But afterwards Antonius hearing that his enfranchised bondman had not burnt his coat-armor with his body, because it was very rich and worth a great sum of money, and that he had also kept back much of the ready money appointed for his funeral and tomb, he also put him to death. [*The Life of Marcus Antonius*, p. 171.]

The Death of Porcia

And for Porcia, Brutus' wife, Nicolaus the Philosopher and Valerius Maximus do write that she, determining to kill herself (her parents and friends carefully looking to her to keep her from it), took hot burning coals and cast them into her mouth, and kept her mouth so close that she choked herself. There was a letter of Brutus found written to his friends, complaining of their negligence, that his wife being sick, they would not help her, but suffered her to kill herself; choosing to die, rather than to languish in pain. Thus it appeareth that Nicolaus knew not well that time, sith the letter (at the least if it were Brutus' letter) doth plainly declare the disease and love of this lady, and also the manner of her death. [*The Life of Marcus Brutus*, pp. 151–52.]

The Character of Caesar

Furthermore, they did not wonder so much at his valiantness in putting himself at every instant in such manifest danger, and in taking so extreme pains as he did, knowing that it was his greedy desire of honor that set him on fire, and pricked him forward to do it: but that he always continued all labor and hardness, more than his body could bear, that filled them all with admiration. For, concerning the constitution of his body, he was lean, white, and soft-skinned, and often subject to headache, and otherwhile to the falling sickness (the which took him the first time, as it is reported, in Corduba, a city of Spain) but yet therefore yielded not to the disease of his body, to make it a cloak to cherish him withal, but contrarily, took the pains of war as a medicine to cure his sick body, fighting always with his disease, traveling continually, living soberly, and commonly lying abroad in the field. [*The Life of Julius Caesar*, p. 57.]

* * *

Furthermore, Caesar being born to attempt all great enterprises, and having an ambitious desire besides to covet great honors, the prosperous good success he had of his former conquests bred no desire in him quietly to enjoy the fruits of his labors; but rather gave him the hope of things to come, still kindling more and more in him thoughts of greater enterprises and desire of new glory, as if that which he had present were stale and nothing worth. This humor of his was no other but an emulation with himself as with another man, and a certain contention to overcome the things he prepared to attempt. [*The Life of Julius Caesar*, p. 93.]

In this journey it is reported, that passing over the mountains of the Alps, they came through a little poor village that had not many households, and yet poor cottages. There his friends that did accompany him asked him merrily, if there were any contending for offices in that town, and whether there were any strife there amongst the noblemen for honor. Caesar, speaking in good earnest, answered: "I cannot tell that," said he, "but for my part I had rather be the chiefest man here than the second person in Rome." Another time also when he was in Spain, reading the history of Alexander's acts, when he had read it, he was sorrowful a good while after, and then burst out in weeping. His friends seeing that, marveled what should be the cause of his sorrow. He answered them, "Do ye not think," said he, "that I have good cause to be heavy, when King Alexander, being no elder than myself is now, had in old time won so many nations and countries: and that I hitherunto have done nothing worthy of myself?" [*The Life of Julius Caesar*, p. 52.]

But the time of the great armies and conquests he made afterwards, and of the war in which he subdued all the Gauls (entering into another course of life far contrary unto the first) made him to be known for as valiant a soldier and as excellent a captain to lead men, as those that afore him had been counted the wisest and most valiant generals that ever were, and that by their valiant deeds had achieved great honor. [*The Life of Julius Caesar*, p. 55.]

* * *

Now Caesar immediately won many men's good wills at Rome, through his eloquence in pleading of their causes, and the people loved him marvelously also, because of the courteous manner he had to speak to every man, and to use them gently, being more ceremonious therein than was looked for in one of his years. Furthermore, he ever kept a good board, and fared well at his table, and was very liberal besides: the which indeed did advance him forward, and brought him in estimation with the people. . . . Thereupon Cicero, like a wise shipmaster that feareth the calmness of the sea, was the first man that, mistrusting his manner of dealing in the commonwealth, found out his craft and malice, which he cunningly cloaked under the habit of outward courtesy and familiarity. "And yet," said he, "when I consider how finely he combeth his fair bush of hair, and how smooth it lieth, and that I see him scratch his head with one finger only, my mind gives me then, that such a kind of man should not have so wicked a thought in his head, as to overthrow the state of the commonwealth." But this was long time after that. [*The Life of Julius Caesar*, p. 45.]

The Characters of Brutus and Cassius

Marcus Brutus came of that Junius Brutus, for whom the ancient Romans made his statue of brass to be set up in the Capitol, with the images of the kings, holding a naked sword in his hand: because he had valiantly put down the Tarquins from the kingdom of Rome. But that Junius Brutus, being of a sour, stern nature not softened by reason, being like unto sword blades of too hard a temper, was so subject to his choler and malice he bore unto the tyrants, that for their sakes he caused his own sons to be executed. But this Marcus Brutus in contrary manner, whose life we presently write, having framed his manners of life by the rules of virtue and study of philosophy, and having employed his wit, which was gentle and constant, in attempting of great things, methinks he was rightly made and framed unto virtue. So that his very enemies which wish him most hurt, because of his conspiracy against Julius Caesar, if there were any noble attempt done in all this conspiracy, they refer it wholly unto Brutus; and all the cruel and violent acts unto Cassius, who was Brutus' familiar friend, but not so well given and conditioned as he. [*The Life of Marcus Brutus*, pp. 105–06.]

He was properly learned in the Latin tongue, and was able to make long discourse in it: beside that he could also plead very well in Latin. But for the Greek tongue, they do note in some of his Epistles that he counterfeited that brief compendious manner of speech of the Lacedaemonians. As, when the war was begun, he wrote unto the Pergamenians in this sort: "I understand you have given Dolabella money: if you have done it willingly, you confess you have offended me; if against your wills, show it then by giving me willingly." Another time again unto the Samians: "Your councils be long, your doings be slow, consider the end." And in another Epistle he wrote unto the Patareians: "The Xanthians, despising my good will, have made their country a grave of despair and the Patareians, that put themselves into my protection have lost no jot of their liberty: and therefore, whilst you have liberty, either choose the judgment of the Patareians, or the fortune of the Xanthians." These were Brutus' manner of letters, which were honored for their briefness. [*The Life of Marcus Brutus*, p. 107.]

They say also that Caesar said, when he heard Brutus plead: "I know not," he said, "what this young man would but what he would, he willeth it vehemently." For as Brutus' gravity and constant mind would not grant all men their requests that sued unto him, but, being moved with reason and discretion, did always incline to that which was good and honest: even so, when it was moved to follow any matter, he used a kind of forcible and vehement persuasion, that calmed not till he had obtained his desire. For by flattering of him man could never obtain anything at his hands, nor make him to do that which was unjust. Further, he thought it not meet for a man of calling and estimation, to yield unto the requests and entreaties of a shameless and importunate suitor requesting things unmeet: the which notwithstanding some men do for shame, because they dare deny nothing: and therefore he was wont to say, "that he thought them ev-

brought up in their youth, that could deny nothing." [*The Life of Marcus Brutus*, pp. 109–10.]

And surely (in my opinion), I am persuaded that Brutus might indeed have come to have been the chiefest man of Rome, if he could have contented himself for a time to have been next unto Caesar, and to have suffered his glory and authority, which he had gotten by great victories, to consume with time. But Cassius, being a choleric man, and hating Caesar privately more than he did the tyranny openly, he incensed Brutus against him. It is also reported, that Brutus could evil away with the tyranny, and that Cassius hated the tyrant: making many complaints for the injuries he had done him; and amongst others, for that he had taken away his lions from him. Cassius had provided them for his sports when he should be aedilis; and they were found in the city of Megara, when it was won by Calenus: and Caesar kept them. The rumor went, that these lions did marvelous great hurt to the Megarians: for when the city was taken, they broke their cages where they were tied up and turned them loose, thinking they would have done great mischief to the enemies, and have kept them from setting upon them: but the lions (contrary to expectation) turned upon themselves that fled unarmed, and did so cruelly tear some in pieces, that it pitied their enemies to see them. And this was the cause (as some do report) that made Cassius conspire against Caesar. But this holdeth no water: for Cassius, even from his cradle, could not abide any manner of tyrants; as it appeared when he was but a boy, and went unto the same school that Faustus, the son of Sulla, did. And Faustus, bragging among other boys, highly boasted of his father's kingdom: Cassius rose up on his feet, and gave him two good wirts on the ear. Faustus' governors would have put this matter in suit against Cassius: but Pompey would not suffer them, but caused the two boys to be brought before him and asked them how the matter came to pass. Then Cassius (as it is written of him) said unto the other: "Go to, Faustus, speak again, and thou darest, before this nobleman here, the same words that made me angry with thee, that my fists may walk once again about thine

ears." Such was Cassius' hot stirring nature. [*The Life o*
Marcus Brutus, pp. 111–12.]

Now Cassius would have done Brutus much honor, a:
Brutus did unto him, but Brutus most commonly prevented
him and went first unto him, both because he was the elde:
man as also for that he was sickly of body. And men repute(
him commonly to be very skillful in wars, but otherwis(
marvelous choleric and cruel, who sought to rule men by fea:
rather than with lenity: and on the other side, he was too fa
miliar with his friends, and would jest too broadly with them
But Brutus, in contrary manner, for his virtue and valiant
ness, was well beloved of the people and his own, esteeme(
of noblemen, and hated of no man, not so much as of his en
emies; because he was a marvelous lowly and gentle person
noble-minded, and would never be in any rage, nor carrie(
away with pleasure and covetousness, but had ever an up
right mind with him and would never yield to any wrong c
injustice; the which was the chiefest cause of his fame, of hi
rising, and of the good will that every man bore him: fc
they were all persuaded that his intent was good. For the
did not certainly believe that, if Pompey himself had ove:
come Caesar, he would have resigned his authority to th
law, but rather they were of opinion that he would still kee
the sovereignty and absolute government in his hands, takin
only, to please the people, the title of Consul, or Dictator, c
of some other more civil office. And as for Cassius, a ho:
choleric, and cruel man, that would oftentimes be carrie(
away from justice for gain, it was certainly thought that h
made war and put himself into sundry dangers, more to hav
absolute power and authority than to defend the liberty of hi
country. For they that will also consider others that were e:
der men than they, as Cinna, Marinus, and Carbo, it is out c
doubt that the end and hope of their victory was to be th
lords of their country, and in manner they did all confess th
they fought for the tyranny and to be lords of the Empire (
Rome. And in contrary manner, his enemies themselves di(
never reprove Brutus for any such change or desire. For
was said that Antonius spoke it openly divers times, that h
thought, that of all them that had slain Caesar, there wa

none but Brutus only that was moved to do it, as thinking the act commendable of itself: but that all the other conspirators did conspire his death for some private malice or envy that they otherwise did bear unto him. [*The Life of Marcus Brutus*, pp. 129–30.]

The Character of Antony

Now Antonius being a fair young man, and in the prime of his youth, he fell acquainted with Curio, whose friendship and acquaintance (as it is reported) was a plague unto him. For he was a dissolute man, given over to all lust and insolency, who, to have Antonius the better at his commandment, trained him on into great follies and vain expenses upon women, in rioting and banqueting: so that in short time he brought Antonius into a marvelous great debt, and too great for one of his years, to wit, of two hundred and fifty talents, for all which sum Curio was his surety. His father, hearing of it, did put his son from him and forbade him his house. Then he fell in with Clodius, one of the desperatest and most wicked tribunes at that time in Rome. Him he followed for a time in his desperate attempts, who bred great stir and mischief in Rome: but at length he forsook him, being weary of his rashness and folly, or else for that he was afraid of them that were bent against Clodius.

Thereupon he left Italy, and went into Greece, and there bestowed the most part of his time, sometime in wars, and otherwhile in the study of eloquence. He used a manner of phrase in his speech called "Asiatic," which carried the best grace and estimation at that time and was much like to his manners and life: for it was full of ostentation, foolish bravery, and vain ambition. [*The Life of Marcus Antonius*, pp. 154–55.]

So was his great courtesy also much commended of all, he which he showed unto Archelaus: for having been his very friend, he made war with him against his will while he lived; but after his death he fought for his body, and gave it honorable burial. For these respects he won himself great fame of them of Alexandria, and he was also thought a worthy man of all the soldiers in the Romans' camp. But besides all this, he had a noble presence, and showed a countenance of one of a noble house: he had a goodly thick beard, a broad forehead, crooked-nosed, and there appeared such a manly look in his countenance, as is commonly seen in Hercules' pictures, stamped or graven in metal. Now it had been a speech of old time, that the family of the Antonii were descended from one Anton, the son of Hercules, whereof the family took name. This opinion did Antonius seek to confirm in all his doings: not only resembling him in the likeness of his body, as we have said before, but also in the wearing of his garments. For when he would openly show himself abroad before many people, he would always wear his cassock girt down low upon his hips, with a great sword hanging by his side and upon that some ill-favored cloak. Furthermore, things that seem intolerable in other men, as to boast commonly, to jest with one or other, to drink like a good fellow with everybody, to sit with the soldiers when they dine, and to eat and drink with them soldierlike, it is incredible what wonderful love it won him amongst them. And furthermore, being given to love, that made him the more desired, and by that means he brought many to love him. For he would further every man's love, and also would not be angry that men should merrily tell him of those he loved. But besides all this, that which most procured his rising and advancement was his liberality, who gave all to the soldiers and kept nothing for himself: and when he was grown to great credit, then was his authority and power also very great the which notwithstanding himself did overthrow by a thousand other faults he had. [*The Life of Marcus Antonius* pp. 156–57.]

But then in contrary manner, he purchased divers other men's evil will, because that through negligence he would not do them justice that were injured, and dealt very churlishly with them that had any suit unto him: and besides all this, he had an ill name to entice men's wives. [*The Life of Marcus Antonius*, p. 159.]

Now after that Caesar had gotten Rome at his commandment, and had driven Pompey out of Italy, he purposed first to go into Spain against the legions Pompey had there, and in the meantime to make provision for ships and marine preparation, to follow Pompey. In his absence, he left Lepidus, that was praetor, governor of Rome; and Antonius, that was tribune, he gave him charge of all the soldiers and of Italy.... To conclude, Caesar's friends, that governed under him, were cause why they hated Caesar's government (which indeed in respect of himself was no less than tyranny) by reason of the great insolencies and outrageous parts that were committed: amongst whom Antonius, that was of greatest power, and that also committed greatest faults, deserved most blame. But Caesar, notwithstanding, when he returned from the wars of Spain, made no reckoning of the complaints that were put up against him: but contrarily, because he found him a hardy man, and a valiant captain, he employed him in his chiefest affairs, and was no whit deceived in his opinion of him. [*The Life of Marcus Antonius*, pp. 158–59.]

Commentaries

MAYNARD MACK

The Modernity of
Julius Caesar

I

In a tribute composed to introduce the collection of plays
that we now call the *First Folio*, Shakespeare's fellow playwright Ben Jonson spoke of his colleague's works as not of
an age but for all time. Though the compliment was something of a commonplace in Renaissance funerary rhetoric, it
has proved to be remarkably clairvoyant, at least up to the
present hour. And of no play, perhaps, has the continuing relevance been more striking than that of *Julius Caesar*, which
again and again twentieth-century directors and producers
have successfully presented as a parable for our days.

Among the many aspects of the play that contribute to its
modernity, one in particular, to my mind, stands out, and it
is to this exclusively, leaving out much, that I want to call attention here. The place to begin is the second scene.

We have just learned from scene 1 of Caesar's return in

From *Everybody's Shakespeare: Reflections Chiefly on the Tragedies* by
Maynard Mack (Lincoln & London: University of Nebraska Press, 1993), pp.
91–106. Used by permission of the author.

triumph from warring on Pompey's sons. We have seen the warm though fickle adulation of the crowd and the apprehension of the tribunes. Now we are to see the great man himself. The procession enters to triumphal music; with hubbub of a great press of people; with young men stripped for the ceremonial races, among them Antony; with statesmen in their togas: Decius, Cicero, Brutus, Cassius, Casca; with the two wives Calphurnia and Portia; and, in the lead, for not even Calphurnia is permitted at his side, the great man. As he starts to speak, an expectant hush settles over the gathering. What does the great man have on his mind?

Caesar. Calphurnia.
Casca.   Peace, ho! Caesar speaks.
Caesar.   Calphurnia!
Calphurnia. Here, my lord.
Caesar. Stand you directly in Antonius' way
When he doth run his course. Antonius!
Antony. Caesar, my lord?
Caesar. Forget not in your speed, Antonius,
To touch Calphurnia; for our elders say,
The barren, touched in this holy chase,
Shake off their sterile curse.
Antony.   I shall remember.
When Caesar says, "Do this," it is performed.   (1.2.1–10)

What the great man had on his mind, it appears, was to remind his wife, in this public place, that she is sterile; that there is an old tradition about how sterility can be removed; and that while of course he is much too sophisticated to accept such a superstition himself—it is "our elders" who say it—still, Calphurnia had jolly well better get out there and get tagged!

Then the procession takes up again. The hubbub is resumed, but once more an expectant silence settles as a voice is heard.

Soothsayer. Caesar!
Caesar. Ha! Who calls?
Casca. Bid every noise be still; peace yet again!

Caesar. Who is it in the press that calls on me?
I hear a tongue, shriller than all the music,
Cry "Caesar." Speak; Caesar is turned to hear.
Soothsayer. Beware the ides of March.
Caesar.   What man is that?
Brutus. A soothsayer bids you beware the ides of March.
Caesar. Set him before me; let me see his face.
Cassius. Fellow, come from the throng; look upon Caesar.
Caesar. What say'st thou to me now? Speak once again.
Soothsayer. Beware the ides of March.
Caesar. He is a dreamer, let us leave him. Pass.   (12–24)

It is easy to see from even these small instances, I think,
how a first-rate dramatic imagination works. There is no hint
of any procession in Plutarch, Shakespeare's source. "Caesar," says Plutarch, "*sat* to behold." There is no mention of
Calphurnia in Plutarch's account of the Lupercalian race, and
there is no mention anywhere of her sterility. Shakespeare, in
nine lines, has given us an unforgettable picture of a man
who would like to be emperor, pathetically concerned that he
lacks an heir, and determined, even at the cost of making his
wife a public spectacle, to establish that this is owing to no
lack of virility in him. The first episode thus dramatizes in-
stantaneously what I take to be the oncoming theme of the
play: that a man's will is not enough; that there are other
matters to be reckoned with, like the infertility of one's wife,
or one's own affliction of the falling sickness that spoils
everything one hoped for just at the instant when one had it
almost in one's hand. Brutus will be obliged to learn this lesson too.
In the second episode the theme develops. We see again
the uneasy rationalism that everybody in this play affects;
we hear it reverberate in the faint contempt—almost a
challenge—of Brutus's words as he turns to Caesar: "A
soothsayer bids you beware the ides of March." Yet underneath, in the soothsayer's quiet defiance as he refuses to
quail under Caesar's imperious gaze, and in his soberly reit-
erated warning, Shakespeare allows us to catch a hint of
something else, something far more primitive and mysterious, from which rationalism in this play keeps trying vainly

to cut itself away: "He is a dreamer, let us leave him. Pass." Only we in the audience are in a position to see that the dreamer has foretold the path down which all these reasoners will go to their fatal encounter at the Capitol.

Meantime, in these same two episodes, we have learned something about the character of Caesar. In the first, it was the Caesar of human frailties who spoke to us, the husband with his hopeful superstition. In the second, it was the marble superman of state, impassive, impervious, speaking of himself in the third person: "Speak! Caesar is turned to hear." He even has the soothsayer brought before his face to repeat the message, as if he thought that somehow, in awe of the marble presence, the message would falter and dissolve: how can a superman need to beware the ides of March?

We hardly have time to do more than glimpse here a man of divided selves, then he is gone. But in his absence, the words of Cassius confirm our glimpse. Cassius's description of him exhibits the same duality that we had noticed earlier. On the one hand, an extremely ordinary man whose stamina in the swimming match was soon exhausted; who, when he had a fever once in Spain, shook and groaned like a sick girl; who even now, as we soon learn, is falling down with epilepsy in the marketplace. On the other hand, a being who has somehow become a god, who "bears the palm alone," who "doth bestride the narrow world / Like a Colossus" (1.2.135–36). When the procession returns, no longer festive but angry, tense, there is the same effect once more. Our one Caesar shows a normal man's suspicion of his enemies, voices some shrewd human observations about Cassius, says to Antony, "Come on my right hand, for this ear is deaf" (213). Our other Caesar says, as if he were suddenly reminded of something he had forgotten, "I rather tell thee what is to be feared / Than what I fear, for always I am Caesar" (211–12).

Wherever Caesar appears hereafter, we shall find this distinctive division in him, and nowhere more so than in the scene in which he receives the conspirators at his house. Some aspects of this scene seem calculated for nothing other than to fix upon our minds the superman conception, the Big

Brother of Orwell's *1984*, the great resonant name echoing
down the halls of time. Thus at the beginning of the scene:

> The things that threatened me
> Ne'er looked but on my back; when they shall see
> The face of Caesar, they are vanishèd.   (2.2.10–12)

And again later:

> Danger knows full well
> That Caesar is more dangerous than he.
> We are two lions littered in one day,
> And I the elder and more terrible.   (44–47)

And again still later: "Shall Caesar send a lie?" (65) And
again: "The cause is in my will: I will not come" (71).

Other aspects of this scene, including his concern about
Calphurnia's dream, his vacillation about going to the senate
house, his anxiety about the portents of the night, plainly
mark out his human weaknesses. Finally, as is the habit in
this Rome, he puts the irrational from him that his wife's intuitions and her dream embody; he accepts the rationalization
of the irrational that Decius skillfully manufactures, and, as
earlier at the Lupercalia, hides from himself his own vivid
sense of forces that lie beyond the will's control by attributing it to her:

> How foolish do your fears seem now, Calphurnia!
> I am ashamèd I did yield to them.
> Give me my robe, for I will go.   (105–7)

2

So far we have looked at Caesar, the title personage of the
play and its historical center. It is time now to consider Brutus, the play's tragic center, whom we also find to be a divided man—"poor Brutus," to use his own phrase, "with
himself at war" (1.2.46). That war, we realize as the scene
progresses, is a conflict between a quiet, essentially domestic

and loving nature, and a powerful integrity expressing itself in a sense of honorable duty to the commonweal. This duality is what Cassius probes in his long disquisition about the mirror. The Brutus looking into the glass that Cassius figuratively holds up to him, the Brutus of this moment, now, in Rome, is a grave studious private man, of a wonderfully gentle temper as we shall see again and again later on; very slow to passion, as Cassius's ill-concealed disappointment in having failed to kindle him to an immediate response reveals; a man whose sensitive nature recoils at the hint of violence lurking in some of Cassius's speeches, just as he has already recoiled at going with Caesar to the market place, to witness the mass hysteria of clapping hands, sweaty nightcaps, and stinking breath. This is the present self that looks into Cassius's mirror.

The image that looks back out, that Cassius wants him to see, the potential other Brutus, is the man of public spirit, worried already by his uncertainty about Caesar's intentions, lineal descendant of an earlier Brutus who drove a would-be monarch from the city, a republican whose body is visibly stiffening in our sight at each huzza from the Forum, and whose anxiety, though he makes no reply to Cassius's inflammatory language, keeps bursting to the surface: "What means this shouting? I do fear the people / Choose Caesar for their king" (79). The problem at the tragic center of the play, we begin to sense, is the tug of private versus public, the individual versus a world he never made, any citizen anywhere versus the selective service greetings that history is always mailing out to each of us. And this problem is to be traversed by the other tug this scene presents, between the irrational and the rational, the destiny we imagine we can control and the destiny that sweeps all before it.

Through 1.2, Brutus's patriotic self, the self that responds to these selective service greetings, is no more than a reflection in a mirror, a mere anxiety in his own brain, about which he refuses to confide, even to Cassius. In 2.1, we see the public self making further headway. First, there is Brutus's argument with himself about the threat of Caesar, and in his conclusion that Caesar must be killed we note how far his private self—he is, after all, one of Caesar's closest

friends—has been invaded by the self of public spirit. From
here on, the course of the invasion accelerates. A letter
comes, tossed from the public world into the private world,
into Brutus's garden, addressing, as Cassius had, the patriot image reflected in the mirror: "Brutus, thou sleep'st;
awake, and see thyself!" (46). Then follows the well-known
brief soliloquy (which Shakespeare was to expand into the
whole play of *Macbeth*), showing us that Brutus's mind has
moved on from the phase of decision to the inquietudes that
follow decision:

> Between the acting of a dreadful thing
> And the first motion, all the interim is
> Like a phantasma, or a hideous dream.   (63–65)

Brutus anticipates here the dreamlike mood and motion with
which Macbeth moves to the murder of Duncan. What is important to observe, however, is that these lines again stress
the gulf that separates motive from action, that which is interior in man and controllable by his will from that which,
once acted, becomes independent of him and moves with a
life of its own. This gulf is a no man's land, a phantasma, a
hideous dream.

Finally, there arrives in such a form that no audience can
miss it the actual visible invasion itself, as this peaceful
garden-quiet is intruded on by knocking, like the knocking of
fate in Beethoven's Fifth Symphony, and by men with faces
hidden in their cloaks. Following this, a lovely interlude with
Portia serves to emphasize how much the private self, the
private world, has been shattered. There is something close
to discord here—as much of a discord as these gentle people
are capable of—and though there is a reconciliation at the
end and Brutus's promise to confide in her soon, this division in the family is an omen. So is the knock of the late-
comer, Caius Ligarius, which reminds us once again of the
exactions of the public life. And when Ligarius throws off
his sick man's kerchief on learning that there is an honorable
exploit afoot, we may see in it an epitome of the whole
scene, a graphic visible renunciation, like Brutus's (or like
Prince Hal's at about the same time in Shakespeare's career)

of the private good to the public; and we may see this also in Brutus's own exit a few lines later, not into the inner house where Portia waits for him, but out into the thunder and lightning of the public life of Rome. It is not without significance that at our final glimpse of Portia, two scenes later, she too stands outside the privacy of the house, her mind wholly occupied with thoughts of what is happening at the Capitol, trying to put on a public self for Brutus's sake: "Run, Lucius, and commend me to my lord; / Say I am merry" (2.4.44–45).

3

Meantime, at the Capitol, the tragic center and the historical center meet. The suspense is very great as Caesar, seeing the Soothsayer in the throng, reminds him that the ides of March are come, and receives in answer, "Ay, Caesar, but not gone" (3.1.2). More suspense is generated as Artemidorus presses forward with the paper that we know contains a full discovery of the plot. Decius, apprehensive, steps quickly into the breach with another paper, a petition from Trebonius. More suspense still as Popilius sidles past Cassius with the whisper, "I wish your enterprise today may thrive" (13), and then moves on to Caesar's side, where he engages him in animated talk. But they detect no telltale change in Caesar's countenance; Trebonius steps into his assignment and takes Antony aside; Metellus Cimber throws himself at Caesar's feet; Brutus gives the signal to "Press near and second him" (29), and Caesar's "Are we all ready?" (31) draws every eye to Caesar's chair. One by one they all kneel before this demigod—an effective tableau which gives a coloring of priestlike ritual to what they are about to do. Caesar is to bleed, but, as Brutus has said, they will sublimate the act into a sacrifice:

Let's kill him boldly, but not wrathfully;
Let's carve him as a dish fit for the gods,
Not hew him as a carcass fit for hounds.   (2.1.172–74)

In performance, everything in the scene will reflect this ceremonial attitude to emphasize the almost fatuous cleavage between the spirit of the enterprise and its bloody result.

The Caesar we are permitted to see as all this ceremony
is preparing will be almost entirely the superman, for obvious reasons. To give a color of justice to Brutus's act, even
if we happen to think the assassination a mistake as many
members of an Elizabethan audience emphatically would,
Caesar must be seen in a mood of super-humanity at least as
fatuous as the conspirators' mood of sacrifice. Hence Shakespeare makes him first of all insult Metellus Cimber: "If thou
dost bend and pray and fawn for him, / I spurn these like a
cur" (3.1.45–46), and then comment with intolerable pom-
posity—in fact, blasphemy—on his own iron resolution,
which he alleges to be immovable even by prayer and thus
superior to the very gods. Finally, Shakespeare puts into his
mouth one of those supreme arrogances that can hardly fail
to remind us of the ancient adage "Whom the gods would
destroy they first make mad." "Hence!" Caesar cries, "Wilt
thou lift up Olympus?" (74). It is at just this point, when the
colossus Caesar drunk with self-importance is before us, that
Casca strikes. Then they all strike, with a last blow that
brings out for the final time the other, human side of this
double Caesar: *"Et tu, Brutè?"* (77)

And now this little group of men has altered history. The
representative of the evil direction it was taking toward auto-
cratic power lies dead before them. The direction to which it
must be restored becomes emphatic in Cassius's cry of "Liberty, freedom, and enfranchisement!" (81) Solemnly, and
again like priests who have just sacrificed a victim, they
kneel together and bathe their hands and swords in Caesar's
blood. Brutus exclaims:

> Then walk we forth, even to the market place,
> And waving our red weapons o'er our heads,
> Let's all cry, "Peace, freedom, and liberty!"   (108–10)

If the conjunction of those red hands and weapons with this
slogan is not enough to give an audience a start, the next
passage will; for now the conspirators explicitly invoke the

judgment of history on their deed. On the stages of theaters the world over, so they anticipate, this lofty incident will be re-enacted, and

> So oft as that shall be,
> So often shall the knot of us be called
> The men that gave their country liberty.   (116–18)

We in the audience, recalling what actually did result in Rome—the civil wars, the long line of despotic emperors—cannot miss the irony of their prediction, an irony that insists on our recognizing that this effort to control the consequences of an act is doomed to fail. (It is a theme that Shakespeare will touch again in *Macbeth* and *Lear.*) Why does it fail?

One reason why is shown us in the next few moments. The leader of this assault on history, like many another reformer, is a man of high idealism, who devoutly believes that the rest of the world is like himself. It was just to kill Caesar—so he persuades himself—because he was a threat to freedom. It would not have been just to kill Antony, and he vetoes the idea. Even now, when the consequence of that decision has come back to face him in the shape of Antony's servant kneeling before him, he sees no reason to reconsider it. There are good grounds for what they have done, he says; Antony will hear them, and be satisfied. With Antony, who shortly arrives in person, he takes this line again:

> Our reasons are so full of good regard
> That were you, Antony, the son of Caesar,
> You should be satisfied.   (224–26)

With equal confidence in the reasonableness of human nature, he puts by Cassius's fears of what Antony will do if allowed to address the people: "By your pardon: / I will myself into the pulpit first / And show the reason of our Caesar's death" (235–37). Here is a man so much a friend of Caesar's that he is still speaking of him as "our Caesar," so capable of rising to what he takes to be his duty that he has taken on the leadership of those who killed him, so trusting of common decency that he expects the populace will respond to reason, and Antony to honor the obligation laid on him by their permitting him to speak. At such a man, one hardly knows whether to laugh or cry.

The same mixture of feelings is likely to be stirring in us as Brutus speaks to the people in 3.2. As everybody knows, this is a speech in what used to be called the great liberal tradition, which assumes that men in the mass are reasonable. It has therefore been made a prose oration, spare and terse in diction, tightly patterned in syntax so that it requires close attention, and founded, with respect to its argument, on three elements: the abstract sentiment of duty to the state (because he endangered Rome, Caesar had to be slain); the abstract sentiment of political justice (because he had delusions of grandeur, Caesar deserved his fall); and the moral authority of the man Brutus.

As long as that moral authority is concretely before them in Brutus's presence, the populace is impressed. But since even trained minds do not always respond well to abstractions, they quite misunderstand the content of his argument, as one of them indicates by shouting, "Let him be Caesar!" (52) What moves them is the obvious sincerity and the known integrity of the speaker; and when he finishes, they are ready to carry him off on their shoulders on that account alone, leaving Antony a vacant Forum. The fair-mindedness of Brutus is thrilling but painful to behold as he calms this triumphal surge in his favor, urges them to stay and hear Antony, and then, in a moment very impressive dramatically as well as symbolically, walks off on the stage, alone. We see then, if we have not seen before, a possible first answer to the question why the effort to take control of history failed as it so often does, blinkered by its own idealism.

4

When Antony takes the rostrum, we sense a possible second answer. It has been remarked that in a school for demagogues this speech should be the whole curriculum. Antony himself describes its method when he observes in the preceding scene, apropos of the effect of Caesar's dead body on the messenger from Octavius, "Passion, I see, is catching" (3.1.283). A statement that cannot be made about reason, as many of us learn to our cost.

Antony's speech differs from Brutus's as night from day. Brutus formulates from the outset positive propositions about Caesar and about his own motives on no other authority than his own. Because of his known integrity, Brutus can do this. Antony takes the safer alternative of concealing propositions in questions, by which the audience's mind is then guided to conclusions which seem its own:

He hath brought many captives home to Rome,
Whose ransoms did the general coffers fill;
Did this in Caesar seem ambitious?   (3.2.90–92)

You all did see that on the Lupercal
I thrice presented him a kingly crown,
Which he did thrice refuse. Was this ambition?   (97–99)

How well Shakespeare knew crowds becomes clear in the replies to Antony. Brutus, appealing to reason, is greeted with wild outbursts of emotion: "Let him be Caesar!" Antony appeals only to emotion and pocketbooks, but now they say, "Methinks there is much reason in his sayings," and chew upon it seriously.

With equal skill, Antony stirs up impulses only to thwart them. He appeals to curiosity and greed in the matter of the will, but then withholds it teasingly. In the same manner, he stirs up rage against the conspirators while pretending to dampen it: "I fear I wrong the honorable men / Whose daggers have stabbed Caesar; I do fear it" (153–54). Finally, he rests his case, not, like Brutus, on abstractions centering in the state and political justice, but on emotions centering in the individual listener. The first great crescendo of the speech, which culminates in the passage on Caesar's wounds, appeals first to pity and then to indignation. The second, culminating in the reading of Caesar's will, appeals first to curiosity and greed, then to gratitude.

His management of the will is particularly cunning: it is an item more concrete than words, an actual tantalizing document that can be flashed before the eye, as in many a modern political TV sound byte. He describes it at first vaguely, as being of such a sort that they would honor Caesar for it. Then, closer home, as something which would show "how Caesar loved you" (143). Then, with an undisguised appeal to self-interest, as a testament that will make them his "heirs." The emotions aroused by this news enable him to make a final test of his ironical refrain about "honorable men," and finding the results all that he had hoped, he can come down now among the crowd as one of them, and appeal directly to their feelings by appealing to his own: "If you have tears, prepare to shed them now" (171).

The power of this direct appeal to passion can be seen at its close. Where formerly we had a populace, now we have a mob. As a mob, its mind can be sealed against later recoveries of rationality by the insinuation that all reasoning is simply a surface covering up private grudges, like the "reason" they have heard from Brutus; whereas from Antony himself, the plain, blunt friend of Caesar, they are getting the plain, blunt truth and (a favorite trick) only what they already know.

So they are called back to hear the will. Antony no longer needs this as an incentive to riot; the mingled rage and pity he has aroused will take care of that. But, after the lynching when the hangover comes, and you are remembering how that fellow looked, swaying a little on the rope's end, with his eyes bugging out and the veins knotted at his temples, then it is good to have something really reasonable to cling to, like seventy-five drachmas (or thirty pieces of silver) and some orchards along a river.

By this point, we can fully understand that a further ground for the failure of the effort to control history is what has been left out of account—what all these Romans from the beginning, except Antony, have been trying to leave out of account: the phenomenon of feeling, one of many nonrational factors in the life of men, in the life of the world, in the processes of history itself—of which this blind infuriated mob is one kind of exemplification. Too secure in his own fancied suppression of this influence, Brutus has failed altogether to reckon with its power. Thus he could seriously say to Antony in the passage quoted earlier: Antony, even if you were "the son of Caesar / You should be satisfied," as if the feeling of a son for a murdered father could ever be "satisfied" by reasons. And thus, too, urging the crowd to hear Antony, he could walk off the stage alone, the very figure of embodied "reason," unaware that only the irrational is catching.

Meantime, the scene of the mob tearing Cinna the Poet to pieces simply for having the same name as one of the conspirators (3.3) confirms the victory of unreason and gives us our first taste of the chaos invoked by Antony when he stood alone over Caesar's corpse. Now, reconsidering that prediction and this mob, we recognize a third reason who attempts to direct the course of history have usually failed. We have seen already that history is only minimally responsive to noble motives, only minimally responsive to rationality. Now we see clearly what was hinted in the beginning by those two episodes with Calphurnia and the soothsayer—that it is only minimally responsive to conscious human influence of any sort. With all their reasons, the conspirators and Caesar only carried out what the soothsayer foreknew. There is, in short—at least as this play sees it—a degree of determinism in history, whether we call it cultural, fatal, or providential, which *helps* to shape our ends, "Roughhew them how we will" (*Hamlet,* 5.2.11). One of the alternative names of that factor in this play is Caesarism, cult of the ever regenerating Will to Power. Brutus puts the point, all unconsciously, when the conspirators are gathered at his house:

We all stand up against the spirit of Caesar,
And in the spirit of men there is no blood.
O, that we then could come by Caesar's spirit,
And not dismember Caesar! But, alas,
Caesar must bleed for it.   (2.1.167–71)

Then Caesar does bleed for it; but his spirit, as Brutus's own
remark might have told him, proves invulnerable. It is simply
set free by his assassination, and now, as Antony says, "ranging for revenge, . . . Shall in these confines with a monarch's
voice / Cry 'Havoc,' and let slip the dogs of war" (3.1.270,
272–73).

5

The rest of the play is self-explanatory. It is clear all
through Acts 4 and 5 that Brutus and Cassius are defeated
before they begin to fight. Antony knows it and says so at
5.1. Cassius knows it too. Cassius, an Epicurean in philosophy and therefore one who has never heretofore believed in
omens, now mistrusts his former rationalism: he suspects
there may be something after all in those ravens, crows, and
kites that wheel overhead. Brutus too mistrusts *his* rationalism. As a Stoic, his philosophy requires him to repudiate
suicide, but he admits to Cassius that if the need comes he
will repudiate philosophy instead. This, like Cassius's statement, is an unconscious admission of the force of the nonrational in human affairs, a nonrational influence that makes
its presence felt again and again during the great battle. Cassius, for instance, fails to learn in time that Octavius "Is overthrown by noble Brutus' power" (5.3.52), becomes the victim
of a mistaken report of Titinius's death, runs on his sword
crying, "Caesar, thou art revenged" (45), and is greeted, dead,
by Brutus, in words that make still clearer their defeat by a
power unforeseen: "O Julius Caesar, thou art mighty yet! /
Thy spirit walks abroad, and turns our swords / In our own
proper entrails" (94–96). In the same vein, when it is Brutus's
turn to die, we learn that the ghost of Caesar has reappeared,
and he thrusts the sword home, saying, "Caesar, now be
still" (5.5.50).

Among the many topics on which Shakespeare casts a cold
eye in this short play—among them the nature of heroism,
the toll that public life exacts, the legitimacy of power, the
danger of violent change (this last especially relevant in 1599
because of the growing concern for the succession after the

aging Queen should die)—the aspect that seems to me to account best for its hold on audiences in our totalitarian century of putsches, coups, and assassinations is its stress on the always ambiguous relation between humankind and history. During the first half of the play, what we are chiefly conscious of is the human will as a force in history—men making choices, controlling events. Our typical scenes are 1.2, where a man is trying to make up his mind; or 2.1, where a man first reaches a decision and then, with his fellows, lays plans to implement it; or 2.2, where we have Decius Brutus persuading Caesar to decide to go to the senate house; or 3.1 and 3.2, where up through the assassination, and even up through Antony's speech, men are still, so to speak, impinging on history, molding it to their conscious will.

But then comes a change. Though we still have men in action trying to mold their world (or else we would have no play at all), one senses a real shift in the direction of the impact. We begin to feel the insufficiency of noble aims, for history is also consequences; the insufficiency of reason and rational expectation, for the ultimate consequences of an act in history are unpredictable, and usually, by all human standards, illogical as well; and finally, the insufficiency of the human will itself, for there is always something to be reckoned with that is nonhuman and inscrutable—Nemesis, Moira, Fortuna, the Parcae, Providence, Determinism: men have had many names for it, but it is always there. Accordingly, in the second half of the play, our typical scenes are those like 3.3, where Antony has raised something that is no longer under his control or anyone's. Or like 4.1, where we see men acting as if, under the thumb of expediency or necessity or call it what you will, they no longer had wills of their own but prick down the names of nephews and brothers indiscriminately for slaughter. Or like 4.3 and all the scenes thereafter, where we are constantly made to feel that Cassius and Brutus are in the hands of something bigger than they know.

In this light, we can see readily enough why it is that Shakespeare gives Julius Caesar a double character. The dilemma in all violence is that the human Caesar who has human ailments and is a human friend is the Caesar who can be killed. Whereas the marmoreal Caesar, the everlasting Big

Brother, must repeatedly be killed but never dies because he lurks in each of us and all together. Any political system is a potential Rome, and there is no reason for the citizen of any country, when he reads or watches a production of *Julius Caesar*, to imagine that this is ancient history.

COPPÉLIA KAHN

A Voluntary Wound

Brutus, of course, isn't so firm as he appears to his co-conspirators. And it is precisely his reluctance to murder Caesar that brings out the feminine in the play—that gives rise to the famous scene between Brutus and Portia on the eve of the assassination. Here his image of himself as savior of the republic is splintered by those "passions of some difference" he reluctantly alluded to in his first encounter with Cassius, passions now reflected in Portia's observations of his behavior and anxieties about what it portends.

The scene depends on our prior knowledge that, as Portia suspects, Brutus does have "some sick offence within [his] mind." We realize that her intuitions are well founded, for in two brief soliloquies following the long one in which Brutus justifies the murder, he admits—but only to the audience—that his "genius" (immortal spirit) and his "mortal instruments" (his powers as a man) are at war in contemplating "the acting of a dreadful thing" (2.1.61–9), a conspiracy that is "monstrous" (77–85). In taking over the direction of that conspiracy and articulating the republican principles I discussed earlier, Brutus represses these sentiments. But they return in the shape of Portia's fears and specifically, in her wound.

At first Portia urges her husband to confide in her, "within the bond of marriage," asserting "by the right and virtue" of her place as his wife that he ought to tell her what is trou-

From *Roman Shakespeare: Warriors, Wounds, and Women* by Coppélia Kahn (London and New York: Routledge, 1997), pp. 96–105. Used by permission of the author and publisher.

bling him. But then she changes tack, and more delicately
presses a bolder claim:

> I grant I am a woman; but withal
> A woman well reputed; Cato's daughter.
> Think you I am no stronger than my sex,
> Being so fathered, and so husbanded?
> Tell me your counsels, I will not disclose 'em.
> I have made strong proof of my constancy,
> Giving myself a voluntary wound
> Here in the thigh: can I bear that with patience,
> And not my husband's secrets? (2.1.294–302)

Women—untrained in reason, dwellers in the *domus* excluded from the *forum*, and susceptible in the extreme to the
affections—lack access to "constancy," meaning control over
the affections, adherence to rationally-grounded principles
like those of the republic, firmness.[1] It is men who are firm,
women who aren't. Sir Thomas Elyot states that woman's inconstancy is "a natural sickenese."

Constancy, part of the complex of Roman values that constitute *virtus* in this play, can be traced specifically to Stoic
philosophy, which enjoyed a strong presence in English letters, through the prominence of Boethius's *De Consolatione
Philosophiae* as mentioned earlier; the writings of Cicero,
who eclectically assimilated Stoic ideas; and Seneca's *Epistles*, translated by Lodge in 1614. Both Cicero and Seneca
were included in the standard grammar school curriculum
(Baldwin 1944). In addition, translations of the Stoics, beginning with Tiptoft's "englishing" of Cicero's *De Amicitia* in
1481, abounded. The Stoic writers enjoyed a revival in the
1590s, just before the play was written, marked by the appearance of Sir John Stradling's *Two Bookes of Constancie*, a
translation of Justus Lipsius' explication of Stoic philosophy,
De Constantia. As John Anson notes, "for the Elizabethans,

[1]Compare the definition of *consto, constare* (to be constant) in Cooper's *Thesaurus*: glossing a phrase from Cicero, *Per se ipsum constare*, Cooper says, "To
be of himselfe: without any to depende of . . . to be like himselfe: to be always
one," which implies a contrast to the dependency and volatility held typical of
women.

neo-Stoicism resuscitated a distinctly Roman ethos; to be a Stoic meant, in effect, to be a Roman" (Anson 1967: 13).

While neither the Stoics nor their Renaissance mediator Lipsius conceive their philosophy as gender-specific, the terms in which they pose its leading postulates are the same as those in which masculine and feminine were commonly framed (Maclean 1980). Building up parallel oppositions between Reason and Opinion, Soul and Body, Constancy and Inconstancy, Lipsius roots constancy in reason; to obey reason is to be "lord of all lusts and rebellious affections" (Lipsius 1939: 81). In certain Christian discourses, women have ready access to and attain such lordship; in the Latin heritage on which Shakespeare draws, it is rarer and comes harder. As Thomas Lodge writes in the preface of his translation of Seneca, "to subdue passion is to be truely a man" (quoted in Lipsius 1939: 29).

If ever a body of literature, comprising poetry, drama, and history in both verse and prose, inscribed the primacy of man as warrior, ruler, father, and bard, it would seem to be Latin literature. Where do women fit in this world? For the beginnings of an answer, we might turn to Plutarch's life of Julius Caesar. It opens,

> At what time Sylla was made lord of all, he would have had Caesar put away his wife Cornelia, the daughter of Cinna Dictator. But when he saw he could neither with any promise nor threat bring him to it, he took her jointure away from him. The cause of Caesar's ill will unto Sylla was by means of marriage. For Marius the elder married his father's own sister, by whom he had Marius the younger; whereby Caesar and he were cousin-germans.
>
> (*Life of Julius Caesar* 5: 1)

Similarly, in the first few pages of Plutarch's life of Brutus, we learn that Brutus's mother, Servilia, was the sister of Marcus Cato the philosopher, that same Cato who was Portia's father; Brutus too married his "cousin-german." Servilia, Brutus's mother, was thought to have had a love af-

fair with Julius Caesar, whence arose the tradition that Brutus
was Caesar's son (*Life of Marcus Brutus*, 6: 185). Women
held no public offices and only in extraordinary circumstances did they even speak in public, but as objects of exchange
in marriage they were crucial to the weaving of political al-
liances and the continuity of the dynasties which formed the
basis of the Roman power elite. One feminist critic has as-
tutely described them has having "a double status as outsider
within"; excluded from public life, they were essential to its
continuity as wives, mothers, and daughters (Joplin 1990:
10). In *Julius Caesar*, evidences of the exchange of women
are elided (Shakespeare doesn't even mention that Cassius
and Brutus are brothers-in-law); it is a man, not a woman,
who mediates the originary moment of Brutus's emergence
into political agency; and it is men who engage each other's
passions—as friends, as rivals, as Romans on the stage of
history. What is Portia's role, then, in the play's representation of Roman masculinity?

In Rome and in Shakespeare's England, whatever the actual scope of women's activities, home was held to be the
woman's place: the *domus*, from which the word domestic is
derived, a private dwelling set in opposition to the public forum of politics. But the scene between Portia and Brutus
can't be contained within a public–private opposition . . . because though Brutus, ruminating in his orchard, has already
admitted his scruples about killing Caesar, he has done so in
the fully politicized context of the nascent conspiracy.
Rather, since Portia's suspicions echo Brutus's earlier admission that killing Caesar seems "a dreadful thing," her appearance privatizes and more important, feminizes his hesitation.
In terms of "the general good" as Brutus's republicanism de-
fines it, individual moral scruples must be overcome; if such
scruples are associated with a woman, and voiced only in the
home, all the more reason to disregard them. An opposition
between private scruples and public action, however, does
parallel an opposition between feminine fear and masculine
constancy. It is such distinctions that underpin the construction of Brutus as a tragic hero who, though he entertains
moral strictures against killing that are associated with the

feminine and the private, must embrace a man's duty and re-
press them in the name of defending an abstract concept of
the public weal. Portia and Calphurnia worry and warn hus-
bands who actually share at least some of their fears but
who, once those fears are voiced by women, gain as it were
a heroic warrant to override them and act in accordance with
"masculine" virtue. As Linda Charnes states, "Literature is
filled with male heroes who must renounce their 'privacy' in
order to achieve renown" (1993: 96).

In the orchard scene, Portia concedes her inferiority as a
woman, but nonetheless seeks entitlement to the constancy of
a man, first through descent from her father, known for his
rigid morality and for resisting submission to Caesar by killing himself; next, through affiliation with Brutus who, Plutarch notes, "studied most to follow [Cato] of all the other
Romans." Portia shows, as it were, a fine discernment in this
strategy of constructing herself as a man, for as I suggested
earlier, men mutually confirm their identities as Roman
through bonds with each other. Brutus can trust Portia only
as a man.

It is above all by wounding herself that she imitates a
man's constancy. That wound destabilizes the gendered concept of virtue in several ways. First, that this virtue might be
imitated by a woman de-naturalizes it and suggests that it
isn't native to the male gender; it is learned behavior. Portia's
"voluntary wound," as Gail Paster shows, is the opposite of
a quintessentially feminine "inability to stop bleeding which
is one aspect of womanly incontinence" (Paster 1993: 94).
Second, the site of Portia's wound, in her thigh, hints ambiguously at a genital wound—what psychoanalysis would take
to be the wound of castration, signifying that she as a woman
lacks the phallus, symbol of power in a patriarchal society.
Seeking to articulate symbolically the dominant masculine
ideal of constancy, she also evokes symbols of femininity. In
the words of Madelon Sprengnether, "she reveals the underlying paradox of the play, which equates manliness with injury, so that the sign of masculinity becomes the wound"
(1986: 96). Her wound anticipates the suicidal wounds of
Brutus and Cassius. Like hers, they are "voluntary wounds,"

cultural markers of the physical courage, autonomy, constancy that count as manly virtue; but at the same time, they demonstrate the fleshly vulnerability, the capacity to be penetrated, that marks woman. In a discursive operation akin to that of the fetish, constancy is haunted by its feminine opposites, making Portia's wound ambiguously, undecideably feminine *and* masculine. Or, to put it another way, the constitution of manly virtue requires the repression of the feminine, and the repressed returns.

The encounter between Portia and her husband, cut short by the arrival of the last conspirator, ends with his promise to "construe" to her the outward signs of his self-division. Evidently, he does; Portia reappears in act 2, scene 4, distraught and anxious for news of events at the Capitol. Now struggling for the constancy to keep Brutus's dangerous secret, she has been reinscribed into the category of woman, and her distress naturalized: "I have a man's mind, but a woman's might" (2.4.8); "Ay me, how weak a thing / The heart of woman is!" (39–40), she cries. We do not see her onstage again, but she returns to trouble the text and its construction of Brutus in a famous crux. Portia's death is announced twice in act 4, scene 3: first Brutus tells Cassius about it (146–56); then when Messala also broaches it (180–94), Brutus gives no sign that he already knows she is dead.

The longstanding debate over which version is "earlier" or "later," what Shakespeare meant by the supposed revision, and whether it is a revision at all has hinged on the implications of these two moments for the characterization of Brutus—not on what they suggest about Portia (Clayton 1983). Critics who think Brutus either disingenuous or lacking in compassion not to reveal his knowledge of the death to Messala or react emotionally to it argue that the second revelation was meant to be cancelled; critics who see him as admirably self-controlled in true Stoic fashion hold out for "duplicate revelation." The judgment depends not only on how the critic interprets Brutus's character but also on how he (they are all male) values the traits he finds in it. Some want Brutus's first announcement unqualified by what they see as the calculated masking of the second; others welcome a second demonstration of Brutus's self-control. Since the second revelation doesn't necessarily conflict with the first, and since the scene can be read and acted to make sense with both, with one, or with neither, the question is undecidable and the crux functions as a litmus test of the critics and the cultural norms of heroic masculinity they endorse. In any case, in both passages Brutus is restrained, not to say impassive, while Cassius exclaims "O insupportable and touching loss!" Whether one stresses Brutus's constancy or his display of it before his two comrades, both are hallmarks of Roman masculinity.

Not only in the announcement of her death, but also in the "strange manner" of it, Shakespeare abandons his earlier ambiguity and reinscribes conventional sexual difference. Furthermore, though he followed rather closely Plutarch's account of her wound and her struggle to keep Brutus's counsel, Shakespeare edits out the suggestive particulars of her death. Plutarch says that, due to "the weake constitution of her body" she fell sick; then,

> determining to kill herself (her parents and friends carefully looking to keep her from it), [she] took hot burning coals and cast them into her mouth, and kept her mouth so close that she choked herself.
>
> (*Life of Marcus Brutus,* 6: 236)

This account allows her the sort of agency proper to Brutus and Cassius themselves as Stoics and Roman heroes who will allow no man dominion over them. It also seems to parody the constancy Portia tried to claim by her wound, and found so hard to maintain once she learned the secret of the conspiracy; here, indeed, she keeps her mouth "close," and Plutarch commends her "for courage and constant mind" because "she shewed herself as stout in defence of her country, as any of us" (*Life of Marcus Brutus,* 6: 204). Shakespeare, in contrast, has Brutus say only that "she fell distract, / And (her attendants absent) swallow'd fire" (4.3.154–55), depriving her of the agency and dignity that she has in Plutarch.

Her crazed, bizarre act of self-destruction reinserts her firmly into the feminine, while Brutus's suicide signifies his *virtus*.[2]

In the succeeding scene (2.2), Shakespeare reworks the themes of male heroism, female fear, wounds and constancy, now focussing on Caesar. Again a Roman wife confronts her noble husband with her fears; again *virtus* is both constituted through and subverted by the feminine. The terrible portents that frighten Calphurnia first evoke Caesar's serene and eloquent assertion of constancy in the face of "death, a necessary end" (32–37). Then he relents, agreeing to stay home, but vacillates between vaunting that he wills the change and seizing the excuse she offers him. Finally he agrees to call it *her* fear, not his, that keeps him from the Capitol. Again a woman provides the alibi for a man's fearfulness, but here the displacement doesn't serve to validate a heroic commitment to public action, as in Brutus's encounter with Portia.

Rather, Calphurnia's dream-image of Caesar's statue, twice recounted, further ambiguates the multiple, contradictory images of Caesar as both Colossus and sick girl, mighty in his triumph over Pompey, yet childless and deaf. Decius transforms the portentous imagery of bloodshed, betrayal, and hypocrisy in Caesar's account of the dream into an odd but suggestively Roman vision of a nursing mother:

> Your statue spouting blood in so many pipes,
> In which so many smiling Romans bath'd,
> Signifies that from you great Rome shall suck
> Reviving blood.   (85–87)

In this version Caesar's blood doesn't just "run," it spouts; the vigor before attributed to the "lusty Romans" who bathed their hands in it is now imputed to Caesar, who takes Brutus's place as Rome's restorer. Decius's version recalls the legend of Romulus and Remus who, suckled by the she-wolf,

---

[2]Boaistuau (1574) lists among the aberrant appetites of pregnant women the desire to eat "hotte burning coales" (sig. Dix^v). If we take Brutus's reference to Portia's "condition" (2.1.236) to indicate not just her femaleness but a possible pregnancy as well, then the manner of her death emphasizes her gender even more.

were thus enabled to found the Roman state. The feast of the Lupercal, being celebrated as the play begins, was named for and associated with the she-wolf's bounty, according to Plutarch: rituals of purification and fertility evoke the wolf at several points (*The Life of Romulus*, 1: 87–88). The feast was also associated with Romulus's physical strength, which was in turn linked to the earth's fertility. Hence, as in the play, the victors in its games touch barren women to make them bear (1.2.6–8). Plutarch suggests many parallels between Romulus and Caesar: both sought to found a line of kings, slew their rivals, were reputed to be tyrants, and were stellified after death. Caesar revived veneration of Romulus, and even considered taking his name. In Decius's flattering vision, though, Caesar is the nurturing mother, not the suckling king-to-be. Swayed by this image of mammary vigor, the inconstant Caesar reverses himself once again and departs for the Senate and his death. His constancy, like his refusal of the crown, seems transparently an act, a pretense at being the firm Roman, belied by his "feminine" mutability and identification with maternal rather than masculine styles of power.

It is the assassination itself that resoundingly feminizes Caesar.[3] His punctured, bleeding body makes men cry, and Antony likens his wounds to eyes streaming with tears, or "dumb mouths" that "ope their ruby lips" to beg an orator to speak for them, because like women they cannot plead their own cause. In an extravagant image, Antony characterizes himself as that very orator, putting "a tongue / In every wound of Caesar that should move / The stones of Rome to rise and mutiny" (3.2.230–32). Antony's rhetoric, his "tongue," is indeed the phallic instrument that transforms Caesar's inert, passively bleeding body into a vehicle of po-

---

[3]Comparing the imagery of Caesar's bleeding body to the similar description of Lavinia in *Titus Andronicus* as "a conduit with three issuing spouts," and also to a contrasting metaphor of bloodletting as deliberate physical purgation in *Coriolanus*, Gail Kern Paster brilliantly interprets Caesar's corpse as "marked with the shameful stigmata of ambiguous gender, especially the sign of womanly blood" (1993: 94), womanly because his bleeding, like menstruation, is involuntary and uncontrollable. Paster, though, attributes to the conspirators a quasiconscious motivation to feminize him; I see that feminization, rather, as an epiphenomenon of their enactment of republican *virtus* in assassinating him.

litical power. The physical presence of Caesar's corpse is, of course, crucial to the project Antony describes in these lines. Cleverly he first points to the holes in Caesar's mantle made by the individual conspirators, evoking from the crowd "gracious drops" of tears to match the drops of Caesar's blood. Then, when he lifts that mantle, he can use the sight of the wounds themselves to produce the first cries of revenge from the crowd.

Revenge, as Antony evokes and shapes it, has a feminine character. Its matrix is pity and tears, the release of tender and passionate feelings which are then easily transmuted into "Domestic fury and fierce civil strife" reminiscent of the Furies or the crazed female worshippers of Dionysus who, in Euripides' *Bacchae*, are capable of rending their children limb from limb. Antony predicts that

> Blood and destruction shall be so in use,
> And dreadful objects so familiar,
> That mothers shall but smile when they behold
> Their infants quartered with the hands of war,
> All pity choked with custom of fell deeds. (3.1.265–69)

In a familiar Shakespearean sequence (compare Lady Macbeth's image of dashing her baby's brains out, and Volumnia's comparison of giving suck to wounds bleeding), maternal love is the touchstone of a generalized human "pity" seen as the last, failed bulwark against unbounded violence. Unrestrained emotions deaf to the general good and inaccessible to reason overtake the Roman republic and its new leaders. Antony and Octavius ruthlessly eliminate their enemies and exploit their allies. Brutus and Cassius, who in their different ways sought to be constant to the general good, fall to petty quarreling. In answer to Brutus's criticisms, the formerly steely Cassius melodramatically proffers his breast for a death-blow (4.3.99–100), and apologizes for his "rash humour" by saying he got it from his mother. When Caesar, once the embodiment of *virtus* as conqueror of Europe and Asia, victor over Pompey, has been feminized and brought low, the most fearsome and destructive images of the feminine possess Rome. Again, one might say, the repressed returns.

Shakespeare's Brutus is a tragic hero, I believe, in the sense that in him the contradictions embedded in his culture are set at war. In the first place, as a Roman, paradoxically he acts both for the general good and out of emulation, in that he wants to stand above other men—in his devotion to the general good. When Portia voices her fears and scruples, she brings to light a further contradiction. His motives for the murder having already been masculinized in the context of republican ideology, his misgivings about it are feminized when Portia voices them, which allows him to deny them as "feminine" and thus to assert his manly virtue in acting upon his political convictions.

Mark Antony eulogizes Brutus as "the noblest Roman of them all," because "He, only in a general honest thought / And common good to all" murdered Caesar (5.5.68, 71–72). Voicing the same cherished ideal of the republic that Brutus stated when he reasoned his way into the conspiracy, Mark Antony sees him as he saw himself, and as others saw him. Many critics have taken his words as the final word on Brutus, without seeing any irony in them. For Mark Antony is surely guided not by the general good but by vengefulness and ambition, and the triumvirate of which he is a member rules by fiat and terror—yet he too proclaims the idea of the republic as a government of and for "the common good." But perhaps it is more significant that he envisions one man only in that republic who triumphs—in virtue—over all the rest.

Works Cited

Anson, J. S. (1967) "*Julius Caesar:* The Politics of the Hardened Heart," *Shakespearean Studies* 2: 11–33.

Baldwin, T. W. (1944) *William Shakespere's Small Latine and Lesse Greeke*, Urbana: University of Illinois Press, 2 vols.

Boaistuau, P. (1574) *Theatrum Mundi*, J. Alday (transl.). London.

Charnes, L. (1993) *Notorious Identity: Materializing the Subject in Shakespeare*. Cambridge, MA: Harvard University Press.

Clayton, T. (1983) " 'Should Brutus Never Taste of Portia's Death But Once?' Text and Performance in *Julius Caesar*," *Studies in English Literature 1500–1900* 23,2 (spring): 237–55.

Cooper, T. (1969) *Thesaurus Linguae Romanae et Britannicae*. Menston, England: Scolar.

Joplin, P. K. (1990) "Ritual Work on Human Flesh: Livy's Lucretia and the Rape of the Body Politic," *Helios* 17,1: 51–70.

Lipsius, J. (1939) *Two Bookes of Constancie, Englished by Sir John Stradling*, R. Kirk (ed. and intro.). New Brunswick, NJ: Rutgers University Press.

Maclean, I. (1980) *The Renaissance Notion of Women: A Study in the Fortunes of Scholasticism and Medical Science in European Intellectual Life*. Cambridge: Cambridge University Press.

Paster, G. K. (1989) " 'In the spirit of men there is no blood': Blood as Trope of Gender in *Julius Caesar*," *Shakespeare Quarterly* 40,3: 284–98.

Plutarch (1895) *Lives of the Noble Greeks and Romans, Englished by Sir Thomas North*, G. Wyndham (intro.). London: David Nutt.
The Life of Julius Caesar, Lives, vol. 5, 1–71.
The Life of Marcus Brutus, Lives, vol. 6, 182–240.

Rose, M. B. (ed.) (1986) *Women in the Middle Ages and the Renaissance: Literary and Historical Perspectives*. Syracuse: Syracuse University Press.

Sprengnether, M. (1986) "Annihilating Intimacy in *Coriolanus*," in Rose (ed. and intro.), 89–101.

ROY WALKER

From Unto Caesar: A Review of
Recent Productions

   No major play of Shakespeare's has suffered more from
democratic distortion than *Julius Caesar*. It seems improb-
able that the sympathies of the Elizabethan poet and his audience would be hostile to the aging, sick and childless
personal ruler, brutally and treacherously assassinated by
professed friends who then plunge their country into the
dread cycle of civil wars that ends only with the disruption
and downfall of the Republic. Although Hazlitt supposed that
Shakespeare painted an entirely antipathetic portrait of Caesar, it was still possible, before two world wars darkened the
scene, to recognize, as MacCallum did in 1910, that "Shakespeare makes it abundantly clear that the rule of the single
master-mind is the only admissible solution for the problem
of the time."[1] The Hazlitt tradition reached its patriotic peak
in Dover Wilson's 1949 edition of the play. Meanwhile it had
spread to the stage. After Orson Welles' 1937 modern-dress
production (in which, of course, this powerful actor elected
to play Brutus), other modern-dress *Caesar*s in this country,
and most costume productions too, presented the drama as
the democratic doing-in of a diabolical dictator. They could
therefore make nothing of the celestial portents and still less
of the fifth act in which the spirit of the dead dictator incon-
veniently triumphs.
   Now that the dogs of war are on the leash again there are

   From *Shakespeare Survey* XI (1958): 132–35. Reprinted by permission of The
Cambridge University Press.
   [1]M.W. MacCallum, *Shakespeare's Roman Plays* (1910), p. 214.

signs of scholarly reaction on both sides of the Atlantic. In 1953 Virgil Whitaker argued that Shakespeare meant Caesar to seem "a great and good ruler"[2] and in the new Arden edition two years later T. S. Dorsch agreed that "Shakespeare wishes us to admire his Caesar."[3] A similar rehabilitation on the stage was overdue. It was peculiarly appropriate that this should be achieved in the year of the 2000th anniversary of the assassination, and in the Shakespeare Memorial Theatre at Stratford-upon-Avon, where Glen Byam Shaw produced the play. The main interest of this production lay in its bold centralization of Caesar, who became the real as well as the nominal protagonist, and in the means employed to keep this presence dramatically alive on the stage after the actual murder, with a consequent gain in coherency and in the significance of the last act.

Glen Byam Shaw's interpretation began at the beginning of the play. The curtain rose on a stage dominated by a larger-than-life statue of Caesar, raised on a tall plinth in the center of the stage. After the disrobing of this image by the envious tribunes, this statue pivoted backwards out of sight, the two walls of gray stone parted and against the blue sky at the back the living Caesar was acclaimed. The statue might easily have dwarfed the human figure, but the magnificence of the gold-embroidered crimson toga and the majesty of Cyril Luckham's bearing made him the incarnation of an immutable and pivotal principle of order. This ordered Rome was visible in the massive fluted monoliths of light gray stone, ranged outwards from Caesar as their personal center in two symmetrical lines, continued in the tall stone portals flanking the forestage. Here was the wide perspective of Caesar's Rome with Caesar himself the keystone.

When the procession had passed, the center was unfilled while Cassius, effectively played as a "little Caesar," a Corsican upstart, by Geoffrey Keen, maneuvered for the advantage of height with a Brutus (Alec Clunes) who was every inch Caesar's angel in presence and noble innocence. At the end of this scene of lurking disorder, the sky darkened with

[2]Virgil K. Whitaker, *Shakespeare's Use of Learning* (1953), p. 234.
[3]T. S. Dorsch (ed.), *Julius Caesar* (1955), p. xxxviii.

supernatural speed and an ominous patch of crimson appeared above the place where Caesar had stood. Cassius' defiance of the lightning was posed at stage center and met with a crackling blaze of white light from heaven, a warning which went unheeded by the arch-plotter.

The foremost monoliths converged again to close the main stage and leave the forestage for Brutus' orchard, but the central niche where Caesar's image had been was now eloquently empty while Brutus struggled to put away loyalty and friendship. When this orchard wall parted to reveal the interior of Caesar's house, the central entrance was hung with a divided crimson curtain, behind which was visible a head of Caesar, now isolated on a pedestal of his own height. The front walls converged again and Artemidorus paused before the empty niche to read over his warning to Caesar. They reopened on the Senate, with a raised central throne, its back a solid sheet of gleaming gold, on which Caesar took his place with his head high against the blue sky beyond. As he fell to the assassins' swords there was a fierce crackle of lightning from the clear sky, which was then rapidly overcast.

When the scene changed to the Forum, the two lines of monoliths had fallen back in disorder, leaving a wider gap in the center. Caesar's central throne had now given place to the popular pulpit from which successive demagogues harangued the changeable many who lined the front of the stage in dark silhouette, as though under a sinister shadow that had fallen on all Rome. Caesar's catafalque, the body shrouded with the crimson, gold-ornamented robe, was laid on the center of the forestage, below the pulpit. As Antony (Richard Johnson) passionately roused the mob to blood, the sky reddened, and at the climactic cry "Here was Caesar! when comes such another?" he was standing a little off-center in front of the now empty pulpit, his right arm thrust straight up to heaven; and suddenly in the true center of the sky the northern star shone out alone. After the tumultuous exit the stage was empty and silent for a moment with the star shining distantly down. The poet Cinna half turned his head toward it as he entered, saying "I dreamt tonight that I did feast with Caesar." Back surged the mob, now bearing lighted torches, bobbing and blazing symbols of disorder, the wandering fires of an earth from which the unmoved mover had been withdrawn. The interval arrived with an unforgettable stage picture of the murdered poet, flopped brokenly over the front of the pulpit like a discarded glove-puppet, and the star, blazing brighter in a sky that turned from blue to black, shining down in silent comment on the grim scene of chaos come again.

The second half opened with the triumvirate standing apart with their backs to a huge suspended map of the Mediterranean. Antony was in front of Italy, Octavius before the Balkans, Lepidus over against Asia Minor; the stretches of sea between the actors subtly suggested the space that always separated them, and the pattern of civil wars to come. Rome was now gone without a trace, and it was in a blood-red tent near Sardis that Brutus contended with Cassius and saw Caesar's ghost, which materialized in the open mouth of the tent, against the sky. When this tent was struck the bare stage was broken only by a low ridge of fissured rock which rose to a slight eminence a little off-center. It was from here that Octavius and Antony, with their troops and standards, saw Brutus and Cassius coming down to battle in the plains where dusty death awaits them. Cassius fell, then Brutus, their own swords turned against them by friendly hands, in the same central area and general posture as Caesar was, but further downstage, on a lower level. When Brutus came upon Cassius' body and exclaimed "O Julius Caesar, thou art mighty yet!", the northern star suddenly appeared again. There it remained, so that the final curtain recalled and resolved the first-half curtain. The dead body of the tragically deluded liberator lay in the center of the stage, not in Rome but in the wilderness he had helped to make of Rome, and high above him shone out the star of whose true-fixed and resting quality there is no fellow in the firmament.[4]

    [4]It is necessary for the reviewer to disclose an interest. The present writer suggested to Mr. Byam Shaw the parallel between "that bright Occidental star," as the Jacobean translators of the Bible called the Queen, and the Caesar whose soul was taken up and made a star in the climax of Ovid's *Metamorphoses*, an episode to which Shakespeare refers in the opening scene of *1 Henry VI*. He also suggested that the northern star speech in *Julius Caesar* draws poetically on that Ovidian climax, and that the promise that the ghost will appear again at Philippi may have been kept by displaying an emblematic star in "the heavens." (For a

more elaborate staging of the transfiguration of a soul into a star on the stage, see the stage direction for the death of Hercules in Thomas Heywood's *The Brazen Age*.) Ways in which a comparable effect might be provided for modern audiences with present-day lighting equipment were also discussed. But a suggested interpretation is one thing; imaginative transformation is another. Mr. Byam Shaw transmuted the argument into his own art. If I am open to suspicion of being prejudiced in favor of the result, I may at least point out that the general opinion of responsible critics was that the production was conspicuously successful in its rendering of the true values of the play.

RICHARD DAVID

A Review of *Julius Caesar*
(Royal Shakespeare, 1972)

At the opening of *Julius Caesar* the trumpets blared out, and a gigantic red carpet spinningly unrolled from the back of the stage to the very front. This was the cue for a production in which parade and panoply bulked large. These are features of our own received ideas of the Grandeur that was Rome, and I have already suggested that it would be particularly difficult to insulate *Julius Caesar*, of all subjects, from these habitual associations. There are other associations that may tend to color the play at least for the over-forties in a modern audience. The commentators never stop telling us that its real subject is dictatorship, and that is a phenomenon of which some of us have had experience. For us Caesar can fall readily into the posture of Hitler or Mussolini, and this production with its heel-clicking and leather garments and fascist salutes strongly encouraged the connection.

Now this, while it adds resonance to the play, may be dangerous. Hitler and Mussolini, parodied as they have been by themselves as well as by others, are in one light too clownish for comparison even with that Caesar to whose failings Shakespeare gave some comic enlargement (he is pompous, hard of hearing, liable to fits, and the stories that Cassius tells against him are Shakespeare's deliberate distortions of incidents that Plutarch relates to his credit). In another light our modern dictators are too palpably and too seriously evil. Caesar must not be seen either as a comic monster or as a

From *Shakespeare in the Theatre* by Richard David. Cambridge: Cambridge University Press, 1978.

black tyrant. Only the lesser conspirators regard him as an unmitigated evil. Brutus sees in him a potential not an actual danger, and the other witnesses testify only to the good that his greatness has brought to Rome. He is another equipoise of right and wrong, and Shakespeare summed up his paradox in the line so mocked by Ben Jonson, which appears to have been edited out of the Folio in deference to that mockery, and which in this production I was glad to hear restored: "Caesar did never wrong but with just cause."

Fortunately Dignam's performance deftly preserved that balance and counteracted any undue pressure from the Hitlerian allusions. For his Caesar appeared a ruler of vision; a just judge if self-consciously so; and essentially a companionable man though too minded of his public position. He perfectly matched Cicero's account, in a private letter, of how the historical Caesar struck a contemporary. The masterly vignette of his call at Cicero's villa was engagingly translated in the theater program: "Nerve-racking—but it passed off tolerably. He was in a very good humor. The talk at table was all of literature, and serious subjects were avoided. Just a quiet man-to-man talk. Still, he wasn't the sort of guest to whom you'd say 'Look me up when you're passing this way again.' Once is enough." There you have the man whose public image has so engulfed the private person that personal relationships are no longer comfortable. The same dichotomy was in this production well conveyed by the introduction of Caesar's colossal statue into the one scene of his domestic life. Standing uneasily in the shadow of his public image Caesar cannot act naturally to his friends or even to his wife. I was not so happy about the continuous presence of this statue in the latter scenes of the play. The intention was good. The most significant irony of the play is that Brutus, regretting that in order to destroy the public Caesar he must kill the private one, ends by recognizing that although the private friend has been duly killed, the public Caesar persists indestructibly. This is the lesson repeatedly voiced by the characters and embodied in the visitation of Caesar's spirit to Brutus' tent on the night before the conspirators are finally liquidated at Philippi. For this visitation the statue, terrifyingly heralded by the nightmare cries of the sleepers, served well; but its later presence was incongruous. It is difficult enough to give reality to the battles without having them take place in a museum of sculpture.

The presentation of Caesar as a positive rather than a negative figure was enhanced by the treatment here given to his opponents. In passing let me call attention to the economy of brushwork with which Shakespeare fixes the conspirators for us. Brutus has a full-length portrait, Cassius a three-quarter-length. Casca gets a vivid head-and-shoulders; and I found Gerald James' hard-bitten black comedian refreshing and convincing in place of the usual bluff hearty. Ligarius is picked out by his illness, Decius is the smooth one who is set to appease Caesar's doubts while Trebonius heads off Antony, Cimber has the banished brother and Cinna the poet namesake. More to my present purpose, however, is the emphasis placed by Shakespeare, and fully but fairly brought out in this production, on the incompetence and fatuity of the conspirators as a group. It is not only Brutus who is at fault here, though his blunders are the most obvious and are pinpointed by Cassius' comments. Brutus spares Antony's life, allows him to speak, and to have the last word at Caesar's funeral, marches out of his secure defensive position above Philippi, and gives the order to attack too soon. Cassius has no sooner killed Caesar ostensibly for dictatorially fixing government appointments by influence and bribes than he sees himself, with Antony, fixing future appointments and his taking of bribes is the cause of his quarrel with Brutus. The muffled conspiracy that visits Brutus' house is the height of amateurishness and the near-hysteria of the assassins shows them intoxicated by what they have done but utterly unprepared for what is next to do. The Citizens are eager to nullify the conspirators' action by making Brutus Caesar, and the triumvirate pledged to avenge Caesar at once demonstrate that they will resume all his political techniques and use them even more ruthlessly. Incidentally I was sorry that the director tacked this scene on to the funeral, before the interval. One need not pay too much attention to the purely editorial dispositions of the Folio, but it is, I think, pertinent that the Folio makes Octavius, Antony, and Lepidus open Act 4 rather than end Act 3. The first movement of the play con-

cludes with Brutus and Cassius riding like madmen out of
Rome. Their enterprise has failed, but it should not yet be
clear what is to happen next. The emergence of the opposition is the start of the second movement. But the implication
of the scene, wherever it is placed, is clear enough and was
confirmed at the end of the play when, just before the curtain
calls, the great red carpet again unrolled itself to signify that
dictatorship had been reestablished as if the conspirators had
never existed.

With this general structure of the play in mind, we may
consider its central problem, Brutus. I will say at once that
I found John Wood's continuously inventive and persuasive
character study quite enthralling. I must add that I could not
make it blend with the rest of the production. To put it in an
epigram, he was more a Dane than an antique Roman. To
this one might reply, why not? Brutus has often been seen as
a preliminary study for Hamlet, and clearly at that moment
in his career Shakespeare was mesmerized by something that
the two have in common. The answer is that Brutus the Dane
would be well enough if the whole play could be translated
into, say, the Renaissance, but that the ties, actual and imag-
ined, with classical Rome are too strong for this, and the introduction of Hamlet into classical Rome produces an effect
on the audience like that of double vision. This is naturally
less intrusive in those scenes in which the contrasting characters are few or none, and in such scenes the richness of the
interpretation could be relished without qualms. In the soliloquy "It must be by his death," in which, before ever the
conspirators arrive to persuade him, Brutus works out for
himself the necessity of assassinating his best friend, the elu-
cidation of the thought was so clear and the expression so
limpid that one wondered how anyone could have found the
speech difficult. When, at the end of the same night scene,
Portia comes to upbraid Brutus for not sharing with her the
secrets that so torture him, both the understanding between
husband and wife and the irritability of one wracked by intolerable anxieties were movingly genuine. So, too, were
Brutus' gentle courtesy to the officers bidden to share his
tent on the night before Philippi, and to his sleepy servant.
Chief among these intimate scenes is the quarrel between

Brutus and Cassius, and this quarrel was a fizzer. . . . Because Brutus had usurped the lean and hungry look and the thinking too much, Cassius had to fall back on other characteristics that certainly exist in the part, such as impetuosity and a quick temper. The violence of his anger was electrifying and he literally whipped the scene to its climax as, seizing Brutus' truncheon, he laid about him in his fury and beat the papers from the council table. With an equally characteristic gesture, Brutus, toward the end of the scene, signaled the extinction of the fires by going quietly about to pick up the scattered papers and restore them to their place. It seemed in keeping, too, that Brutus' fury should break out at the suspected mockery of the "poet" (here a masquerading soldier) while Cassius, now calm, could laugh at the joker. The end of the scene brought a beautiful touch. There is a famous crux here. Brutus, having revealed Portia's death to Cassius, pretends to Messala that he has heard nothing of it. The commentators on the whole have found it impossible to believe that Shakespeare can have meant to show the noble Brutus as so disingenuous, and before Cassius too, who knows that he is play-acting to Messala. The passage with Messala has therefore been written off as an alternative version that has accidentally remained uncanceled in the printed text, and it is usually cut in performance. Here it was retained and turned to advantage. As Messala speaks of Portia, Brutus signals to Cassius to keep silence. His dialogue with Messala is a public shield against the privacy of his grief being further invaded, and Cassius is the one sharer of the secret of Brutus' prior knowledge and real feelings. This second, personal conspiracy seals the bond of brotherhood that has just been renewed between them.

It was in the big public scenes that the difference in kind between Brutus and the others became disconcerting. That Brutus does differ in kind is of course part of the point of the play. The director must not be blamed for bringing this point out, and that he was deliberately seeking to do so was plain. For example, there was no need to dress Brutus in a severe personal uniform that made of him a Roundhead rather than a Roman general. But the gap can be too wide, so that even credibility suffers: impossible to accept that a Caesar as hard-bitten as this one could have so close an attachment to a dreaming don, or that even such incompetent conspirators as these could think that they needed this Brutus to impress even so gullible a crowd as these citizens. It was not easy to believe that this Brutus would follow the example of his Roman associates and decide "not to be." A pity that the scene was cut in which Lucilius prepares us for the suicide, warning Antony in the fine words (taken over from North): "When you do find him, or alive or dead, He will be found like Brutus, like himself."

The Brutus is not to be blamed for the comparative failure of the biggest public scene of all, Caesar's funeral. The grouping was awkward. The rostrum was, perhaps inevitably, stage-center, and the people were crowded around it, backs to the audience. Between those backs and the audience was Caesar's bier. This was clumsy and created a double focus to the scene until Antony turned the people to look at Caesar's corpse. In addition all were in dingy colors. Perhaps this was to signify mourning, but it looked rather as if the artisans (who still apparently made up the whole populace of Rome) had not changed their clothes since Coriolanus' time. (Yet the tipsy revelers of the first scene had been quite gay.) As a result the whole scene had a clogged and muddy effect that gave Richard Johnson little chance to show his paces.

RALPH BERRY

On Directing Shakespeare: An Interview with Trevor Nunn, Director of the Royal Shakespeare Company

RB: I found your *Julius Caesar* startlingly original in at least two major ways, in terms of character presentation. Your Caesar was the first I've ever seen who's really struck me as being dangerous, an enemy to the state. Every other Caesar has appeared to me as a sort of company chairman, who's a little bit over the top, and the Board are getting rather restive about him. He doesn't really seem that much of a problem. He does in your production. And the other is Brutus. Every other production I've seen takes at face value the adjective that is applied to him constantly throughout the play, "the noble Brutus." Your production questions this. And taken together, this sheds a flood of light on the play for me.

TN: Yes. Brutus himself questions his nobility. He questions himself and his own actions constantly. When at the height of the tent scene Brutus turns on Cassius and says, "I shall be glad to learn of *noble* men," it's a vicious taunt at Cassius, but I also think it's an indication of the self-revulsion that is in him. We were able to find a complete continuity for the character by questioning that endlessly repeated adjective. Viewed through Cassius' (myopic) eyes, Caesar is fundamentally *ignoble* in wishing to retain and

From *On Directing Shakespeare: Interviews with Contemporary Directors* by Ralph Berry. (New York: Harper and Row, 1977), pp. 64–68.

consolidate power. The aristocratic tradition is otherwise, a commitment to preserve the idea of equality and freedom—as John Wood (who played Brutus) once pointed out, freedom for Cassius to dislike Caesar publicly without fear of arrest. Both Brutus and Cassius die amidst uncertainty, but they know that a whole era has come to an end. "It is *impossible* that Rome shall ever breed thy fellow"—because Rome has changed. "Our day is gone," says Titinius. The opportunists and Empire builders have taken over. So far as Caesar is concerned—I was reading recently a review by Bernard Crick who, writing about the plays, lamented that we had chosen a simple and naïve Mussolini-like solution for the character, and pointed out that the problem Shakespeare is dealing with is less obvious than that. It seems to me he has put his finger on the difficulty with the play in performance. If one *doesn't* suggest that Caesar is fast becoming a military dictator—I mean, that after the civil war he has total control of the army, and therefore cannot be removed—he can't be *voted* out, and he's not going to move over, to let somebody else enjoy that power he has fought for—if one doesn't suggest that military power supports him, and if he doesn't in some way embody that military power, then obviously we get to the moment of his assassination and we just think that it's dreadfully unfair and dreadfully unnecessary that so many people should set upon a harmless defenseless senator.

There's a great deal of evidence in the play that Caesar has reached a point of dangerous insanity. Not only the number of times that he refers to himself in the third person, and as an institution, not only in the terrifying "Northern Star" speech just before the assassination, but in little references like from Casca, "there was more foolery yet . . ." What happens to the two tribunes? This is something that I haven't picked up in any previous production—maybe that's because I wasn't concentrating—but Casca says that Marullus and Flavius, the tribunes of the people, "for pulling scarfs off Caesar's images, are put to silence." Surely he means they've been executed. It's been very sudden. Two men in high office have been executed and all they did was to pull down a decoration off an image which until last year no one was allowed to put up in the first place. Now that's deeply sinister and deeply disturbing, the cult of the individual leader has arrived, Fascist control has happened. It can be argued that it's a tiny reference to it, but I believe that what Shakespeare is trying to do at the moment is to suggest that these things cannot be *openly* discussed; and why Brutus has to pluck Casca by the sleeve, is because it is no longer possible to go openly up to Casca and say, "Hey, what just happened?" It has to be secret, cloak and dagger. A police state is either in existence or is imminent, everybody is going to report on everybody else. Can Cassius trust Brutus, who after all when the play begins is a chief adviser to the supremo? Can Casca be trusted? Where does Artemidorus get his information from? So I think one *has* to be that graphic in a stage production. On the other hand, we did try very hard to show Caesar's humanity—wherever it exists in the text. Again, it seems to me it's not Shakespeare's primary concern—at the beginning of the play we tried to present a relationship with Antony from the little suggestions of "you and I like plays and Cassius doesn't" or "you and I laugh a lot and Cassius doesn't," but actually there are no opportunities in the play for Caesar to laugh a lot. He's constantly disturbed by soothsayers, by prophecies and by premonitions of one sort or another, he is decidedly unrelaxed, fainting, angry, disputatious.

RB: You worked in too that nice line that Jonson reports, "Caesar did never wrong, but with just cause."

TN: I'm sure that's the original. If one does take that to be the line, it's the ultimate statement of the power-obsessed dictator. Papal infallibility, etc.

RB: I'm glad you replaced that line. It was too good to be taken out just because Jonson laughed at it.

TN: I get the feeling that something like that must have happened.

RB: And *Coriolanus*?

TN: *Coriolanus* really is my favorite play, and I am annoyed that I can't get it as clear and as good in performance as I want it. Here is the example of the mature Shakespeare adopting every possible point of view through his characters, approving of nobody, but rejecting nobody—and so allowing a complex debate to occur.

RB: How did your actors experience the problems of the

Roman plays? How did they react to the text and its difficulties? What did you find to be the major difficulties at the rehearsal stage?

TN: We began in ideal circumstances. We had a four-week period in London with a totally available company, which is rare, a large bare rehearsal room, and no restrictions on the scheduling of rehearsals or undue pressures of time. So we talked and we improvised a great deal. We improvised every single situation in *Coriolanus*, we improvised a lot of *Julius Caesar*, nothing more memorably than the assassination. I only wish I could have recaptured what happened in the rehearsal room when some of the actors were using texts and some of the actors, overwhelmed, were using the only words that occurred to them at the moment.

RB: If I can speak as a member of the audience here, something special unquestionably did come through. What was particularly powerful about the assassination as you staged it was that the emotional effect came after the killing, rather than the event itself. The reactions of the assassins to the deed that they had done was the most powerful stroke of theater.

TN: That's exactly what happened at the improvisation. The incident was quick, many people had no time to move, and some people genuinely thought that some joke was being played. We discovered why it could be possible for the Senate area to be surrounded by guards, yet for none of them to prevent the killing. The four guards were positioned quite close to Caesar. They had been told that their job on which their lives depended was to prevent any harm happening to Caesar at any time, but they still didn't move. We conducted a series of interviews after the event to try to find out from people, as it would be TV reporters trying to find out; what did they feel? What happened? Give us your version. And the guards were agreed that it wasn't their place to go into the middle of the Senate floor. That's where the politicians went, that's where the great speeches were given. Whatever happened there, it was not for them to interfere. But then we also discovered that once the assassination had happened, there was a long, stunned time, when nobody said or felt anything. Then there was pandemonium, which of course is exactly noted in the text. Shakespeare's naturalistic writing amazes me. He is so accurate. In improvisation John Wood desperately required to be able to say to everybody, "stand still," he needed to impose some order or pattern. And then contradictorily, he had the feeling that everybody else must go away, for the double reason that the responsible people must now deal with the immediate aftermath, and if people were going to get hurt it should be himself and his colleagues and not innocent people. In the improvisation it became absolutely clear how different the assassins' attitudes were. Cassius just couldn't stop stabbing at Caesar. That's a much more emotive part of the improvisation process, but since there is more of a personal vendetta between Cassius and Caesar—this was the moment when it really got expressed. Cassius was crazed, frenzied, and Brutus stopped him. In the tent scene Cassius threatens Brutus, with "I may do that I shall be sorry for" and Brutus replies, "You have done that you should be sorry for." That always seemed to us to be a paralyzing moment. Brutus is talking about the assassination, and what Cassius has revealed of his motives. I am not saying that is unarguably the meaning of the line, but in performance it could only mean that one thing to the actors.

RB: These improvisations that you practice are obviously superbly effective at bringing out the inner truth of the lines, the energies of the drama if you like. How did you deal with the more obviously technical problems of the text—I think of matters like verse/prose distinctions, and the like?

TN: In the Royal Shakespeare Company, we're very fortunate in having John Barton, who is a Shakespeare scholar, and who is specially talented in teaching actors and helping actors with difficult texts. Consequently, at the beginning of rehearsals for the Roman plays, we had verse classes and a great deal of Barton-led text work. Our attitude to the text has to vary from play to play, as Shakespeare's language varies from play to play—sometimes our attitude has to vary from scene to scene, because Shakespeare's language varies from scene to scene. We mustn't *generalize*. The modern actor confronted with a complex Shakespearean text generalizes. He tries to suck out its emotional meaning; he re-presents the text with a generalized coloring of the words which he believes will somehow communicate that emotional meaning. And he won't be specific, he won't coin language at the very moment when it is emotionally necessary.

PEGGY GOODMAN ENDEL

Julio Cesar:
The 1986 Florida Shakespeare Festival

Julio Cesar. *An original adaptation of* Julius Caesar, *by John Briggs and R. H. Deschamps. Presented at Vizcaya Museum by the Florida Shakespeare Festival, Miami, 27 February–6 April 1986. Director, John Briggs; Set Design, Kenneth Kurtz; Costumes, Robin Murray; Lighting, David Martin Jacques.* CAST: *Calpurnia, Carol Cadby; Casca, Michael Mauldin; Cassius, Daniel Oreskes; Decius, Barry Mann; Emmanuel Sanchez, John Delaney; Julio Cesar, Cal Winn; Marco Antonio, Roger Pretto; Metellus, Rudolpho Marrocco; Octavius, Tom Ehas; Portia, Marilyn Downey; Santera / Cinna the poet, Claudia Robinson; Trebonius, Joe Gargiulo; Waitresses, Kathleen Brant / Polly Stone.*

Set in the Renaissance gardens of Villa Vizcaya, the Florida Shakespeare Festival burst into full flower in its 1986 season. In a city less combustible, in an atmosphere less heavy with political intrigue, and in a less exotic playing space, the Festival's adaptation of *Julius Caesar*—one of three plays in rotating repertory—might have failed; in Miami, however, *Julio Cesar* was galvanizing political theatre. Although in 1969 the Guthrie Theatre set its production of *Julius Caesar* in South America, the prototype for *Julio Cesar* seems to be Orson Welles's controversial production of 1937, a revival calculated to touch a nerve in an audience perceived as a sensitive political body. Building on the strong, antifascist currents in his New York audiences,

From *Shakespeare Quarterly* 38 (1987): 214–16. Used by permission of the author and of *Shakespeare Quarterly*.

Welles subtitled Shakespeare's play "Death of a Dictator," costumed his actors in Fascist uniforms, and created the longest run in *Julius Caesar*'s American stage history. Like Welles, Guest Director John Briggs and co-adapter Robert Deschamps would maintain that *Julius Caesar* thematizes the relation between the past and the future; consequently, they have approached *Julio Cesar* as a serious exploration of Cassius's open question:

> How many ages hence
> Shall this our lofty scene be acted over
> In states unborn and accents yet unknown!

> (3.1.111–13)

The "lofty scene" to which Cassius refers is, of course, the savage spectacle of Caesar's assassins bathing their hands in their fallen leader's blood. In Miami this spectacle brought the audience to its feet.

Staged in a city whose population includes 850,000 expatriates from Latin America and Cuba, *Julio Cesar* frankly played to anti-Castro sentiment. The adaptation relied on actor Cal Winn's Cesar *qua* Fidel Castro, heavily bearded, in army fatigues, a cigar held characteristically between forefinger and thumb. But the focus of the production was not so much on character as on place. Literally conceived as a state unborn, Shakespeare's Rome became "Corba"—a quasi-mythical, Latin American republic beset by political turmoil in the year 1994.

In the program notes and the slides that preceded Act 1, Briggs embellished his conceit, contriving an intricate plot more Byzantine than Roman; the national debt of Latin America has brought the West to the edge of bankruptcy; in an effort to avert disaster, the debtor nations have elevated the Corban leader Julio Cesar to Supreme Commandante of the Latin American countries; to the north, the United States responds by appointing its first Spanish-American Secretary of State, a right-wing politician named Emmanuel Sanchez; convinced that Cesar and Mark Antony will pack cards with Sanchez and betray Latin American interests to North American policy, Cassius and Brutus conspire Cesar's death.

As a framing device, this scenario interfered little with Shakespeare's text, and signaled the audience that *Julio Cesar* aspired to be more than just another *Julius Caesar* in modern dress.

Immediacy, the dangerous climate of conspiracy, atmosphere, a sense of the uncanny—these were the overarching strengths of a production that explored the idea of "Corba" much as Shakespeare explores the idea of Rome. In 1599, Shakespeare's Elizabethan Romans, costumed in hats, cloaks, and doublets, queried the antique and pagan past about regicide, the efficacy of humanistic ideals, and the limits of natural reason, all issues destined to become palpable fifty years later at the execution of Charles I. The idea of Rome frees Shakespeare to speculate widely on a future that men cannot yet read: in *Julius Caesar* ghosts merely squeak and gibber; and, despite auguries, portents, dreams, and prodigies, men can only construe things after their fashion.

For *Julio Cesar*, Set Designer Kenneth Kurtz magnified this disjunctive relation between past and future with sixty slides projected onto large, blank screens placed at either side of the stage: when the house lights faded, Latin music and the noises of war precede emotion-laden images of the Cuban Revolution, Castro's headquarters, and landmarks of pre-Revolutionary Cuba, all set against discomfiting images and headlines that presaged a future containing the imminent fall of Nicaragua and El Salvador, the eventual collapse and unification of the South American-Caribbean bloc, and, amid global panic, the ultimate triumph of Cesar. The last visual image prior to the beginning of Act 1 was that of the actor representing the newly appointed Secretary of State, a small man dwarfed by the flags projected on either side of him, an orator standing mute behind his rostrum, himself a blank in the glare of white lights.

Conspiracy inhabits the first two acts of *Julius Caesar* as tangibly as any character in the play; because Briggs could depend on his audience linking Miami with vice, particularly vice of a conspiratorial stripe, the early scenes of *Julio Cesar* were among the strongest in the production. At the opening of Act 1, the revellers of Carnaval who spilled over the outdoor stage instantly fell silent before the jackbooted menace of Flavio (Flavius) and Marula (Marullus), militaristic bully boys wielding truncheons. Put to silence themselves, this monstrous pair leaves the play to a brand of conspiracy which, as Brutus says, cloaks its "monstrous visage" in "smiles and affability."

As staged in *Julio Cesar*, the scene in which Cassius draws Casca into the conspiracy to kill Cesar (1.3) might have recurred that same evening at any outdoor café in Miami. Framed by the live oaks in the gardens of Vizcaya, a setting that merged with slide projections of leafy, half-familiar streets, the stage set consisted of ornate lampposts placed at the four corners of the stage and a round table with chairs where Casca sat, an attaché case held across both knees. The scene belonged to Michael Mauldin, an affable Casca with one foot out the door should trouble arise. A civilian among soldiers, costumed in white trousers and jacket, an open-necked shirt, white shoes, and a white fedora, wearing wire-rimmed glasses and with a cigarette dangling from his mouth, this Casca fell exactly midway between nattiness and sleaze.

Everything about this excellent scene was dangerously plausible: the conspirators were at home in a restaurant where the headwaiter evidently knew them and where soft, Latin music played; they greeted each other comfortably with a word or two of Spanish; and they discussed the work in hand almost sociably over a bottle of rum. These men were old acquaintances, powerful associates proceeding out of mixed motives. All might have seemed rather too quotidian were it not for the unseasonable weather that bedeviled *Julio Cesar*: while in repertory, the play seemed to attract every tropical storm of an otherwise balmy winter season, so that lines like Casca's "Who ever knew the heavens menace so?" were accompanied on cue by lightning, winds, and rain driven in from the ocean. Such atmospherics contributed to the overwhelming sense that all was both familiar and strange, that this threatening "Corba" was the South conceived as the Other, and that one had drifted close to the edge of the uncanny.

Any production of *Julius Caesar* must accommodate not only the natural and the unnatural, but the supernatural as

well; in his thoughtful review of the 1983 Shakespeare season at Stratford-on-Avon (*SQ*, 34, 451), Roger Warren observes that although the political concerns of *Julius Caesar*
invite a contemporary treatment, other features of the play,
particularly the belief in auguries, seem to militate against
contemporary staging. *Julio Cesar* brilliantly capitalized on
the very difficulty that Warren observes, chiefly by transla-
ting the Soothsayer of *Julius Caesar* into the Roman augur-
er's regional counterpart, an electrifying Santera.

Coached by local Santeras, Haitian-born actress Claudia
Robinson read the future in coury shells, chanted in Yoruba,
and communed on a ritual mat with objects that were discon-
certingly mundane: a railroad spike, horseshoes, coconut
shells, a lighted cigar, rum, raw meat, paper bags. To com-
pound the sense of foreboding that precedes Caesar's murder,
Briggs intermixed Brutus's taking leave of Portia with
Cesar's taking leave of Calpurnia, and ratified Calpurnia's
fears with the Santera's anguished cries. At either side of the
stage stood two couples engaged in the business of bidding
one another farewell, to the one side Calpurnia pleading with
Cesar, to the other side Brutus arming himself in a bullet-
proof vest; and between them sat a modern-day Caribbean
banshee, gaunt, turbaned, draped in white, grieving over the
doom foretold in her coury shells.

As Cesar's death drew nearer, the Santera became more
agitated, her language more hermetic. She had twice warned
Cesar to beware the Ides of March, first in Spanish, then in
English. When it became apparent that Cesar would disregard all portents and premonitions, she retreated into the re-
cesses of archaic Yoruba, a sealed language that comes as
close as any to accents yet unknown. Accompanied by the
Santera's unearthly invocations to *Elegua*, god of revenge,
Cesar's death was reenacted at the base of an historical piece
of Cuban statuary, a monument fashioned out of sheaves of
sugar cane and beaten copper, and inscribed, *"Independen-
cia, Libertad, Y Paz."* Lest butchery be mistaken for sacrifice, as Cesar fell, the stage turned blood red; darkened
silhouettes encircled Cesar's corpse; and, in slow motion, the
conspirators hacked the body with machetes.

SYLVAN BARNET

Julius Caesar on Stage and Screen

How many ages hence
Shall this our lofty scene be acted over
In states unborn and accents yet unknown!

(3.1.111–13)

Thus speaks Shakespeare's Cassius a moment after he and others assassinate Julius Caesar; and indeed Shakespeare's lofty scene has for four hundred years been acted, often in tongues unknown to him, with only a few noticeable intervals. In the United States, the play was long a safe choice for all new theater groups, probably because at least until recently every schoolchild knew something about Julius Caesar. A version of *Julius Caesar* was among the first televised Shakespeare plays, and when the American Shakespeare Festival opened its new theater at Stratford, Connecticut, in 1955, *Julius Caesar* was its choice. But of course the play has not meant the same thing to every age. For instance, looking at Shakespeare's *Julius Caesar* the late seventeenth century saw a play about a heroic Brutus, the first half of the eighteenth century saw a play celebrating republican liberty, but (to skip to our recent past) the mid-twentieth century saw a play about fascism. For a painstaking discussion of most of the famous productions up to recent times, the reader is advised to consult John Ripley's *"Julius Caesar" on Stage in England and America, 1599–1973.* The following brief essay is deeply indebted to information in Ripley's book.

If the first thing to say is that throughout its history
the play has been almost continuously popular on the stage
(this can be said of only a minority of Shakespeare's plays),
the second thing to say is that it has been ignored by some
of England's most notable actors; Olivier, for example, never
played in it. Doubtless, part of the problem is that Caesar
gets killed in the third act, and though generations of teach-
ers have patiently urged their students to believe that Caesar's spirit dominates the entire play, actors have felt
otherwise. The parts of Brutus and Cassius are substantial,
of course, but the play is named after Caesar. Nevertheless
. . . what leading actor wishes to die before the middle of
the play? Moreover, some actors have seen unusual difficulties in the play. In *Early Stages*, one of his autobiographies,
John Gielgud (who has played Antony, Cassius, and
Caesar—but never Brutus) offers an actor's comment on *Julius Caesar*.

The verse pitched, almost throughout, in a lofty, rhetorical style,
is very tiring and difficult for the actors to sustain without mo-
notony in a large theater. There is little prose to vary it, and it is
difficult for the leading characters to keep continuously alive
against the mass of restless citizens, senators, and soldiers who
must continually revolve and shout around them. There is little
feminine interest to give the play domestic warmth and relaxa-
tion. The classical costumes, though becoming and graceful to
players of fine physique, can be ridiculous and hampering to men
who are too short, too tall, too thin or too fat. There is always a
danger of the effect of a lot of gentlemen sitting on marble
benches in a Turkish bath. There may be something to be said for
experimenting with a production in Elizabethan dress, and yet it
might only be confusing to see a Brutus looking like Guy
Fawkes, or a Caesar crowned with laurel, wearing a beard and
dressed in doublet and hose, thus adding further anachronisms to
those which Shakespeare has already provided in his text. Unlo-
calized scenery—balconies, rostrums, and bare boards—may
serve well enough for Roman streets, the Forum and the senate-
house, but they will hardly serve to conjure up Brutus's orchard,
his tent, and Philippi fields, even though Shakespeare's audiences

may have found no difficulty in so imagining them on the open stage of the Globe three hundred years ago. The play bristles with hazards of all kinds both for actors and directors, even on the stage.

Hazards or not, the play has, we have noted, an almost continuous stage history. The first reference to a performance was by a Swiss visitor to London (see above, page lxiii) in 1599; references to specific performances in the next few decades are scarce, but general allusions to the play make it clear that *Julius Caesar* was popular. In the late seventeenth century, when (after the restoration of Charles II in 1660) several of Shakespeare's plays were drastically adapted to appeal to the new taste, *Julius Caesar* survived virtually unchanged. The evidence for this assertion is a barely modified text of the play (for instance, a few speech prefixes are altered), printed at least six times between 1684 and 1691, which proclaims that it gives the play "as it is now acted at the Theatre Royal." Presumably acting in this virtually uncut text, Thomas Betterton performed the role of Brutus from at least 1684 until 1707. Twentieth-century viewers of the play, used to seeing Brutus portrayed as a stuffed shirt or a muddled idealist, may be surprised to learn that Betterton portrayed him as a philosophic man, in contrast to the passionate Cassius. An eye witness—though one who gave his report years after the fact—spoke of

the unruffled temper of his Brutus. . . . When the Betterton Brutus was provoked in his dispute with Cassius, his spirit flew only to his eye; his steady look alone supplied that terror which he disdained an intemperance in his voice should rise to. Thus, with a settled dignity of contempt, like an unheeding rock he repelled upon himself the foam of Cassius.

The almost unaltered text of 1684 gave way to a somewhat more altered text of the play published in 1719. This text bore the claim that it was *The Tragedy of Julius Caesar: With the Death of Brutus and Cassius; Written Originally by Shakespeare, And since alter'd by Sir William*

Davenant and John Dryden late Poets Laureate. As it is now Acted by His Majesty's Company of Comedians at the Theatre Royal. The attribution to Davenant and Dryden (both of whom were safely dead) is almost certainly false, but the text probably does give us a good idea of how the play was done in the eighteenth century after the first decade or so. The departures from the original (if we contrast them with the massive departures made in *King Lear*) are minor. In keeping with the period's idea of decorum, a few words that seemed absurd for one reason or another were cut, for instance Caesar's boast (2.2.44–48) that he and "Danger" are "two lions littered in one day." Brutus's remark (3.1.171) that his pity for Rome prevented him from feeling pity for the Caesar whom he helped to murder—"As fire drives out fire, so pity pity"—was also deleted, perhaps because it seemed detrimental to Brutus's character. The most substantial cut was that of the horrifying scene (3.3) showing the murder of Cinna the Poet. One other sort of change should be noted: a few lines were added, for instance four lines in which Brutus reflects on his first interview with the Ghost, a bit of dialogue between Brutus and the Ghost at Philippi (added because Shakespeare's Ghost promises to appear again at Philippi but doesn't), and in Brutus's dying speech some lines emphasizing Brutus's patriotism.

This version, or something very close to it, was staged in London almost every year in the second quarter of the eighteenth century; in the second half of the century performances of *Julius Caesar* were fewer, partly because David Garrick, the greatest actor of the period, never chose to do the play. It is probably fair to say, however, that throughout the eighteenth century *Julius Caesar* was regarded as a patriotic play showing the heroic Brutus nobly opposing the tyrannical Caesar. In the early nineteenth century John Philip Kemble continued along the same line. Because of this emphasis, Kemble omitted these world-weary lines that Brutus utters near the end of the play:

> So fare you well at once, for Brutus' tongue
> Hath almost ended his life's history.

Night hangs upon mine eyes; my bones would rest,
That have but labored to attain this hour.   (5.5.39–42)

Instead, Kemble adopted the passage that had been added in the 1719 version attributed to Davenant and Dryden, and he made some further alterations. The effect was to heighten the patriotic note:

This was the justest cause that ever men
Did draw with swords for; and the gods renounce it.
Disdaining life, to live a slave in Rome,
Thus Brutus strikes his last—for liberty!
Farewell,
Beloved country!—Caesar, now be still;
I killed not thee with half so good a will.

Abundant evidence indicates that Kemble depicted Brutus not as a self-deceived figure but as a noble stoic. Only in 4.3., when Brutus tells Cassius of the death of Portia, did he seem to have the weaknesses of other mortals. A stoic hero suited Kemble's style of acting which was what today we would call highly formal. "Statuesque" is a word often used to describe Kemble's style. The Roman grandeur of the style was supplemented by classical costume and an attention to grand pictorial effects, gained, for instance, by the use of masses of supernumeraries who set off the major figures. Ludwig Tieck, however, who attended a performance in 1817, saw in the formality not high seriousness but a "pretentious solemnity" that disguised the butchery of the assassination. Kemble's style, which of course also implies his interpretation of the role, dominated the interpretation both in England and in the United States until William Macready, playing Brutus in 1838, introduced a more intimate or (to use the word of a contemporary commentator) "amiable" note. The underlying idea now was that Shakespeare's Romans were not simply classical heroes but were also endowed with the strengths and weaknesses of all mortals. The assassination scene now was not the solemn ritual that Brutus intends, but the scene of shocking violence that it in fact becomes.

Macready kept experimenting with the role from 1838 to 1851, but always in the direction of emphasizing Brutus's humanity.

Other actors, of course, also performed the role in the nineteenth century, notably Edwin Booth in the United States, and Samuel Phelps and (at the very end of the century) Herbert Beerbohm Tree in England. Edward Booth inherited the role from his father, Junius Booth, who had performed it in the 1830s. In 1864, a year before Lincoln was assassinated, three Booths—Junius, Edwin, and Edwin's brother John Wilkes—performed in *Julius Caesar*, taking the roles, respectively, of Brutus, Cassius, and Antony. Edwin Booth's productions were known for their historical accuracy and also for the splendor of the scenery and costumes, but since the period of Julius Caesar—and age of the Roman Republic—seemed a bit drab, Booth followed Kemble in setting it later, in the more opulent Augustan period of Imperial Rome. Thus, instead of white buildings, he showed buildings of tawny marble, with crimson columns and colored friezes. For a text, he relied chiefly on Kemble's version, which cut some two hundred lines from the play, but he did not use the lines Kemble had added to the play. And in his interpretation of the role he apparently conveyed not only Kemble's heroism but a sense of psychological complexity (even a deep love for Portia) associated less with Kemble than with Macready.

Although *Julius Caesar* had been popular during the first two-thirds of the nineteenth century, when Herbert Beerbohm Tree staged it in London in 1898 it had not been done there (except occasionally by a touring company) for more than thirty years. Tree's highly successful production, often repeated during the next eighteen years, was influenced by a visit that the Saxe-Meiningen company had made to London in 1881. The Meiningen Players, a German company formed by the Duke of Saxe-Meiningen, were renowned for their emphasis on the relationship between the setting and the actors. For instance, they performed not on a uniformly flat platform but divided the surface of the stage floor into different levels and deployed the actors meaningfully on these levels. The company was also known for its handling of crowd scenes, so that the crowd in effect became another personage in the drama. (In fact, Macready had earlier achieved fame for his handling—orchestration, we might say—of the crowd in the forum scene.) Antony, the patrician who is attuned to the crowd, was the star in the Meiningen production, and Beerbohm Tree played this role in his production. A letter to his wife is revealing: "I like Brutus best—and he is so much deeper—but I still feel Antony has the color—the glamor of the play." Tree made the role more sympathetic by cutting the proscription scene (4.1.) in which Antony, Lepidus, and Octavius lightly consent to executing various enemies, and in which, after Lepidus departs, Antony speaks scornfully of Lepidus. Although *Julius Caesar* is short enough to be staged uncut, because Antony's role is not especially prominent after the forum scene, Tree made heavy cuts in lines spoken by others in the second half of the play. He cut, for instance, the whole of Cassius's birthday speech in 5.1. 70–88. Tree performed the play in three acts, which John Ripley says might well have been called "Antony Introduced, Antony Contriving, and Antony Triumphant." The sets (Republican Rome, with some picturesque touches of Imperial Rome) and costumes were designed by Sir Lawrence Alma-Tadema, who gave Antony a splendid scarlet toga, steel helmet, and plume for the final act. The romantic portrayal of Antony established by Tree—more precisely, established by the Meiningen players—was continued by F. R. Benson, who, like Tree, played a dashing Antony and cut the discreditable proscription scene. Benson had, in fact, played Antony as early as 1890, that is, even before Tree did, and he continued to play the role until 1933 when he was seventy-five.

Tree and Benson worked well into the twentieth century, but their productions, with their splendid pictorial sets, are unmistakably of the nineteenth. What of productions born in the twentieth century? We can glance at some relatively recent productions in modern dress in England and in the United States, then will go back to Orson Welles's immensely influential New York production of 1937, and

at last will end with a look at a Hollywood film made in
1953.

In 1963 John Blatchley produced the play with the Royal
Shakespeare Company, at Stratford-upon-Avon. Stratford in
the sixties, reacting against "museum theater," was much
taken with the ideas of Artaud, Beckett, and Brecht, which
means that the directors strongly imposed rather dark ideas
on the production. Earlier interpretations had seen nobility
and heroism and sometimes even warm humanity in Brutus;
Blatchley's Brutus, played by Tom Fleming, was physically
unprepossessing, and although this Brutus meant well he had
little idea of what was happening. Antony's sensuality was
evident, but reviewers found him unappealing. The set, regarded by many as equally unappealing, consisted of a ramp,
some staircases, and a cloth for Brutus's tent. The costumes
combined World War I uniforms with motorcycle togs and
togas, chiefly grays, browns, and blacks.

The play is a tragedy, of course, but it has long been seen
as a political play. At least as early as the late eighteenth
century it was regarded as a display of Brutus's libertarian
patriotism. That is, the tragedy was given a political interpretation that was seen as relevant to the audience. In 1770, for
example, a group called the American Company performed
the play in Philadelphia, saying that it showed "the noble
struggles for Liberty by that renowned patriot Marcus Brutus." The political elements in the play lend themselves to
those who wish to make statements about democracy and
about political assassination. Three essays reprinted in this
volume bring up the question of the political implications in
the play—the two essays by Ralph Berry and by Richard David on Trevor Nunn's Royal Shakespeare Company's production of 1972, and the essay by Peggy Goodman Endel on
Julio Cesar, in Miami in 1986. But here we can add that not
all spectators who saw Trevor Nunn's production agreed on
what they saw. Richard David found Caesar moderately sympathetic, but Peter Thomson (in a review in *Shakespeare Survey* [26]) reported that Caesar's appearance was "cold and
cruel," and that "there was nothing attractive about this Caesar, except perhaps to the National Front." Thomson also ob-

served that this "Caesar's Rome was a police state, with black-armored soldiers to enforce the law" (page 145).

A production at Stratford, Connecticut, in 1979 somewhat similarly used modern dress in order to emphasize the political (and supposedly contemporary) aspects of the tragedy: Caesar was a Latin American dictator in the uniform of a general; Flavius and Marullus wore trench coats; soldiers wore fatigues and fought with guns (which made one wonder why in this play people committed suicide with swords). In a 1982 production at Ashland, Oregon, a roll of barbed wire was suspended across the rear of the stage; Arab and military gear suggested the contemporary Near East. The director, Jerry Turner, said he was influenced by the assassination of Egyptian President Sadat. Brutus was depicted as a serious but muddleheaded professor, Casca was a female revolutionary, and the Soothsayer—always a problem in productions set in modern times—was a bag lady. For at least one reviewer, this effort to make the play familiar served also to make it small, something routine rather than awesome. For a 1986 anti-Castro version, see the essay by Peggy Goodman Endel on page 201.

The father of modern political interpretations of the play was the production by John Houseman and Orson Welles in New York in 1937, with Welles (then twenty-two years old) as Brutus. (Strictly speaking, Houseman and Welles had been anticipated by a modern-dress production at the Delaware Federal Theater in 1937, but the Delaware production did not attract the attention that Houseman and Welles received.) The set showed neither Republican Rome nor Augustan Rome; rather, the blood-red brick back wall of the Mercury Theatre, fire extinguishers and steam pipes and all, was the backdrop. The main playing area, the apron fourteen feet deep, rose gently to meet a set of shallow steps that ran the full width of the stage. The steps led to an eight-foot plateau, and the stage then rose again with another set of steps. Thus, this bare stage was not at all as simple as it looked, for it offered a variety of playing areas. (Houseman describes the stage in detail in *Run-through: A Memoir*.) Without scenery to change, the play moved rapidly; columns of light illuminated a playing space, then faded out and were replaced by

others. The players wore modern dress (Caesar—played by
an actor who strongly resembled Mussolini—wore a military
tunic and breeches, Brutus a double-breasted pin-stripe suit),
and there was a good deal of striding about and of saluting
with uplifted right arms. Welles claimed that the bare stage
and the contemporary costumes were in keeping with Elizabethan methods, but obviously his concern was to emphasize
the contemporary (1930s) aspects of the play.

Welles's *Julius Caesar* ran for an hour and forty-nine min-
utes, without an intermission. It was fairly heavily cut—no
ghost of Caesar, no proscription scene, almost no Octavius,
and almost no battle, for instance—but one scene (3.3) that
for two centuries had been absent from most productions was
restored: the murder of the luckless Cinna the Poet, which
Time said (November 22, 1937) became "a minor tragedy."
Cinna, pathetic in his innocent protestations, caught in a ring
of light, finds himself surrounded by hoods; the crowd closes
in, the ring of light diminishes, and suddenly there is black-
ness. (For a photograph, see John Ripley's *"Julius Caesar"
on Stage*, page 229. For Houseman's discussion of the scene,
which in the early rehearsals seemed so unsuccessful that it
was almost dropped, see *Run-through*, pages 310–12.) *Time*
also found other aspects of the production impressive:

Lighting sets the mood and changes the scene. Notable effects:
the giant backwall shadow of Antony, speaking over Caesar's
body; a cross-hatching of light and shadow high up in the loft,
unintentionally giving the impression of crossed fasces; the climax, patterned after *Life*'s pictures of last summer's Nazi Congress at Nürnberg, vertical shafts of light stabbing up through the
darkness as background for the eulogy of the noblest Roman of
them all.

Subtitled *Death of a Dictator*, this production was widely
regarded as antifascist—witness the reference in *Time* to
the Nürnberg rallies. But Welles said the play was not antifascist; it was, he said, about Brutus. Brutus, he informed
the theatergoer (in a statement reprinted in Ripley, page
223), is

the classical picture of the eternal, impotent, ineffectual, fumbling liberal; the reformer who wants to do something about things but doesn't know how and gets it in the neck in the end. He's dead right all the time, and dead at the final curtain. He's Shakespeare's favorite hero—the fellow who thinks the times are out of joint but who is really out of joint with his time. He's the bourgeois intellectual, who, under a modern dictatorship, would be the first to be put up against the wall and shot.

In a newspaper interview Welles referred to the mob as "the hoodlum element you find in any big city after a war." It is this hoodlum element, not any fascistic ideal, that tears apart Cinna the Poet, and so, though Welles and Houseman related the play to current events in Europe, the production scarcely made a coherent political statement about fascism.

This production, the most revolutionary and the most discussed version of our century, came close to being not so much a staging of Shakespeare's play as an independent work. Perhaps we should end, then, with a brief comment on a more traditional version, the 1953 MGM film produced by John Houseman and directed by Joseph Mankiewicz, with Louis Calhern (Caesar), James Mason (Brutus), John Gielgud (Cassius), and Marlon Brando (Marc Antony). Houseman, we have noticed, had already had some experience with Shakespeare; in addition to having been codirector of *Julius Caesar* in New York with Welles, he had directed *King Lear* on Broadway. Houseman in *Films in Review*, April 1953, and again in an autobiography entitled *Front and Center*, mentions that his conception of the play owes something to newsreels showing political figures signing pacts and making speeches, especially Hitler at Nürenberg—again, a *Julius Caesar* for our day—but the idea is not pressed, and the film is fairly true to the text.

If not precisely exciting, it nevertheless is a highly competent film. (In *Front and Center*, Houseman discusses some of the problems of turning Shakespeare's play into a film.) Movie buffs appreciate the fact that this is no mere filmed production of the play; it is a highly cinematic work, one that shows affinities with such films as *Double Indem-*

nity and *The Asphalt Jungle*, that is, with the *film noir* of the 1940s and fifties, films emphasizing urban corruption. Furthermore, the film was shot (like *film noir*) in black and white—not, however, to save money but because Mankiewicz and Houseman saw the story as something intense, even gritty, to be told without the allure of color. The litter in the streets, the graffiti on the walls, and the menacing nighttime imagery of *film noir* appear here too, for instance in the scene in which Casca—played by Edmond O'Brien, who usually played detectives or crooked lawyers—encounters Cassius (1.3.) in the public square as a storm gathers. With its shots of dark alleys and rickety tenements, this was a Rome never before thought of as part of *Julius Caesar*. Possibly Calhern's performance as Caesar was overly indebted to *film noir*, in which he had played cultivated crooks, for instance a dishonest lawyer in *The Asphalt Jungle*. In any case, some viewers found his Caesar suave rather than dangerous—but most viewers found his performance impressive, and there is general agreement that Mason (Brutus) and Gielgud (Cassius) were excellent. Gielgud had already played (under Anthony Quayle's direction) a bitter, vehement Cassius at Stratford-upon-Avon in 1950, and he now repeated his performance. Brando's Marc Antony is more controversial; his appearance was appropriately athletic and voluptuous, but his delivery of the lines (despite abundant coaching from Gielgud) left something to be desired.

The text for this film is fairly complete, but some cuts were made, notably the scene with Cinna the Poet, and the final speech of Octavius. (The scene with Cinna was filmed, but it appeared anticlimactic after the powerful forum scene, and so it was dropped.) The battle scenes near the end were reduced to a paltry ambush in a ravine. Houseman explains, in *Front and Center*, that although in the stage production Welles had omitted the battles and no one had noticed, the film audience would expect a good battle, possibly in the tradition of Olivier's *Henry V*. The budget, however, prohibited anything more than a perfunctory battle. The result was a battle that, although infinitely beyond what an Elizabethan audience could hope for, was vastly disappointing to a movie audience. In other respects, however, the film is impressive.

It is good to have so strong a version captured on film, but of course the film version does not make subsequent performances superfluous. The "lofty scene"—the assassination of Caesar—that Cassius speaks of continues to be acted around the world; that Caesar so often bleeds is a sign that the play is healthy.

Bibliographical Note: In addition to the works cited within this essay, consult *Shakespeare Quarterly* and *Shakespeare Studies* for reviews of contemporary productions. For briefer comments on the play in production, see the books listed in Section 4, Shakespeare on Stage and Screen, in the Suggested References, page 220.

Suggested References

The number of possible references is vast and grows alarmingly. (The *Shakespeare Quarterly* devotes one issue each year to a list of the previous year's work, and *Shakespeare Survey*—an annual publication—includes a substantial review of biographical, critical, and textual studies, as well as a survey of performances.) The vast bibliography is best approached through James Harner, *The World Shakespeare Bibliography on CD-Rom: 1900–Present.* The first release, in 1996, included more than 12,000 annotated items from 1990–93, plus references to several thousand book reviews, productions, films, and audio recordings. The plan is to update the publication annually, moving forward one year and backward three years. Thus, the second issue (1997), with 24,700 entries, and another 35,000 or so references to reviews, newspaper pieces, and so on, covered 1987–94.

Though no works are indispensable, those listed below have been found especially helpful. The arrangement is as follows:

1. Shakespeare's Times
2. Shakespeare's Life
3. Shakespeare's Theater
4. Shakespeare on Stage and Screen
5. Miscellaneous Reference Works
6. Shakespeare's Plays: General Studies
7. The Comedies
8. The Romances
9. The Tragedies
10. The Histories
11. *Julius Caesar*

The titles in the first five sections are accompanied by brief explanatory annotations.

1. Shakespeare's Times

Andrews, John F., ed. *William Shakespeare: His World, His Work, His Influence,* 3 vols. (1985). Sixty articles, dealing not only with such subjects as "The State," "The Church," "Law," "Science, Magic, and Folklore," but also with the plays and poems themselves and Shakespeare's influence (e.g., translations, films, reputation)

Byrne, Muriel St. Clare. *Elizabethan Life in Town and Country* (8th ed., 1970). Chapters on manners, beliefs, education, etc., with illustrations.

Dollimore, John, and Alan Sinfield, eds. *Political Shakespeare: New Essays in Cultural Materialism* (1985). Essays on such topics as the subordination of women and colonialism, presented in connection with some of Shakespeare's plays.

Greenblatt, Stephen. *Representing the English Renaissance* (1988). New Historicist essays, especially on connections between political and aesthetic matters, statecraft and stagecraft.

Joseph, B. L. *Shakespeare's Eden: the Commonwealth of England 1558–1629* (1971). An account of the social, political, economic, and cultural life of England.

Kernan, Alvin. *Shakespeare, the King's Playwright: Theater in the Stuart Court 1603–1613* (1995). The social setting and the politics of the court of James I, in relation to *Hamlet, Measure for Measure, Macbeth, King Lear, Antony and Cleopatra, Coriolanus,* and *The Tempest.*

Montrose, Louis. *The Purpose of Playing: Shakespeare and the Cultural Politics of the Elizabethan Theatre* (1996). A poststructuralist view, discussing the professional theater "within the ideological and material frameworks of Elizabethan culture and society," with an extended analysis of *A Midsummer Night's Dream.*

Mullaney, Steven. *The Place of the Stage: License, Play, and Power in Renaissance England* (1988). New Historicist analysis, arguing that popular drama became a cultural institution "only by . . . taking up a place on the margins of society."

Schoenbaum, S. *Shakespeare: The Globe and the World*

(1979). A readable, abundantly illustrated introductory book on the world of the Elizabethans.

Shakespeare's England, 2 vols. (1916). A large collection of scholarly essays on a wide variety of topics, e.g., astrology, costume, gardening, horsemanship, with special attention to Shakespeare's references to these topics.

2. Shakespeare's Life

Andrews, John F., ed. *William Shakespeare: His World, His Work, His Influence,* 3 vols. (1985). See the description above.

Bentley, Gerald E. *Shakespeare: A Biographical Handbook* (1961). The facts about Shakespeare, with virtually no conjecture intermingled.

Chambers, E. K. *William Shakespeare: A Study of Facts and Problems,* 2 vols. (1930). The fullest collection of data.

Fraser, Russell. *Young Shakespeare* (1988). A highly readable account that simultaneously considers Shakespeare's life and Shakespeare's art.

———. *Shakespeare: The Later Years* (1992).

Schoenbaum, S. *Shakespeare's Lives* (1970). A review of the evidence and an examination of many biographies, including those of Baconians and other heretics.

———. *William Shakespeare: A Compact Documentary Life* (1977). An abbreviated version, in a smaller format, of the next title. The compact version reproduces some fifty documents in reduced form. A readable presentation of all that the documents tell us about Shakespeare.

———. *William Shakespeare: A Documentary Life* (1975). A large-format book setting forth the biography with facsimiles of more than two hundred documents, and with transcriptions and commentaries.

3. Shakespeare's Theater

Astington, John H., ed. *The Development of Shakespeare's Theater* (1992). Eight specialized essays on theatrical companies, playing spaces, and performance.

Beckerman, Bernard. *Shakespeare at the Globe, 1599–1609* (1962). On the playhouse and on Elizabethan dramaturgy, acting, and staging.

Bentley, Gerald E. *The Profession of Dramatist in Shakespeare's Time* (1971). An account of the dramatist's status in the Elizabethan period.

———. *The Profession of Player in Shakespeare's Time, 1590–1642* (1984). An account of the status of members of London companies (sharers, hired men, apprentices, managers) and a discussion of conditions when they toured.

Berry, Herbert. *Shakespeare's Playhouses* (1987). Usefully emphasizes how little we know about the construction of Elizabethan theaters.

Brown, John Russell. *Shakespeare's Plays in Performance* (1966). A speculative and practical analysis relevant to all of the plays, but with emphasis on *The Merchant of Venice*, *Richard II*, *Hamlet*, *Romeo and Juliet*, and *Twelfth Night*.

———. *William Shakespeare: Writing for Performance* (1996). A discussion aimed at helping readers to develop theatrically conscious habits of reading.

Chambers, E. K. *The Elizabethan Stage*, 4 vols. (1945). A major reference work on theaters, theatrical companies, and staging at court.

Cook, Ann Jennalie. *The Privileged Playgoers of Shakespeare's London, 1576–1642* (1981). Sees Shakespeare's audience as wealthier, more middle-class, and more intellectual than Harbage (below) does.

Dessen, Alan C. *Elizabethan Drama and the Viewer's Eye* (1977). On how certain scenes may have looked to spectators in an Elizabethan theater.

Gurr, Andrew. *Playgoing in Shakespeare's London* (1987). Something of a middle ground between Cook (above) and Harbage (below).

———. *The Shakespearean Stage, 1579–1642* (2nd ed., 1980). On the acting companies, the actors, the playhouses, the stages, and the audiences.

Harbage, Alfred. *Shakespeare's Audience* (1941). A study of the size and nature of the theatrical public, emphasizing the representativeness of its working class and middle-class audience.

Hodges, C. Walter. *The Globe Restored* (1968). A conjectural restoration, with lucid drawings.

Hosley, Richard. "The Playhouses," in *The Revels History of Drama in English*, vol. 3, general editors Clifford Leech and T. W. Craik (1975). An essay of a hundred pages on the physical aspects of the playhouses.

Howard, Jane E. "Crossdressing, the Theatre, and Gender Struggle in Early Modern England," *Shakespeare Quarterly* 39 (1988): 418–40. Judicious comments on the effects of boys playing female roles.

Orrell, John. *The Human Stage: English Theatre Design, 1567–1640* (1988). Argues that the public, private, and court playhouses are less indebted to popular structures (e.g., innyards and bear-baiting pits) than to banqueting halls and to Renaissance conceptions of Roman amphitheaters.

Slater, Ann Pasternak. *Shakespeare the Director* (1982). An analysis of theatrical effects (e.g., kissing, kneeling) in stage directions and dialogue.

Styan, J. L. *Shakespeare's Stagecraft* (1967). An introduction to Shakespeare's visual and aural stagecraft, with chapters on such topics as acting conventions, stage groupings, and speech.

Thompson, Peter. *Shakespeare's Professional Career* (1992). An examination of patronage and related theatrical conditions.

———. *Shakespeare's Theatre* (1983). A discussion of how plays were staged in Shakespeare's time.

4. Shakespeare on Stage and Screen

Bate, Jonathan, and Russell Jackson, eds. *Shakespeare: An Illustrated Stage History* (1996). Highly readable essays on stage productions from the Renaissance to the present.

Berry, Ralph. *Changing Styles in Shakespeare* (1981). Discusses productions of six plays (*Coriolanus, Hamlet,*

Henry V, Measure for Measure, The Tempest, and *Twelfth Night*) on the English stage, chiefly 1950–1980.

―――. *On Directing Shakespeare: Interviews with Contemporary Directors* (1989). An enlarged edition of a book first published in 1977, this version includes the seven interviews from the early 1970s and adds five interviews conducted in 1988.

Brockbank, Philip, ed. *Players of Shakespeare: Essays in Shakespearean Performance* (1985). Comments by twelve actors, reporting their experiences with roles. See also the entry for Russell Jackson (below).

Bulman, J. C., and H. R. Coursen, eds. *Shakespeare on Television* (1988). An anthology of general and theoretical essays, essays on individual productions, and shorter reviews, with a bibliography and a videography listing cassettes that may be rented.

Coursen, H. P. *Watching Shakespeare on Television* (1993). Analyses not only of TV versions but also of films and videotapes of stage presentations that are shown on television.

Davies, Anthony, and Stanley Wells, eds. *Shakespeare and the Moving Image: The Plays on Film and Television* (1994). General essays (e.g., on the comedies) as well as essays devoted entirely to *Hamlet, King Lear,* and *Macbeth*.

Dawson, Anthony B. *Watching Shakespeare: A Playgoer's Guide* (1988). About half of the plays are discussed, chiefly in terms of decisions that actors and directors make in putting the works onto the stage.

Dessen, Alan. *Elizabethan Stage Conventions and Modern Interpretations* (1984). On interpreting conventions such as the representation of light and darkness and stage violence (duels, battles).

Donaldson, Peter. *Shakespearean Films/Shakespearean Directors* (1990). Postmodernist analyses, drawing on Freudianism, Feminism, Deconstruction, and Queer Theory.

Jackson, Russell, and Robert Smallwood, eds. *Players of Shakespeare 2: Further Essays in Shakespearean Performance by Players with the Royal Shakespeare Company*

(1988). Fourteen actors discuss their roles in productions between 1982 and 1987.

———. *Players of Shakespeare 3: Further Essays in Shakespearean Performance by Players with the Royal Shakespeare Company* (1993). Comments by thirteen performers.

Jorgens, Jack. *Shakespeare on Film* (1977). Fairly detailed studies of eighteen films, preceded by an introductory chapter addressing such issues as music, and whether to "open" the play by including scenes of landscape.

Kennedy, Dennis. *Looking at Shakespeare: A Visual History of Twentieth-Century Performance* (1993). Lucid descriptions (with 170 photographs) of European, British, and American performances.

Leiter, Samuel L. *Shakespeare Around the Globe: A Guide to Notable Postwar Revivals* (1986). For each play there are about two pages of introductory comments, then discussions (about five hundred words per production) of ten or so productions, and finally bibliographic references.

McMurty, Jo. *Shakespeare Films in the Classroom* (1994). Useful evaluations of the chief films most likely to be shown in undergraduate courses.

Rothwell, Kenneth, and Annabelle Henkin Melzer. *Shakespeare on Screen: An International Filmography and Videography* (1990). A reference guide to several hundred films and videos produced between 1899 and 1989, including spinoffs such as musicals and dance versions.

Sprague, Arthur Colby. *Shakespeare and the Actors* (1944). Detailed discussions of stage business (gestures, etc.) over the years.

Willis, Susan. *The BBC Shakespeare Plays: Making the Televised Canon* (1991). A history of the series, with interviews and production diaries for some plays.

5. Miscellaneous Reference Works

Abbott, E. A. *A Shakespearean Grammar* (new edition, 1877). An examination of differences between Elizabethan and modern grammar.

Allen, Michael J. B., and Kenneth Muir, eds. *Shakespeare's Plays in Quarto* (1981). One volume containing facsimiles of the plays issued in small format before they were collected in the First Folio of 1623.

Bevington, David. *Shakespeare* (1978). A short guide to hundreds of important writings on the subject.

Blake, Norman. *Shakespeare's Language: An Introduction* (1983). On vocabulary, parts of speech, and word order.

Bullough, Geoffrey. *Narrative and Dramatic Sources of Shakespeare*, 8 vols. (1957–75). A collection of many of the books Shakespeare drew on, with judicious comments.

Campbell, Oscar James, and Edward G. Quinn, eds. *The Reader's Encyclopedia of Shakespeare* (1966). Old, but still the most useful single reference work on Shakespeare.

Cercignani, Fausto. *Shakespeare's Works and Elizabethan Pronunciation* (1981). Considered the best work on the topic, but remains controversial.

Dent, R. W. *Shakespeare's Proverbial Language: An Index* (1981). An index of proverbs, with an introduction concerning a form Shakespeare frequently drew on.

Greg, W. W. *The Shakespeare First Folio* (1955). A detailed yet readable history of the first collection (1623) of Shakespeare's plays.

Harner, James. *The World Shakespeare Bibliography*. See headnote to Suggested References.

Hosley, Richard. *Shakespeare's Holinshed* (1968). Valuable presentation of one of Shakespeare's major sources.

Kökeritz, Helge. *Shakespeare's Names* (1959). A guide to pronouncing some 1,800 names appearing in Shakespeare.

———. *Shakespeare's Pronunciation* (1953). Contains much information about puns and rhymes, but see Cercignani (above).

Muir, Kenneth. *The Sources of Shakespeare's Plays* (1978). An account of Shakespeare's use of his reading. It covers all the plays, in chronological order.

Miriam Joseph, Sister. *Shakespeare's Use of the Arts of Language* (1947). A study of Shakespeare's use of rhetorical devices, reprinted in part as *Rhetoric in Shakespeare's Time* (1962).

The Norton Facsimile: The First Folio of Shakespeare's

Plays (1968). A handsome and accurate facsimile of the first collection (1623) of Shakespeare's plays, with a valuable introduction by Charlton Hinman.

Onions, C. T. *A Shakespeare Glossary*, rev. and enlarged by R. D. Eagleson (1986). Definitions of words (or senses of words) now obsolete.

Partridge, Eric. *Shakespeare's Bawdy*, rev. ed. (1955). Relatively brief dictionary of bawdy words; useful, but see Williams, below.

Shakespeare Quarterly. See headnote to Suggested References.

Shakespeare Survey. See headnote to Suggested References.

Spevack, Marvin. *The Harvard Concordance to Shakespeare* (1973). An index to Shakespeare's words.

Vickers, Brian. *Appropriating Shakespeare: Contemporary Critical Quarrels* (1993). A survey—chiefly hostile—of recent schools of criticism.

Wells, Stanley, ed. *Shakespeare: A Bibliographical Guide* (new edition, 1990). Nineteen chapters (some devoted to single plays, others devoted to groups of related plays) on recent scholarship on the life and all of the works.

Williams, Gordon. *A Dictionary of Sexual Language and Imagery in Shakespearean and Stuart Literature*, 3 vols. (1994). Extended discussions of words and passages; much fuller than Partridge, cited above.

6. Shakespeare's Plays: General Studies

Bamber, Linda. *Comic Women, Tragic Men: A Study of Gender and Genre in Shakespeare* (1982).

Barnet, Sylvan. *A Short Guide to Shakespeare* (1974).

Callaghan, Dympna, Lorraine Helms, and Jyotsna Singh. *The Weyward Sisters: Shakespeare and Feminist Politics* (1994).

Clemen, Wolfgang H. *The Development of Shakespeare's Imagery* (1951).

Cook, Ann Jennalie. *Making a Match: Courtship in Shakespeare and His Society* (1991).

Dollimore, Jonathan, and Alan Sinfield. *Political Shake-speare: New Essays in Cultural Materialism* (1985).

Dusinberre, Juliet. *Shakespeare and the Nature of Women* (1975).

Granville-Barker, Harley. *Prefaces to Shakespeare*, 2 vols. (1946–47; volume 1 contains essays on *Hamlet, King Lear, Merchant of Venice, Antony and Cleopatra,* and *Cymbeline*; volume 2 contains essays on *Othello, Coriolanus, Julius Caesar, Romeo and Juliet, Love's Labor's Lost*).

———. *More Prefaces to Shakespeare* (1974; essays on *Twelfth Night, A Midsummer Night's Dream, The Winter's Tale, Macbeth*).

Harbage, Alfred. *William Shakespeare: A Reader's Guide* (1963).

Howard, Jean E. *Shakespeare's Art of Orchestration: Stage Technique and Audience Response* (1984).

Jones, Emrys. *Scenic Form in Shakespeare* (1971).

Lenz, Carolyn Ruth Swift, Gayle Greene, and Carol Thomas Neely, eds. *The Woman's Part: Feminist Criticism of Shakespeare* (1980).

Novy, Marianne. *Love's Argument: Gender Relations in Shakespeare* (1984).

Rose, Mark. *Shakespearean Design* (1972).

Scragg, Leah. *Discovering Shakespeare's Meaning* (1994).

———. *Shakespeare's "Mouldy Tales": Recurrent Plot Motifs in Shakespearean Drama* (1992).

Traub, Valerie. *Desire and Anxiety: Circulations of Sexuality in Shakespearean Drama* (1992).

Traversi, D. A. *An Approach to Shakespeare,* 2 vols. (3rd rev. ed, 1968–69).

Vickers, Brian. *The Artistry of Shakespeare's Prose* (1968).

Wells, Stanley. *Shakespeare: A Dramatic Life* (1994).

Wright, George T. *Shakespeare's Metrical Art* (1988).

7. The Comedies

Barber, C. L. *Shakespeare's Festive Comedy* (1959; discusses *Love's Labor's Lost, A Midsummer Night's Dream, The Merchant of Venice, As You Like It, Twelfth Night*).

Barton, Anne. *The Names of Comedy* (1990).

Berry, Ralph. *Shakespeare's Comedy: Explorations in Form* (1972).

Bradbury, Malcolm, and David Palmer, eds. *Shakespearean Comedy* (1972).

Bryant, J. A., Jr. *Shakespeare and the Uses of Comedy* (1986).

Carroll, William. *The Metamorphoses of Shakespearean Comedy* (1985).

Champion, Larry S. *The Evolution of Shakespeare's Comedy* (1970).

Evans, Bertrand. *Shakespeare's Comedies* (1960).

Frye, Northrop. *Shakespearean Comedy and Romance* (1965).

Leggatt, Alexander. *Shakespeare's Comedy of Love* (1974).

Miola, Robert S. *Shakespeare and Classical Comedy: The Influence of Plautus and Terence* (1994).

Nevo, Ruth. *Comic Transformations in Shakespeare* (1980).

Ornstein, Robert. *Shakespeare's Comedies: From Roman Farce to Romantic Mystery* (1986).

Richman, David. *Laughter, Pain, and Wonder: Shakespeare's Comedies and the Audience in the Theater* (1990).

Salingar, Leo. *Shakespeare and the Traditions of Comedy* (1974).

Slights, Camille Wells. *Shakespeare's Comic Commonwealths* (1993).

Waller, Gary, ed. *Shakespeare's Comedies* (1991).

Westlund, Joseph. *Shakespeare's Reparative Comedies: A Psychoanalytic View of the Middle Plays* (1984).

Williamson, Marilyn. *The Patriarchy of Shakespeare's Comedies* (1986).

8. The Romances (*Pericles, Cymbeline, The Winter's Tale, The Tempest, The Two Noble Kinsmen*)

Adams, Robert M. *Shakespeare: The Four Romances* (1989).

Felperin, Howard. *Shakespearean Romance* (1972).

Frye, Northrop. *A Natural Perspective: The Development of Shakespearean Comedy and Romance* (1965).

Mowat, Barbara. *The Dramaturgy of Shakespeare's Romances* (1976).

Warren, Roger. *Staging Shakespeare's Late Plays* (1990).

Young, David. *The Heart's Forest: A Study of Shakespeare's Pastoral Plays* (1972).

9. The Tragedies

Bradley, A. C. *Shakespearean Tragedy* (1904).

Brooke, Nicholas. *Shakespeare's Early Tragedies* (1968).

Champion, Larry. *Shakespeare's Tragic Perspective* (1976).

Drakakis, John, ed. *Shakespearean Tragedy* (1992).

Evans, Bertrand. *Shakespeare's Tragic Practice* (1979).

Everett, Barbara. *Young Hamlet: Essays on Shakespeare's Tragedies* (1989).

Foakes, R. A. *Hamlet versus Lear: Cultural Politics and Shakespeare's Art* (1993).

Frye, Northrop. *Fools of Time: Studies in Shakespearean Tragedy* (1967).

Harbage, Alfred, ed. *Shakespeare: The Tragedies* (1964).

Mack, Maynard. *Everybody's Shakespeare: Reflections Chiefly on the Tragedies* (1993).

McAlindon, T. *Shakespeare's Tragic Cosmos* (1991).

Miola, Robert S. *Shakespeare and Classical Tragedy: The Influence of Seneca* (1992).

———. *Shakespeare's Rome* (1983).

Nevo, Ruth. *Tragic Form in Shakespeare* (1972).

Rackin, Phyllis. *Shakespeare's Tragedies* (1978).

Rose, Mark, ed. *Shakespeare's Early Tragedies: A Collection of Critical Essays* (1995).

Rosen, William. *Shakespeare and the Craft of Tragedy* (1960).

Snyder, Susan. *The Comic Matrix of Shakespeare's Tragedies* (1979).

Wofford, Susanne. *Shakespeare's Late Tragedies: A Collection of Critical Essays* (1996).

Young, David. *The Action to the Word: Structure and Style in Shakespearean Tragedy* (1990).

————. *Shakespeare's Middle Tragedies: A Collection of Critical Essays* (1993).

10. The Histories

Blanpied, John W. *Time and the Artist in Shakespeare's English Histories* (1983).

Campbell, Lily B. *Shakespeare's "Histories": Mirrors of Elizabethan Policy* (1947).

Champion, Larry S. *Perspective in Shakespeare's English Histories* (1980).

Hodgdon, Barbara. *The End Crowns All: Closure and Contradiction in Shakespeare's History* (1991).

Holderness, Graham. *Shakespeare Recycled: The Making of Historical Drama* (1992).

————. ed. *Shakespeare's History Plays: "Richard II" to "Henry V"* (1992).

Leggatt, Alexander. *Shakespeare's Political Drama: The History Plays and the Roman Plays* (1988).

Ornstein, Robert. *A Kingdom for a Stage: The Achievement of Shakespeare's History Plays* (1972).

Rackin, Phyllis. *Stages of History: Shakespeare's English Chronicles* (1990).

Saccio, Peter. *Shakespeare's English Kings: History, Chronicle, and Drama* (1977).

Tillyard, E. M. W. *Shakespeare's History Plays* (1944).

Velz, John W., ed. *Shakespeare's English Histories: A Quest for Form and Genre* (1996).

11. *Julius Caesar*

In addition to the readings listed above in Section 9, The Tragedies, see the following:

Bonjour, Adrien. *The Structure of "Julius Caesar"* (1958).

Charney, Maurice. *Shakespeare's Roman Plays* (1961).

Dean, Leonard, ed. *Twentieth Century Interpretations of "Julius Caesar"* (1968).

Dorsch, T. S., ed. *Julius Caesar* (1955).

Honigmann, E. A. J. *Myriad-Minded Shakespeare: Essays, Chiefly on the Tragedies and Problem Comedies* (1989).

———. *Shakespeare: Seven Tragedies* (1976).

Knight, G. Wilson. *The Imperial Theme* (1951).

Leggatt, Alexander. *Shakespeare's Political Drama: The History Plays and the Roman Plays* (1988).

Levitsky, Ruth M. " 'The elements were so Mix'd . . .' " *PMLA* 88 (1973): 240–45.

MacCallum, M. W. *Shakespeare's Roman Plays and Their Background* (1910).

Mahood, M. M. *Bit Parts in Shakespeare's Plays* (1992).

Miola, Robert S. "Shakespeare and His Sources: Observations on the Critical History of *Julius Caesar*." *Shakespeare Survey* 40 (1988): 69–76.

———. *Shakespeare's Rome* (1983).

Palmer, John. *Political Characters of Shakespeare* (1945).

Paster, Gail Kern. " 'In the spirit of men there is no blood': Blood as Trope of Gender in *Julius Caesar. Shakespeare Quarterly* 40 (1989): 284–98.

Richmond, Hugh M. *Shakespeare's Political Plays* (1967).

Ripley, John. *"Julius Caesar" on Stage in England and America, 1599–1973* (1980).

Sinfield, Alan. *Faultlines* (1992).

Stewart, J. I. M. *Character and Motive in Shakespeare* (1949).

Stirling, Brents. *Unity in Shakespearian Tragedy* (1956).

Thomas, Vivian. *Julius Caesar* (1992).

Velz, John W. *The Tragedy of Julius Caesar: A Bibliography to Supplement the New Variorum Edition of 1913* (1977).

Wilson, Richard. *Will Power* (1993).

WITHDRAWN

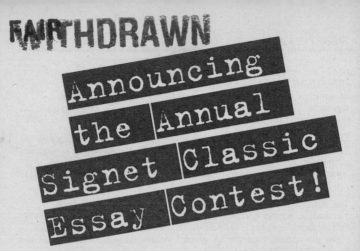

Announcing the Annual Signet Classic Essay Contest!

$5,000 in Scholarships
for high school Juniors and Seniors!

Win a Signet Classic library
for your high school!

Write an essay on a literary classic!

For more information write to:
Signet Classic Scholarship Essay Contest
375 Hudson Street, New York, NY 10014,
or request via e-mail at academic2@penguin.com.

Full details are available on Penguin's
website at www.penguin.com

Signet Classic

Penguin Putnam Inc. Mass Market